V O I C E S

THE UNIVERSITY OF
WINCHESTER

R O M

B A C K

A I R S

Voices

from the Back Stairs

Interpreting

Servants' Lives

at Historic House

Museums

Jennifer Pustz

NORTHERN ILLINOIS UNIVERSITY PRESS *DeKalb*

© 2010 by Northern Illinois University Press

Published by the Northern Illinois University Press, DeKalb, Illinois   60115

Manufactured in the United States using postconsumer-recycled, acid-free paper.

All Rights Reserved

Design by Julia Fauci

Library of Congress Cataloging-in-Publication Data

Pustz, Jennifer.

Voices from the back stairs : interpreting servants' lives at
historic house museums / Jennifer Pustz.

    p.   cm.

Includes bibliographical references and index.

ISBN 978-0-87580-622-8 (clothbound : alk. paper)

1. Historic house museums—Interpretive programs—United States.

2. Historic sites—Interpretive programs--United States.

3. Domestics—United States—History—19th century. 4. Domestics—
United States—History—20th century. 5. Domestics—United States—
Social conditions. 6. Domestics—United States—Social life and customs.

7. Households—United States—History. 8. United States—Social life and
customs—1865–1918. 9. United States—Social conditions—1865–1918.

10. United States—History, Local. I. Title.

E159.P867 2009

973—dc22

To my parents for giving me the courage to start

To Matt for giving me the strength to continue

Contents

Acknowledgments

This work began its life as a dissertation, a typically solitary endeavor. However lonely the process is overall, the end result is always achieved because of the involvement of other individuals. As teachers and mentors, the members of my dissertation committee all made a positive impact on the progress of this work. My thesis supervisors, John Raeburn and Joni Kinsey, were especially helpful throughout the entire process and provided essential encouragement and editorial assistance. Jane Desmond, Lauren Rabinovitz, and Allen Steinberg also contributed their academic talents and insights.

Throughout the process of my research and writing I have had the extremely good fortune to be able to work in the environment about which I write and to work alongside extraordinary colleagues. My work at Brucemore initially inspired this work and gave me my first insight into the practical side of public history and my current experiences as the museum historian for Historic New England continue to provide enlightenment. I especially wish to thank Peggy Whitworth, former executive director of Brucemore, for her constant support, flexibility, and encouragement. She gave me extraordinary opportunities to pursue various aspects of interpreting domestic service and other subjects of interest, and her enthusiasm for the subject matter made her a wonderful partner in these endeavors. James Kern, the current executive director, deserves thanks for answering many follow-up questions after my departure for New England and for facilitating image and permission requests. Former Brucemore staff members David Janssen and Melanie Alexander were instrumental in several early projects concerning domestic service at Brucemore, specifically in the conception and production of the exhibition "Help Wanted: Working at Brucemore, 1907–1937" and the Teaching with Historic Places lesson plan. I am also thankful to Brucemore's volunteers, especially the tour guides, who completed a survey regarding their interpretation of servants and talked with me on numerous occasions about their experiences. My new colleagues at Historic New England have also supported my interest in this topic, and I wish to thank several whose assistance and support helped me complete the manuscript: Carl R. Nold, Diane Viera, Peter Gittleman, Lorna Condon, and Emily Gustanis.

I also wish to thank those who provided images for this work: Tara Marsh, Brucemore; Jeanne Gamble, Historic New England; Diana Carey, The Schlesinger Library, Radcliffe Institute, Harvard University; Kathy Garrett-

Cox, Maymont Foundation; Lisa Marine, Wisconsin Historical Society; Steve Woit, and Meghan Hughes, Valentine Richmond History Center.

I am also fortunate to have had the support of many professionals in the historic house museum field, especially the over 350 people that filled out and returned my survey about interpreting domestic service. Conversations with colleagues in person and via e-mail have also been invaluable. Thank you to Susan Schreiber, former director of Interpretation and Education at the National Trust for Historic Preservation for her early assistance with my research and for providing materials from "The View from the Kitchen" workshop. I am deeply grateful to Patricia Walker for sharing a copy of her research with me. Mark Heppner provided me with extensive information about the tours and domestic service research at Stan Hywet Hall & Gardens, Akron, Ohio. Craig Johnson, site administrator, James J. Hill House, St. Paul, Minnesota, and Michael Douglass, site administrator, Villa Louis, Prairie du Chien, Wisconsin, met with me early in the project about their interpretations of domestic service and generously provided follow-up information during the preparation of the manuscript. I especially wish to thank Elizabeth O'Leary and Dale Wheary of Maymont in Richmond, Virginia, for taking the time to talk with me in detail about the restoration of the domestic service wing and for giving me tours of the restoration in its early and complete stages, in addition to answering numerous questions. The incredible support and enthusiasm that my colleagues have shown for this project is perhaps the best evidence of the great interest in the interpretation of domestic servants. However, any errors committed are mine alone.

Thanks are also due to the staff at the Northern Illinois University Press for their assistance in turning this work from a dissertation into a publication. I am grateful to Melody Herr and Sara Hoerdeman for their encouragement and feedback and to Lisa Williams for her careful copy editing.

My family and friends have been towers of strength for me during what has been occasionally a strenuous journey. Thank you to my parents, David and Teresa Mach, for always believing in me and for their unfaltering emotional (and occasionally, financial) support. My husband, Matt, deserves special thanks for his steady support. He has been my companion during most of my site visits, and the inevitable discussions we had after house tours gave me a terrific sounding board for my ideas. I am grateful for the time he spent reading and commenting on the written work, and the hours he contributed to stuffing, labeling, and sealing envelopes for my mail questionnaire. Most of all, he always believed in my ability to see the project through to completion.

VOICES

FROM

THE BACK

STAIRS

Introduction

"Is it original?" Between my experiences as a museum visitor and tour guide I have probably heard this question a thousand times. Perhaps the first time I considered the authenticity of historic objects was during a family vacation. These trips were never very long or extravagant and usually involved visiting museums and historic sites within reasonable driving distance. My dad, in particular, enjoyed going to Lincoln sites, so during a week-long driving trip from our home in western Illinois to Nashville, we stopped at Abraham Lincoln's birthplace in Hodgenville, Kentucky. After viewing the orientation film in the visitor center, we were all excited to see the spring Lincoln played in as a child, the tree he sat under, and the celebrated log cabin in which this famous president began his life.

What we found was quite different: the spring was dry, the tree had succumbed to disease and was now a stump, and the cabin was made of logs that "may have been" those of Lincoln's cabin. I remember feeling let down because we expected to encounter these authentic artifacts of the early life of a legendary man. Like many visitors to historic sites, we had in mind an ideal and largely mythic vision of the subject of our visit and a desire to see the "real" things closely associated with him. In retrospect, I understand the spring and tree sites as having authentic connections to Lincoln. However, at the time the reality did not match our expectations, and because we lacked the tools to fully interpret these artifacts, we were disappointed. Despite this fact, for years my family has remembered and talked about this trip many times, and in some ways this complicated encounter with authenticity probably made a greater impact on my later thinking than if we had been able to see the bubbling spring, the living tree, and the authentic logs of Lincoln's cabin.[1]

During my early years in graduate school, I worked as a guide at the Old Capitol Museum on the University of Iowa campus, and for the first time I was on the receiving end of the question "Is it original?" The training manual focused heavily on the building's furnishings, most of which were from the period or reproductions. The interiors were beautifully restored, from the spotless ivory-painted walls to the shiny wood floor. I remember feeling conflicted about how to interpret this building and its contents. The structure itself was "original," but the inside was much different than I imagined it had been when it served as the capitol, considering that horse stalls had been present in the lower level, the stoves would have produced a layer of black soot on the walls and ceiling, and unpaved roads would have made for masses of muddy footprints on the wood floor, not to mention the use of spittoons by the building's occupants. Since most visitors marveled at how beautiful and well kept the place was, I constructed my tour around the story of Old Capitol's well-documented restoration. I also addressed some of the activities that took place in the building, the use and history of some of the objects, and how the reality would likely have been different than what visitors saw. However, I felt most comfortable telling a story about why the interiors looked the way they did by describing the discovery of architectural features and selection of the furnishings. Using the story of the building's restoration gave me an opportunity to talk to visitors about not only the objects on display but the choices behind them. This preservationist/curatorial detective story allowed me to interpret the "original" aspects of the museum while acknowledging and explaining the somewhat ideal contemporary appearance.[2]

While working at the Old Capitol, I started my PhD in American studies and anticipated that I would write my dissertation on the botanical artist who was the subject of my art history master's thesis. My experiences at the Old Capitol Museum convinced me that a museum career was in my future, but it was my work at Brucemore, a National Trust Historic site in Cedar Rapids, Iowa, that gave me a passion for historic house museums. I started at Brucemore as a summer intern doing research to help their staff put the story of the George Bruce Douglas family into its local, regional, and national contexts. One of the interpretive themes the staff were developing related to the family's relationship with technology, both in their business ventures and in their home. Among the objects that could be used to interpret this theme was a circa 1927 refrigerator. Studying the refrigerator and the history of domestic technology led me to histories of domestic service. The more I read, the more I wondered about how the *entire* household had functioned during Brucemore's interpretive period, 1915–25. Fortunately, during the eight years I spent at Brucemore as their historian, I had the opportunity to delve deeper into this subject. When I started, site staff had recently launched a rehabilitation of the carriage house into a visitor center, which allowed current staff offices to be moved out of the servants' wing and gave visitors greater access to spaces once used and lived in by the Douglases' servants. The spaces themselves became critical to telling the servants' story. Although Brucemore's servants are relatively well-documented, there are no extant servants' furnishings or possessions to parallel the "real" things that were key to interpreting their employers.

By this time, I had started rethinking my dissertation topic, and a visit to another historic house gave me a new idea. While visiting my in-laws one Christmas season, my husband and I visited a former president's home. At some point during the tour, I asked what they knew about the servants who worked there. The guide's defensive response to my inquiry launched a series of internal questions about how well historic house museums tell the stories of their domestic servants, if they approach the subject at all. I also became aware, as I toured more and more house museums, that when guides did share the stories of servants, they said little about the household's complex social system, which involved multiple ethnicities and social classes under one roof. Servants were often described as "like one of the family," an idealized description, which even if true on some levels, I suspected was only one side of a more nuanced story. These experiences launched a new dissertation topic and an ongoing desire to find new ways to authentically interpret the lives of people whose presence at historic houses is often ephemeral but are as significant as those who employed them.

Working at Historic New England, an organization that has nearly a century of history in the preservation of the region's built environment and which owns and operates thirty-six historic houses, I now contemplate a wider range of issues related to authenticity. Shortly after I started as the museum historian, I toured one of the organization's properties, Rundlet-May House in Portsmouth, New Hampshire, during an all-staff outing. Built in 1807, the house was far older than any I had toured during my life in the Midwest. The house had been home to several generations of the same family before it was donated to what was then known as the Society for the Preservation of New England Antiquities (SPNEA). Each generation had preserved the architecture and furnishings of the previous owners, while updating and adding as technology and taste changed. For example, the kitchen features a rare and innovative Rumford Roaster, installed by the family who built the house, as well as a modern stove used by the final residents. Several of Historic New England's properties feature similar layers of history, which can be challenging to interpret but offer another version of authenticity because the whole life span of the house as a residence has been preserved.

Looking back, it seems that authenticity has been a perpetual concern of mine, whether it has been as a visitor, scholar, or museum professional. Visiting historic places is still my primary leisure activity and where I look for inspiration. Now relocated to the Boston area, my husband and I entertain ourselves by spending our weekends and time off walking the Freedom Trail and the Battle Road and touring a seemingly endless bounty of historic houses and history museums. We enjoy these experiences, but as a scholar I have high expectations for the intellectual, academic, and historical rigor of historic sites. On the other hand, my professional experiences have made me sympathetic to the challenges and limitations of historic house museums and historic sites in general. I regularly contemplate how to make historic sites more authentic by presenting the stories of those we know were present but for whom we have little "real" material culture evidence. Having experienced the pressure of working with limited budgets, training guides, and compromising with coworkers on the wording of labels, the choice of images and artifacts for exhibits, and the content of tour scripts, I am sensitive to the fact that, despite an institution's best intentions, powerful interpretations often are diluted by the time they reach the visitor.

Therefore, I approach this work with enthusiasm but also a full understanding of reality. During the course of my graduate studies and the first decade of my museum career, I have been regularly impressed and inspired by the efforts many history museums have taken to make their collections and historic sites engaging and meaningful in ways that go beyond the objects in display cases and the recitations of inventories. On the other hand, I am sometimes disappointed by exhibitions and tours that have great potential to share important authentic stories but fail to be bold enough to trust that their audiences will appreciate complex or controversial material. I fully agree with historian Eric Foner's recent statement that "we owe it to visitors to give them the most up-to-date, complex history that we can, and that's where museums have sometimes fallen down in the past. The history presented has been oversimplified and too bland." I do, however, understand why museums err on the side of caution and end up putting forth interpretations that will not offend but, as a result, will not inspire.[3]

All of these concerns deal on some level with the issue of "authenticity," a concept that is an important part of the museum experience. It is at the core of what makes museums special, especially in an era of "virtual" entertainment and highly realistic simulations. A survey of Americans' uses of the past, which became the basis for Roy Rosenzweig and David Thelen's book *The Presence of the Past: Popular Uses of History in American Life* (1998), revealed that museums are considered the most trustworthy sources for information about history, because they provide an unmediated experience with authentic objects. Respondents noted that they enjoy making personal connections with the artifacts on display. A recent survey of outdoor museum visitors by Reach Advisors found that to some visitors authenticity means "everything." For the majority of these survey respondents, authenticity included addressing difficult issues like slavery, racism, and religious intolerance openly, although some respondents preferred more delicate approaches to such topics. Unlike Disney World or other attractions loosely based on historical people, places, or events, only museums can deliver authentic objects, structures, and built environments. It is our mission to preserve and interpret them, and it is our responsibility to do so accurately.[4]

The importance of the "real" and "authentic" remains central to history museum practice, but simply exhibiting collections has diminished as sites' primary function. The influx of academically trained historians on museum staffs and the subsequent influence of social history on exhibitions and interpretation have resulted in a broader definition of authenticity that can encompass the whole truth, warts and all, and the history of all Americans. The civil rights and feminist movements inspired historians in the academic community to research previously ignored participants in American history—women, African Americans, immigrants, and working people. This new awareness was slower to take root in the museum profession, but when the saturated job market of the 1970s sent many newly minted PhDs in search of other opportunities, a boom in museum growth (encouraged by bicentennial patriotism) provided them.

These scholars, some of the first to be influenced by the "new social history," made an important impression on institutions traditionally associated with local elites and volunteer history buffs. As professional historians took the helm at history museums and historic sites and granting agencies encouraged or required their consultation on major exhibitions, museums increasingly became places where average Americans could find their own histories treated with the same respect formerly given only to those deemed great or extraordinary. The input of these historians also resulted in exhibitions that were more academically rigorous and held to higher standards of historical accuracy. After a long period during which little had changed in museum practice, the civil rights and feminist movements, the increased number of academic historians working in museums, an overall professionalization of the field, and growing interest in a broader sense of local history challenged the established order. Museum methodology has slowly shifted from a traditionally formalist, object-centered approach to an idea-centered one that more readily embraced the interpretation of people who left behind less in terms of documents and material evidence. However, these changes have also been slow to fully take root and blossom, and the adoption of social history and an idea-centered approach has been uneven. Carol Kammen recently wrote that

> visitors ask for, and are interested in, authenticity. They ask about the wallpaper and the quilts because they want to know and because we have successfully taught them to wonder about such things. . . . And yes, these things are important, but to me, they are not the lesson—or perhaps question—I would like to have the visitor learn or ask. I would prefer that the visitor wonder about who ran the shop and was she married, and I would like people to think about the customers in it. . . . I would like visitors to think about such things rather than about carpets and dishes, which are the background against which life was lived—against which history for that place was made.

Museum professionals may have adopted many aspects of the academic approach to history, but we must continue to encourage audience members to define authenticity beyond the physical object.[5]

Many scholars and museum professionals have engaged in public discourse about the impact of social history on museum practice. Of these many musings, two in particular have been influential in my approach to thinking about authenticity and the interpretation of domestic servants. In their essay "Locating Authenticity: Fragments of a Dialogue," Spencer R. Crew and James E. Sims, curator and designer of the Smithsonian exhibition "Field to Factory: Afro-American Migration, 1915–1940," describe some of the challenges related to creating exhibitions in the era of social history. Since history museums have traditionally collected primarily high-quality objects with well-documented histories, their collections have over-represented the well-to-do. Everyday objects and those owned by lower- and middle-class Americans, which would create the foundation for most social history exhibitions, were less likely to survive, let alone land in the Smithsonian's collection. The focus on social history over the past twenty years has probably already led to significant changes in collecting practices; Crew and Sims mention an aggressive collecting campaign launched to find artifacts with African American provenance for their exhibition. However, they argue, the museum should not wait until objects with the exact provenance are available to tell important stories in exhibitions. Instead, curators should look to the "idea-driven" exhibition.[6]

According to Crew and Sims, "in idea-driven exhibitions, objects remain one of the most important vehicles for transmitting the themes of the exhibition. . . . But in this model, objects do lose their preeminence as the primary source of authority in the presentation; they no longer control the discussion. More importance is given to the research done by scholars affiliated with the exhibition team." They also suggest that for exhibitions on nineteenth- and twentieth-century subjects, mass-produced objects, which are less tied to region, can offer more flexibility. The authors respect the power of authentic objects, but by using them accurately in period settings, they are allowed to tell stories that are more inclusive. The strategy of allowing ideas or themes to drive a narrative supported by objects (some original, and others of the period) has become increasingly common in house museum tours.[7]

Some elements of "Field to Factory" were reproductions that facilitated the display of "authentic" objects or the experience of specific emotions. Recreated scenes from stages of the journey, complemented by oral histories and photographs, added dimension to the story. The exhibition was not particularly interactive, with one significant exception. To enter the train station to get transportation north, visitors chose one of two doors, one marked "White" and the other "Colored." It was a simple, but effective, component. Although it was a reconstruction, the curators argued that it was indeed an "authentic" experience: "At the doors of the Ashland station, the condition of legal segregation is authentic. The object is a reproduction, somewhat diagrammatic in form but not metaphorical." The Ashland station component not only suggests that a recreated scene can offer a powerful "real" experience, but also is a reminder of the importance of engaging visitors in a kinesthetic learning experience. For example, the simple act of leading a tour group down a long, steep, servants' staircase sometimes makes a greater impact on visitors than anything I could tell them about the physical demands of domestic service.[8]

Richard Handler and Eric Gable's fieldwork at Colonial Williamsburg, which culminated in the book *The New History in an Old Museum: Creating the Past at Colonial Williamsburg* (1997), has contributed some of the most thought-provoking critiques of the use of social history in history museums. While I disagree with some of their conclusions, the authors provide useful observations about the function of authenticity at an important living history museum that serves as a model for many others. Handler and Gable argue that Colonial Williamsburg's social historians espouse a "constructivist" approach that acknowledges that history is an interpretation, making facts meaningful based on their use in the context of themes and arguments, in the same way that Crew and Sims argue that objects can be made to tell different stories based on the themes behind an idea-driven exhibition. However, the constructivist approach is undermined "on the ground" by interpreters who choose to focus on an objectivist, "just the facts" approach that foregrounds the institution's desire to continually pursue a more "real" depiction of the past.[9]

Perhaps the most extensive tribute to authenticity in Colonial Williamsburg's history was the reinterpretation of the Governor's Palace between 1975 and 1981. When it opened in the 1930s, the reconstructed palace featured interiors more in line with the Colonial Revival style, which was enjoying popularity due to the bicentennial of George Washington's birth. The curators in charge of the reinterpretation relied on an inventory of 16,500 objects taken at the death of colonial governor Norborne Berkeley, Baron de Botetourt in 1770. Colonial Williamsburg staff members tout the palace as exemplary of their dedication to authenticity, yet conjectural aspects of the reinterpretation are downplayed. Although the inventory supplies a list of artifacts that were present in the palace, some could not be precisely identified, and it does not identify their placement in the rooms, or wallpaper designs and other fixtures. Like most period restorations, the Governor's Palace presents its authenticity as being believable to a person from the period, despite the fact that the inventory represents an incomplete picture of life in 1774.[10]

When it came to interpreting the history of slavery at Colonial Williamsburg, Handler and Gable found that white interpreters regularly distinguished between "fact" and "conjecture," the former used to discuss white inhabitants, the latter to interpret black residents. Some interpreters avoided discussing slavery, because "they believed that black history was, as they often complained, 'undocumented'—it verged on fiction; it never quite had the same just-the-facts authenticity as the stories they could tell about the elite white inhabitants of the town." Even when documents provided "facts" about Williamsburg's black population, such as an inventory of Peyton Randolph's estate, this information was presented one-dimensionally by focusing on the slaves' names, their monetary values, and the concept that slaveowners treated enslaved people well because of what they were worth. Both uses of inventories are one-dimensional because they focus only on the "facts" documented by them. The interpreters take pride in the authenticity that an inventory provided for the reinterpretation of the Governor's Palace, without recognizing the constructivist nature of the restoration and the use of conjecture in creating the final product. The Randolph inventory acknowledges the status of African Americans as property but focuses on only one interpretation of a status that dehumanizes people.[11]

In their conclusion, Handler and Gable suggest that the problem stems from museums' overemphasis on their possession of the "really real": "The dream of authenticity is a present-day myth. We cannot recreate, reconstruct, or recapture the past. We can only tell stories about the past in a present-day language, based on our present-day concerns and the knowledge (built, to be sure, out of documents and evidence) we construct today." I suspect that most museum professionals agree with this statement, but perhaps our actions inadvertently suggest that we care only about creating a more perfect physical re-creation of the past or that we privilege those whose stories we are able to tell with "real" objects and documents. *Conjecture* should not be a dirty word. As William Seale, a historian who specializes in the restoration of historic houses, has aptly pointed out: "Of course, you will face conjecture. This is perfectly all right if your solutions are based on real knowledge of the time and place and possibilities—this is part of the usual work of historians." Used honestly, this approach allows a site to tell a richer and, hopefully, more authentic story.[12]

Standards of authenticity should now apply more broadly to the stories and people interpreted in museums and at historic sites rather than simply as a quality held by objects and buildings. The efforts of social historians have raised the bar for all of us working in the museum profession, thanks in part to the more educated public that has resulted from greater exposure to social history themes. Rex Ellis suggested in his article "Interpreting the Whole House" that because "public access to research is more immediate and more comprehensive than ever before, the public will begin to hold teachers of history in the twenty-first century to ever-higher standards of accuracy and inclusion. Historic house museums will be judged by these standards, as well, and their survival will depend, in many cases, upon the extent and effectiveness of their efforts to interpret their sites more fully."[13]

For historic sites, and historic house museums in particular, it is through interpreting domestic servants that the goal of telling a more complex story of everyday life may be achieved. The first step involves tracing changes in thinking about historic houses from their roles as shrines, collections of antiques, and architectural masterpieces to their more recent roles as sites for educating the public about the everyday lives of people beyond the wealthy male owners. Chapter 2 explores the growing interest in and implementation of domestic service interpretation at historic house museums interpreting the post–Civil War era. A nationwide mail survey I conducted on the interpretation of domestic service will act as a barometer of the current state of such efforts and will identify the challenges involved in their development and implementation. Chapter 3 provides the historical context necessary for developing an interpretation of domestic life based on the "servant problem," a common complaint of women engaged in hiring servants in the nineteenth and early twentieth centuries. I address the fragmentary evidence that most house museum staff face when they set out to interpret the lives of servants and demonstrate the value of period resources in creating a rich story built upon site-specific material. Chapter 4 focuses on how to populate the whole historic house with servants and how to use the "servant problem" to incorporate domestic servants into the general tour given to everyday visitors. The final chapter offers case studies that illustrate responses to specific interpretive challenges and creative approaches to interpreting servants beyond the standard tour.

My goal is to help historic house museum staff reach the objective of telling the whole history of their sites through interpretation of domestic servants in a rich and complex fashion that favors the "real" over the "ideal." Although many of my general recommendations are applicable to house museums interpreting servants in any period of American history, the focus of my research has primarily been on the period between 1870 and 1920. For those who have not yet begun the process of interpreting servants this book will offer a toolbox to get them started. For those whose sites are already telling the stories of domestic servants, which based on my research is a number that is already large and growing, I will offer encouragement to push this interpretation to a level of greater complexity. Conversations about why and how historic house museums should interpret domestic service have been taking place in the field for at least twenty years. Much has been accomplished, and there is much left to do. I hope to provide a progress report, constructive criticism, and the foundation for the next stage of the conversation.

Shrines, Slave Quarters, and Social Relevance

The Changing Historic House Museum

New Solutions for House Museums. New Audiences for Old Houses. "Future Options for Historic House Museums." These titles are from a book currently on my bookshelf, a symposium I attended in 2007, and a session I attended at a conference addressing sustainability in the field of public history in June 2008. They also summarize the current "hot issue" in the field of historic house museums. In recent years, much of the news about these institutions has been grim. As of this writing, the Mark Twain House and Edith Wharton's home, The Mount, are fighting to keep their doors open due to financial strains. Panels about house museums at recent annual meetings of the American Association of State and Local History (AASLH) have focused on sustainability and the steps failing institutions should take to continue protecting historic buildings if they must close their doors as museums. Studies have been released that indicate that the audience for historic sites is shrinking. A major "summit" known as the Forum on Historic Sites Stewardship in the 21st Century convened by the American Architectural Forum, American Association of Museums (AAM), AASLH, and the National Trust for Historic Preservation (NTHP) initiated a conversation about historic site sustainability.[1]

The question of whether the United States has too many history museums started appearing in the professional literature around the turn of this century. In 2002, shortly after the first meeting of the aforementioned forum, Gerald George, a special projects associate for the Council on Library and Information Resources and former director of AASLH, described a "historic house museum malaise." George cited presentational redundancies, declines in maintenance and interpretation, and lack of community involvement with these institutions as endemic. Historic house museums have the power to "employ unique educational tools and processes, preserving human experience, encouraging empathy by explaining lives and emotions in other eras, and helping visitors understand their own relationships to larger communities." However, despite their potential educational value, house museums "often fail to connect with [their communities]. Efforts are inadequate to tap into new constituencies or keep up with the needs and interests of old ones."[2]

The early twenty-first century may indeed see a contraction in the number of house museums after years of rapidly increasing numbers. As heart-wrenching as it may be, there is great value in assessing the health of house museums as a subgroup of the history museum field, and in individual institutions determining whether their current tours and programs meet community needs and interests. Although my own work is not a full answer to the sustainability question, essentially it addresses a core concern of the "new solutions for historic house museums" debate—change—which may come in the more dramatic forms of closing, merging, or changing missions, or conservative changes focused on new programming or tour offerings.

Change occurs slowly in the historic house museum field, and an overview of the history of these institutions offers one window into the difficulties associated with it. The origins of any house as a public historic site play an important role in the development of the story that guides tell its visitors. Material culture scholar Thomas J. Schlereth has observed, "A historic house possesses at least two histories: its past as an actual residence and present life as a house museum." For some sites, preservation and restoration often become an important part of their narratives. In many cases, the original reasons for preserving a site affect the subsequent interpretation. Early preservation criteria, for example, favored birthplaces or residences of important individuals and sites of significant events, and consequently skewed representation of the past in favor of the elites and solidified the "sacred" associations of the sites themselves. Their stories are a product of their eras—for many, the times have changed, but their stories remain the same. The most successful house museums and preservation organizations have adapted both their interpretation and preservation strategies to suit a more diverse audience and have become increasingly socially relevant.[3]

The preservation movement initiated the concept of saving houses for use as museums, so as a result, the histories of house museums and historic preservation have been intertwined. The first house museums in the United States were connected with George Washington. The Hasbrouck House in Newburgh, New York, which served as the headquarters of his Continental Army between 1782 and 1783, became the first house museum, in 1850. Later that decade, "Southern matron" Ann Pamela Cunningham began her crusade to save Mount Vernon and open it as a shrine to the first president. While her effort was initially confined to southern women, it became clear that the campaign would have to expand north to raise the necessary funds. Cunningham then appealed to both northern and southern women in the midst of growing sectional tensions. In 1854, she suggested that through preservation of Mount Vernon, women could set an example of rising above the conflict: "'We neither desire nor intend sectionality. . . . If ever in the future period of our national history, the Union should ever be in serious danger, political storms rocking it to its base, or rendering it in twain, there will be such a moral grandeur . . . in the mere fact that the tomb of Washington rests secure under the flag of his native state, enshrined in the devotional reverence of the wives, mothers, and daughters of the Union.'"[4]

Cunningham's eventual success laid the groundwork for preservation of other houses, serving as an example of volunteer leadership and a national effort spearheaded by women. As a result, other women's groups, including the Daughters of the American Revolution and the National Society of Colonial Dames, began campaigns to save historic buildings. Such activities were considered appropriate for women, because they were related to the domestic sphere. Women's groups continued to focus on saving the homes of founding fathers as secular shrines. The Association for the Preservation of Virginia Antiquities, for example, saved and restored the home of Mary Ball Washington and erected a sign on the property reading, "Home of Mary, Mother of George, Shrine Open Daily." The parallel with Christ's mother, "Mary, Mother of God," was surely intentional. Crusaders hoping to save these sites often presented the buildings as holy places worthy of pilgrimage: "We hope that this appeal will strike the keynote of patriotism and that in a very few years the home of Andrew Jackson, the beautiful Hermitage, will be the Mecca of all true patriots in the United States and of historic interest to the touring stranger."[5]

The women's groups that saved these houses used them to promote specific values or ideologies, most often patriotism or appropriate roles for women. The early years of historic preservation, for example, coincided with major demographic changes in the United States due to immigration, which prompted groups such as the DAR to promote historical landmarks as instruments in the Americanization of immigrants and their children. Other ideological goals involved the advocacy of specific concepts of morality or gender roles. To achieve these ideals, one aspect of a resident's life could be used to create the desired message. For example, the founders of Louisa May Alcott's Orchard House, the Concord Women's Club, provided a shrine to the characters of *Little Women* to teach domesticity, ignoring Alcott's suffragist sentiments. The result was a simplification of both the novel and its author. Patricia West explains that the "genius of *Little Women* was that it preserved the deeply felt values of domesticity through the insular warmth of the March cottage, while simultaneously expressing Jo's rebellion against its restrictions. . . . Just as Alcott 'invented' her own life story in *Little Women,* the Concord Women's Club 'invented' the history of Orchard House." Although Orchard House preserved the home of a famous woman instead of a founding father, the emphasis on traditional values was similar.[6]

A slightly different approach to preservation criteria was established by William Sumner Appleton, a wealthy Bostonian who became actively involved with historic preservation in 1905 through a campaign to save the Paul Revere House. In 1910, he founded the Society for the Preservation of New England Antiquities (SPNEA), which expanded the criteria of significance to include architecture, and emphasized a more scientific approach to preservation based on connoisseurship, photographic documentation, and measured drawings. Houses saved by the society were opened for public exhibition, but despite Appleton's contemporaries' interest in period room installations, most of SPNEA's early historic house museums were sparsely furnished, allowing the architecture to take center stage. Appleton also acknowledged that historic houses could be used as more than museums and sought alternative uses for them, either allowing them to remain residences or to be used for tearooms and other commercial purposes, so long as their architectural character was preserved. Appleton espoused a conservative preservation philosophy, claiming, "What is left today can be changed tomorrow, whereas what is removed today can perhaps never be put back."[7]

Appleton's interest in preserving New England's architectural past was part of a larger antiquarian phenomenon focused on reclaiming the region's history, which was increasingly disappearing in the post–Civil War industrial landscape. Collecting antique books and furniture became popular pastimes, and interest in old buildings increased. Appleton's wealth permitted him to pursue preservation as a full-time vocation, but he was one of many wishing to save New England's "antiquities" in the shadow of the modern urban and industrial city.[8]

SPNEA continued to grow and evolve while remaining true to Appleton's principles. The house museum collection has expanded and contracted over time in the interest of being able to maintain its properties to the best of the organization's abilities. When historic properties were deaccessioned from the collection in the 1970s and 1980s, they were sold into private ownership with protective easements held by the organization, essentially following Appleton's belief that old homes could remain residences as part of a successful preservation strategy. The Stewardship Program is one of the first comprehensive preservation easement programs and has served as a model for others. Today the organization preserves and interprets over 350 years of architectural and social history representing a range of building styles, including rustic seventeenth-century homes, the elegant Federal era Otis House, a pink Victorian cottage, and Walter Gropius's modern masterpiece. The organization also cares for large and diverse material culture and archival collections that expand the preservation of New England heritage beyond the walls of its building collection. The organization has also embraced new public uses of its historic properties. Pierce House, an underperforming house museum in a working-class neighborhood in Dorchester, Massachusetts, has been successfully revitalized as a center for school programs. At Casey Farm in Saunderstown, Rhode Island, a community-supported agriculture (CSA) program meets local demand for organic, locally grown produce, while preserving the region's agricultural history. Another farm, the Spencer-Peirce-Little Farm, in Newbury, Massachusetts, has established a successful partnership with the Massachusetts Society for the Prevention of Cruelty to Animals by serving as a foster farm for rescued animals. The sheep, chickens, turkey, and other resident animals have made the site a family-friendly place with increasing attendance and repeat visitors. In 2004, the organization concluded a rebranding initiative with the introduction of a new name, Historic New England, "to better reflect a renewed commitment to its mission of serving the public by preserving and presenting New England's heritage for today's audiences."[9]

The preservation efforts of women's organizations and Appleton's SPNEA were all private endeavors, and this model continues to be the most prevalent despite the later activities of federal and state agencies. The first federally controlled historic house was Arlington House, seized in 1861 as a spoil of the Civil War, since it had belonged to Confederate general Robert E. Lee. However, the United States government's involvement with historic preservation did not accelerate until well into the twentieth century. The National Park Service (NPS) was created in 1916 as a branch of the Department of the Interior to supervise natural sites, but by 1933, it had expanded to maintain historic battlefields previously maintained by the War Department. The federal government's entry into preservation coincided with the concern that the nation's past was disappearing and with the creation of New Deal projects that documented the diversity of American culture. Programs such as the Historic American Building Survey (HABS), Federal Writers Project state guides, and the Index of American Design made lasting contributions to the history of architecture and preservation. Works Progress Administration workers constructed visitor centers for many of the NPS sites, some of which are still in use.[10]

The passage of the Historic Sites Act in 1935 further involved the federal government in historic preservation. It "called for the creation of a national survey of historic sites; it encouraged cooperative agreements with private and governmental bodies for the maintenance of those sites; and it empowered the secretary of the interior to accept properties as part of a system of national historic sites." At the National Park Service, the park historian and his staff drew up standards for federal historic sites by designating three types of areas considered worthy of federal support: those that "clearly illustrated an important theme in the history of the nation," sites associated with famous Americans, and sites of specific historical events. Today, the NPS continues to maintain a variety of sites, including battlefields, parks, and historic homes, but it is increasingly active in preserving and interpreting historic sites that reflect the nation's diversity, such as Manzanar, one of ten Japanese internment camps; the Brown vs. Board of Education National Historic Site in Topeka, Kansas; the home of Maggie Lena Walker, the first female African American bank president; and the textile mills of Lowell, Massachusetts.[11]

After World War II, the number of historic house museums in the United States continued to increase substantially. The National Trust for Historic Preservation was chartered by Congress in 1949 with an original charge to "receive donations of sites, buildings, and objects significant in American history and culture, to preserve and administer them for the public benefit." The National Trust began creating its own "collection" of historic properties with Woodlawn Plantation in Mount Vernon, Virginia, the home of Eleanor Parke Custis Lewis, who was raised by her grandparents, George and Martha Washington. Most of the early properties were the southern and northeastern homes of great men and artists such as James Madison, Frank Lloyd Wright, and Daniel Chester French.[12]

In recent years, however, the National Trust has expanded the scope of its collection and interpretation, both geographically and thematically. Houses in the Midwest, California, and Texas have joined the early sites. In the past two decades, the organization has been a driving force in encouraging more diversity in the preservation movement, both in the types of structures saved and in the community of preservationists. Three of its recent acquisitions and affiliate sites—the Lower East Side Tenement Museum (New York City), the Gaylord Building (Lockport, Illinois), and Touro Synagogue (Rhode Island)—show an interest in telling stories related to America's diverse immigrant heritage and the commercial and religious aspects of the American experience. The National Trust has held interpretation workshops on historic landscapes, domestic service, and childhood to educate house museum professionals about new angles of interpretation. The organization has recently moved beyond its original focus on collecting historic properties to become a vocal opponent of urban sprawl and a catalyst for preservation of neighborhoods and Main Streets, including those in ethnic and low-income areas.[13]

"Shrines" connected with presidents and well-known personalities continue to open. For example, the interpretive themes of the First Home of President William J. Clinton in Hope, Arkansas, include "A young boy of a single mother in the rural south can achieve the American dream to become President of the United States." However, these places of pilgrimage are balanced by the reinterpretation of the homes of "great men" and new historic house museums that focus on stories of lesser-known figures, women, and minorities. These changes are related to the increasing presence of social historians, but they are also responses to the need and desire to attract new audiences. *Relevance* has also been a buzzword in the discussion of the sustainability of historic sites. Two important changes in the historic house museum field, the interpretation of slavery and the preservation and interpretation of a New York City tenement, provide lessons for all house museum professionals as they seek to tell more relevant stories.[14]

Some of the first historic sites and house museums to consider a broader approach to their interpretation were sites with a history of slavery. These efforts have met with varying levels of success. For most southern plantations, a long-standing focus on the owning family is difficult to change. The myths of the "Old South" and the "lost cause" continue to drive the mystique of plantation sites. However, human bondage and ownership, violence, abuse, and racism are but some of the issues that need to be addressed to provide a full picture of life on a plantation. Some sites have made important steps toward a balanced representation of white owners and enslaved people at plantations, but many others continue to ignore the issue or represent it inaccurately. The successes and challenges experienced by sites grappling with the very difficult task of telling these stories are instructive for interpreters of free domestic workers.

The history of slavery is a very difficult subject to present in a public venue, and interpreters face challenges in addition to the difficult content. Most guided tours average one hour, which may not be enough time to give a balanced house tour that addresses slavery in the most meaningful and accurate ways. That isn't to say that slavery can't be discussed honestly and directly during a one-hour experience, but these presentations often suffer from lack of detail because slavery is one of many topics that tend to be covered. James Oliver Horton, a scholar with great sensitivity to the challenges of public history, has written that the "history of slavery and its role in the formation of the American experience is one of the most sensitive and difficult subjects to present in a public setting. At historic plantation sites and historic houses, in museum exhibitions, in film productions, and in historic parks, public historians and historical interpreters are called upon to deal with this unsettling but critical topic, often under less than ideal teaching conditions. Moreover, they are asked to educate a public generally unprepared and reluctant to deal with a history that, at times, can seem very personal." The average visitor likely comes to a house museum expecting to experience the romance of an elegant setting. While today's visitors are perhaps better prepared for the discussions of slavery that should be part of tours at plantation sites, guides are in the difficult position of not knowing how much background their audience has on the subject or the perceptions they bring to the experience.[15]

In the eyes of many academics, the overall interpretation of slavery at plantations is still unsatisfying, despite the significant improvements of the past twenty years. Sites receiving accolades for their progress seem to be the exception rather than the rule. Jennifer L. Eichstedt and Stephen Small's *Representations of Slavery: Race and Ideology in Southern Plantation Museums* (2002) provides a detailed analysis of how slavery is or is not discussed on plantation tours in Virginia, Georgia, and Louisiana. Their research used participant observation as the primary tool. Without identifying themselves as scholars, the authors and their students collectively took hundreds of house tours to gather their information. Their findings indicate that even when slavery is interpreted at plantations, its educational value is often diminished by poor interpretive techniques.[16]

Eichstedt and Small's research resulted in the most critical and detailed analysis of slavery interpretation to date by developing a typology of four representational/discursive strategies used by plantation museums to interpret slavery and African Americans: symbolic annihilation and erasure, trivialization and deflection, segregation and marginalization, and relative incorporation. These strategies are used singly and in combination. Eichstedt and Small argue that overall "these sites work to construct and maintain public white (male-dominated) racial identities that both articulate with and bolster a sense of (white) pride in a partial history of freedom, democracy, and hard work. In this story, slavery and African Americans are presented as almost incidental to the growth of the South and, by extension, the United States." These typologies are useful tools to apply to all sites where domestic workers, enslaved or free, were present.[17]

Symbolic annihilation and erasure wipe away the existence of enslaved people and their work. It is defined as interpretation that focuses exclusively on the material and social life of the plantation owners; neglects to mention, acknowledge, or discuss slavery, the enslaved, or African Americans; mentions the enslaved or free blacks in fleeting ways that lack details or context; uses euphemisms such as "servants" or "servitude"; uses the passive voice or neutral pronouns to discuss enslaved people; and uses universal or ahistorical statements that refer only to white experiences. Twenty-five percent of the 122 sites in the study "failed to mention slavery or the enslaved in *any way* whatsoever," and nearly 83 percent used symbolic annihilation as one of their primary strategies. A common way to erase the presence of slaves or other workers is to draw the visitor's attention to another aspect of the house. The tendency of tour guides to focus on details such as furnishings and decorative arts is typical at many house museums, but Eichstedt and Small quantify just how unbalanced such interpretation is. First, they tracked the number of references to both furniture and slavery/enslaved people. From this data, they determined that sites using symbolic annihilation refer to furniture thirty-one times as often as they did to slavery or the enslaved. This tendency has been reversed at Somerset Place, a restored plantation in Creswell, North Carolina. Director Dorothy Spruill Redford, whose ancestors were enslaved at Somerset, teaches interpreters to "'mention slavery within the first twenty sentences and to keep talk about furniture to a minimum.'"[18]

Small's description of his visit to Nottaway Plantation in Louisiana illustrates many elements of symbolic annihilation. In the main hall, the guide described nearly every object *except* two 8.5-feet-tall statues of black servants. She noted that the family acquired three hundred slaves and fifty-seven household servants over the years but kept her tour's focus on the owner's business prowess and ingenuity. When the guide did mention slaves (usually referred to as "servants"), she used the passive voice. Small inquired about a compact, severely neglected barn-type building on the grounds and was told that it was "just an old building . . . an old slave building." At other plantation museums, the scholars found slave quarters turned into restrooms or bed-and-breakfast units. A docent at a different Louisiana site even said, "I wish we had some [slave cabins]; they would make pretty little bed-and-breakfast rooms."[19]

The devices of symbolic annihilation are not unique to southern plantations. Former slave sites in the North have also been negligent in acknowledging or interpreting the presence of enslaved people. At the John Brown House in Providence, Rhode Island, Brown's involvement in the slave trade was addressed only minimally until pressure from community members forced the site's staff to consider how this information could be incorporated into a tour that had focused heavily on decorative arts. House museums that were once the home and worksite for free domestic workers also engage in a similar symbolic annihilation when they fail to mention servants when they are known to have been present or when they refer to servants in the passive voice.[20]

Sites using trivialization and deflection as their primary strategies are described as those where slavery and those enslaved are mentioned, but in ways that trivialize their experiences, often by using humor. Eichstedt and Small identify two categories of this strategy. One suggests that slavery was not that bad, and even beneficial for the enslaved, citing happy and loyal slaves. The other emphasizes whites and whiteness over blacks and enslavement. Trivialization and deflection often coexist with symbolic annihilation.[21]

Eichstedt and Small offer several examples of this approach in action. In some cases, guides mention that enslaved people were sometimes better off than poor whites. This point was made by the guide when we took the "Other Half" tour at Colonial Williamsburg in 2003, but she reminded the group that the big difference was that even poor whites had more rights than those enslaved, because they were *free*. The myth of the happy or grateful slave enforces stereotypes of Africans as childlike; Eichstedt and Small heard these stories at 19 percent of sites. James Loewen has also commented that depictions of happy or grateful slaves trivialize the horrors of slavery: "No antebellum house shows that slavery was a penal system resting ultimately on force and threat of force. Never have I seen on display a whip, whipping post, chains, fetters, branding iron, or any of the advanced technology of mobile human confinement that owners devised." An example from Rosedown Plantation in Louisiana shows how the loyal slave and good master can be packaged together on the tour. Tours at Rosedown are self-guided and use taped narrations in various parts of the house. In the kitchen, "Henrietta, the slave cook" talks about the benevolence of her master:

Miss Martha, we all love her, she is good and kind. . . . You know, once a week, Massa give each slave, men, women, girls, and boys, when they's old enough to go to the field, five pounds of good clean bacon, one quart of molasses, and as much meal for bread as they want and one pint of coffee. . . . the worst times we ever had were when the Yankee men came through. . . . The war over now, and we free now. We ain't have no celebration after we's freed. We ain't even know we was freed until a good while after. After that, Miss Martha let all the slaves go, 'cept for me, I stayed.

Eichstedt and Small do not indicate the source of the cook's story, whether it is a complete fiction or loosely based on an actual Rosedown slave.[22]

Identifying the master as a "good owner" valorizes whiteness. Thirty-five percent of all sites, even those whose interpretation fits the rhetorical strategy of relative incorporation, presented the master as a positive figure. Guides described slaves as "like family" or as an "investment" that should not be damaged. Sites emphasized whiteness by representing the owner-enslavers as industrious and hard workers in their own rights, as seen in an exhibit panel at Stratford Hall Plantation in Virginia: "The story of the colonial planter is the story of a great occupational versatility and unremitting toil. The planter was relieved of some of his physical toil by the widespread use of slave labor, but he assumed complete supervisory control of this agricultural and mercantile enterprise." Such interpretations misplace the bulk of the labor as the burden of the white owner, thus trivializing the enslaved people who endured the hardest work without the benefit of freedom. The description of slaves as "like family" is especially problematic in a system where one person owned another, but it can also be a misleading statement when applied to free domestic servants. As I will demonstrate in later chapters, in some cases domestic workers seem to have established mutually affectionate relationships with their employers. However, such relationships were not fully equal, and the community belowstairs often constituted a distinct world in its own right that was intertwined with that of the upstairs realm.[23]

At some plantations, slavery is discussed using the strategy Eichstedt and Small identify as segregated knowledge, in which it is interpreted separately from the traditional, white-focused information. Sites that offer special tours focused on slavery or African American history engage in this practice. The main problem with such tours is that only a small percentage of visitors take them, due to limited availability. They are usually offered on a regular basis only during peak seasons (generally April through October), and vary from being monthly to daily or multiple times daily. On the Mount Vernon slave life tours taken by Eichstedt and Small, the guide noted that the content would be limited to what was known about slavery at the site and would not address slavery in general. By avoiding the big picture, docents could evade the overall unpleasantness of slavery as an institution and would not have to compare George Washington to other owner-enslavers. In isolation, Washington could be depicted as a man "'born into a society that accepted slavery,'" who provided good quarters, plenty of food, and Sundays and holidays off. The staff does discuss slave rebellions, but qualifies them by explaining that they rebelled against their captivity, not their enslaver (even though he participated in the system that enslaved them). At other sites, Eichstedt and Small found separate exhibits about slavery that provided specific examples of the master's brutality, but were balanced by examples of the good master. A more accurate way to "balance" the evils of slavery would be to describe the ways that enslaved people created strategies for survival and self-preservation in spite of their conditions. That enslaved Africans and their descendents survived enslavement had less to do with the benevolence of their masters than with the strength of their own characters and communities.[24]

Another way that information about slavery is segregated is based on the location in which it is discussed. An African American interpreter at Arlington House observed that visitors were more likely to discuss slavery in the slaves' quarters than in the main house. Visitors were comfortable learning about the work but were less interested in slave–master relationships. This type of interpretation is common at sites interpreting both enslaved and free domestic servants, where servants are discussed only in kitchens and the servants' wing, despite the fact that their work took them into all areas of the house, including the most private spaces.[25]

When given by a knowledgeable guide, slave life tours can be a valuable part of a visit to a plantation site. Since these programs and interpretation have developed primarily in the past twenty years, they are more likely to be the product of trained historians and more sound in terms of scholarship. Special slave life tours may create "segregated knowledge," but they also have positive aspects. They direct visitors' attention to specific subject matter and provide a more detailed interpretation, because they have a narrower focus. One may wonder, though—if a site has enough information about enslaved people to create a special tour—why isn't more of this information in the standard, everyday tour? The answer is usually a lack of time—so much to see, so little time to talk about it all. To extend the length of a standard tour or make special slave life tours part of every visitor's experience, sites would most likely have to increase their guide staff or offer fewer tours each day, neither of which is feasible for institutions with tight budgets. The varied attention spans of visitors must also be considered; a one-hour guided tour tends to be a comfortable length for most. However, the information developed for plantation tours often does benefit the standard tours. During her interviews with experienced interpreters at Thomas Jefferson's Monticello, Lois Horton learned that the amount of general information about slavery on the house tour increased after the debut of the plantation tour.[26]

Only 3.3 percent the plantation museums in Eichstedt and Small's study were identified as practicing relative incorporation. These sites provided information about slavery throughout the tour that was not degrading, discussed specific slaves, and indicated that learning about enslavement at their property has importance. They acknowledged that the ability of one race to live at a higher standard was based on the subjugation of another, and presented a more complicated interpretation of the master-enslaver and his family, instead of simply focusing on their hospitality, benevolence, and other positive characteristics.[27]

Eichstedt and Small identified Montpelier, the home of James Madison in Orange, Virginia, as a site where relative incorporation is the primary rhetorical strategy. Montpelier has undergone dramatic changes since the publication of their book; all later additions to Madison's structure have been removed, allowing the site to focus their interpretation on the Madison era. At the time of Eichstedt and Small's study, visitors toured the house with an Acoustiguide, a handheld listening device with a keypad. Each location is assigned a number that the visitor enters to hear the interpretation. At Montpelier, most locations featured four or more narrations, allowing the visitor to choose to listen to the more general interpretations in addition to information about specific themes or personalities. In terms of the overall content, slavery was consistently part of the narrated tour, and enslaved workers were credited with performing the labor necessary to maintain the lifestyle of the Madisons. The narration also described the social lives of the enslaved at Montpelier, including their right to Sundays off and their additional production of food and baked goods for trade with other enslaved people or white masters. The character of the "good master" was not absent, but it was balanced by information about documented slave resistance and rebellion and the acknowledgment that the true feelings of those enslaved toward their masters are difficult to know. One segment in particular spoke to the ambiguity of most sources: "It is difficult to know with accuracy how Montpelier's slaves felt toward their masters. Visitor Margaret Bayard Smith noted of a maid who was helping her: 'Nany, you have a good mistress.' And Nany replied, 'Yes, the best I believe in the world. I am sure I would not change her for any mistress in the whole country.' It is not possible to know whether this statement reflected Nany's true feelings."[28]

Montpelier's staff was willing to address the complicated personality of the white enslaver, something that might be particularly difficult when discussing one of the founding fathers. Eichstedt and Small found that Montpelier tours present Madison as "a statesman, generous host, and so on, but recognized him as someone who enslaved other people. Further his 'comfortable existence' is credited to the labor of enslaved people." The use of the Acoustiguide as an interpretive tool plays a significant role in the success of this well-rounded interpretation. It gives the site staff more control over content and consistency, while giving visitors some liberties to choose their own path and tailor the tour somewhat to their interests (although based on Eichstedt and Small's experiences, it seems that it is more difficult to "segregate" information about slavery). However, this option may be out of the price range for most historic house museums, and some museum staff find its impersonal approach less appealing than the warmth and personality provided by a human being.[29]

Monticello, Thomas Jefferson's home in Charlottesville, Virginia, faces similar challenges in terms of interpreting a founding father as a slave owner. This site has made significant improvements in the interpretation of Jefferson as a statesman, a slave owner, and the probable father of slave Sally Hemings's children. Eichstedt and Small identify Monticello as one of the 9.8 percent of sites they describe as "in-between," which are defined as sites that "attempt to incorporate the discussion of enslavement throughout their tours—or at least some docents do. At the same time they also occasionally lapse back into trivializing practices or, depending on the docent, into symbolic annihilation." The visitor encounters the topic of slavery during the house tour, in self-guided portions of the estate, and through a special tour of Mulberry Row, a row of excavated work buildings and slaves' quarters. Monticello's Web site provides additional background information about the lives of enslaved residents, and publications by research staff provide scholarly treatments of the subject. Staff at Monticello make it clear through their tours, programs, publications, and Web site that history is a continually evolving story, and they are dedicated to research that will help contemporary people understand the complexities of Jefferson and his world.[30]

Monticello's reputation for interpreting slavery has not always been so good. Only twenty years ago, guides referred to enslaved people as "servants" and described Jefferson in the active voice and the actions of slaves in the passive voice. Staff did not suggest the possibility that Jefferson had fathered the children of Sally Hemings. In 1993, Monticello staff started giving "plantation tours." Historical and archaeological research revealed the remains of the plantation's slave village, and with the assistance of university and public historians, staff began to take a more scholarly approach to their interpretation of slavery. Visitors to Monticello today are more likely to hear about Jefferson's slaves on their tour and have several opportunities to learn more while on site.[31]

When I toured Monticello in 2003 and 2005, I learned about Jefferson's enslaved workers throughout my visits. At the beginning of the guided tour of the main house, the guide mentioned that Jefferson's butler, Burwell Colbert, greeted visitors at the front door and asked them to wait in the Indian Hall. Throughout the tour, the guide pointed out examples of Jefferson's ingenuity in creating various gadgets, elements of his architectural style, and his voracious appetite for knowledge. However, the guide did not neglect the activities of the enslaved residents of Monticello during the tour. In the first intimate family space, the study, she pointed out a copy of the Declaration of Independence hanging on the wall, and immediately addressed the contradictory issue of Jefferson's role in obtaining freedom for white Americans while remaining a slaveholder. In particular, she noted matter-of-factly that it was very likely that Jefferson was the father of his slave Sally Hemings's children. Throughout the tour she called attention to the craftsmanship of John Hemings, a Monticello slave who made some of Jefferson's mahogany furniture. In the dining room, the guide discussed Edith Fossett, a slave trained in French cooking, who prepared the formal meals. She went on to explain that Jefferson was concerned about privacy while dining and was particularly worried that political conversations overheard by slaves would be repeated to those at other plantations. As a result, Jefferson trusted only Burwell Colbert to be present at mealtime. In the past, Monticello guides discussed only Jefferson's activities in the active voice, and slave actions in the passive voice. During my tour, the guide used enslaved people's names and active descriptions of their activities throughout the house, although she did not discuss the horrors of slavery in general, and most of her comments about Jefferson's enslaved workers were neutral; in other words, he was not painted as a particularly good or bad owner.[32]

The guide of the tour I went on was very knowledgeable and integrated information about the work and lives of slaves into a story that depicted the complexity of Thomas Jefferson as an autodidact, statesman, politician, and slave owner. However, like any guided house tour, Monticello's most likely varies according to the presenter. Since the quality of the guide makes such an impact on the visitor's experience, each group may learn more or less than the last one about Jefferson and the enslaved people at Monticello.

After completing the guided house tour, visitors have the opportunity to take self-guided tours of the rooms in the all-weather passageway, the gardens, and Mulberry Row. A small room in the all-weather passageway houses an exhibit of photographs and artifacts retrieved during archaeological excavations of root cellars and the sites of slave cabins that document the architecture and lifestyles of enslaved people at Monticello. The all-weather passageway also leads to the restored kitchen, the cook's room, and some storage areas, which have been simply furnished based on the study of Jefferson's records and other primary sources. An informative series of "reading rail" panels complement these spaces. In the cook's room, a photograph of the cook's husband, Joseph Fossett, accompanies a relatively detailed biography, which illustrates the depth of knowledge available about some of Monticello's slaves. Touchable squares of cloth provide visitors with a tactile experience of the clothing and blankets used by enslaved residents. A small display of personal items and their labels notes the use of leisure time and the pursuit of literacy: "Despite working from dawn to dusk for their owners and at night for themselves and their families, enslaved people found time for marbles, dominoes, and other games. Slate pencils and writing slates were among the tools that slaves used in learning to read and write. Many Monticello slaves, including some of the Fossetts, were literate as a result of their own efforts." While it would be easy to limit interpretation of Edith Fossett to describing the food she prepared and how she did her job, Monticello chooses a more complete representation. Together, the kitchen and the cook's room provide visitors with a well-rounded picture of Edith Fossett's life at Monticello: her place of work, a biography of her husband and names of her children, the type of clothing she might have worn, and the way she, her family, and other enslaved persons at the plantation educated themselves and spent their precious leisure time.

Between April and October, visitors have the opportunity to take plantation tours of "Mulberry Row," which are offered hourly between 10:00 and 3:00. My first visit to Monticello was a week or two before the tours resumed, which helped me understand Eichstedt and Small's concern about segregated knowledge. During a second visit two years later, I was able to take the plantation tour and found it a welcome addition to the information presented during the house tour. The guide was able to provide more detail about the many types of work performed by enslaved people and made an important distinction between those working on the quarter farms, in the skilled trades of Mulberry Row, and house slaves. She also noted the tension that existed between those working in the house and those outside. The guide described what was known about living conditions and rations, and discussed several of the same people (Edith Fossett and the Hemings family) mentioned in the house, but in more detail. This tour also touched on some of the more unsettling aspects of slavery, such as the sale of slaves into the Deep South as punishment, and the value of female slaves during their reproductive years. In part because the plantation tours are offered only seasonally, fewer visitors take them. Some of the more general information could be incorporated into the house tours to provide greater nuance for the standard visitor experience.[33]

Visitors unable to take the special tour may take a self-guided tour of Mulberry Row, aided by interpretive markers in front of each site and a brochure that is densely packed with information. The brochure in use during my 2003 visit provided general information about Mulberry Row and its slave community, and biographical sketches of slaves Isaac Jefferson, John Hemings, and the Hemings sisters. Although the brochure includes some examples of symbolic annihilation, such as referring to house slaves as "household servants," and employs several passive constructions in describing the work of enslaved people, it also addressed the conflicted nature of Jefferson's views on slavery and acknowledged that he was a slaveholder all his life. He did outlaw the international slave trade to Virginia but was unsuccessful in ending or restricting slavery. Jefferson did not believe a solution would be found in his lifetime, although he advocated resettling slaves outside of the United States. The text also acknowledged Jefferson's paternalism in that he did not think freed slaves would be able to survive in a white world. The Mulberry Row brochure also recognized the likelihood that Sally Hemings was Jefferson's mistress by stating that "historians generally accept the probability of a relationship that produced at least one and perhaps all of Sally Hemings' children listed in Jefferson's records."

The Jefferson–Hemings controversy most likely made Monticello's interpretation better. Due to the very public nature of the issue, interpreters were obliged to understand it and be willing to discuss it. Thomas Jefferson Foundation president Daniel P. Jordan noted in his statement on the DNA evidence that they had "instructed . . . interpreters to initiate conversations with . . . visitors about the study." While my tour guide did bring the topic up without being asked, there wasn't really enough time for any discussion. When visitors asked more specific questions at the end of the tour, she answered them and recommended visiting Monticello's Web site, which has extensive information about the Jefferson–Hemings relationship. In 1999, James and Lois Horton and four graduate students conducted interviews with visitors after Monticello house tours to learn how they felt about the DNA findings, Jefferson's role as a slaveholder, his relationship with Hemings, and the importance of discussing slavery at sites like Monticello. The majority of respondents agreed that information about slavery is important to understanding Monticello and Jefferson, although several visitors constructed narratives about Jefferson as a benevolent slaveholder who was for the most part powerless to free his own slaves or change the system on a national level. Whether these narratives were part of their tour or based on information visitors learned in the past is unclear, but perhaps the important points are that most visitors are open to hearing the information and that greater efforts should be made to counteract myths and preconceived notions about slavery.[34]

The successes and challenges of plantation sites are instructive for the house museum community as a whole. Eichstedt and Small make it clear that mentioning the existence of slaves is not as critical as how they are discussed, and the same is true about free domestic servants. Enslaved and free domestic servants deserve to have their actions described in the active voice. The owners of the house are discussed by name, so when servants' names are known, they should be treated the same way. Information about domestic service is most effective when it is woven through the fabric of the overall interpretation instead of limited to servants' wings and outbuildings. These are the first basic steps any site should take when incorporating domestic workers into tour interpretation. However, as I will demonstrate later, basic information such as names and the duties of servants should be further developed with contextual information that offers a more nuanced interpretation of the relationships between people of different colors, ethnicities, and social classes.

Interpreting the history of slavery has clearly proved challenging for historic houses with long histories that did not open with the intention of discussing the lives of enslaved people. Some house museums that opened in recent decades considered the significance of interpreting race, ethnicity, gender, and class from the beginning. These museums boldly address social history themes beyond domestic work by expanding into the neighborhoods inhabited by working and middle-class people and immigrants. The most prominent and dynamic of these new socially relevant house museums is New York City's Lower East Side Tenement Museum. Chartered in 1988, the museum's mission is "to promote tolerance and historical perspective through the presentation and interpretation of the variety of immigrant and migrant experiences on Manhattan's Lower East Side, a gateway to America." The Lower East Side Tenement Museum is housed in a five-story tenement built in 1863 at 97 Orchard Street. Between 1863 and 1935 it was home to approximately 7,000 people from twenty countries. The lives of six families are currently interpreted: the German Jewish Gumpertz family (1870s), the Russian Levine family (1890s), the

Eastern European Jewish Rogarshevsky family (1900s), the Italian Catholic Baldizzi family (1930s), the Confinos, a Sephardic Jewish family from Turkey (1916), and the Irish Moore family (1869). Some tours are based on themes, which focus on the way two families from different ethnic backgrounds and time periods adjusted to issues like economic depression and working for the garment industry. The fact that the Tenement Museum provides a unique experience that has resonated with many visitors may be demonstrated by steadily increasing attendance numbers. In addition to offering guided tours of the tenement apartments, the museum offers special programs to involve the community and to take an active role in current affairs.[35]

Reviewers of the museum's interpretive tour have been generally complimentary, with perhaps the only quibble being the lack of coal dust and other dirt that once likely existed. In all fairness, there are some aspects of tenement life that are impossible to depict accurately due to modern health codes and other regulations. In his column "The Abusable Past," R. J. Lambrose asked whether the museum would "install backyard privies, . . . and then clog them? Will it supply tubercular interpreters to work the sewing machines . . .?" While these and other situations would be impossible to re-create, visitors do pass hallway bathrooms added in 1905 to comply with the Tenement Act, complete with torn newspaper hanging above the seats for use as toilet paper. Tuberculosis and the treatment known as "cupping" are discussed in the Rogarshevsky apartment, which is interpreted in the context of Abraham Rogarshevsky's death from tuberculosis and the subsequent Jewish mourning ritual of sitting shiva. Although the museum does not provide the "time travel" experience that Lambrose describes, the fact that sanitation and disease are even discussed is a major step in the right direction for house museums.[36]

In addition to interpreting the immigrant experience of the past, the museum offers programs that focus on their contemporary counterparts. In 1996, the staff hosted a roundtable discussion with recent New York City immigrants of various ages and backgrounds. The participants discussed the expectations they had of the city and the successes and disappointments that resulted from their migration. Ruth Abram, museum president, noted that that program "gives us the opportunity to draw a connection between the immigration saga of the past, which we are interpreting, and the ongoing." Many of the participants made these connections as they viewed the apartments, remarking that the issues of immigration had changed little. The museum offers walking tours of adjacent neighborhoods to further make connections between past and present immigration.[37]

One particularly innovative step the Tenement Museum has taken is to change the visitor experience by encouraging dialogue among visitors. House museum tours traditionally follow the lecture format, and although many museum professionals promote inquiry-based tour methods that require active visitor participation, such techniques are employed primarily with children. In 2004, the museum launched "Kitchen Conversations," a dialogue program that draws on the tour experience as a starting point for discussing past and present immigration issues. As Ruth Abram described in her article "Kitchen Conversations: Democracy in Action at the Lower East Side Tenement Museum," the program has had mixed success thus far in terms of the number of visitors who participate, but those who do seem to leave the museum with a deeper understanding of their own immigration stories and how they compare to those of today.[38]

The Tenement Museum also offers assistance of various kinds to new immigrants. The staff holds classes in English for Speakers of Other Languages and uses primary source documents in the curriculum. This class generated the *Immigrant Resource Guide*, a free publication available in several languages, which contains stories of immigrants past and present, names of organizations that assist them, and answers to common questions. The Lower East Side Tenement Museum has created dynamic programs that take the role of museums to a further level, not only interpreting the past, but playing an active role in creating knowledgeable citizens and empowering immigrants in the present.[39]

The topics addressed at the Lower East Side Tenement Museum could be part of any house museum tour, and their success is proof that museum audiences are receptive to them. Mansions had bathrooms; their residents got sick; and the many immigrants who lived in the servants' quarters brought their own ethnic traditions into the homes of upper-class Anglo-Americans. While visitors may not come expecting such stories, house museum staff may be surprised to find that the humanity depicted by these everyday subjects is of great interest. In his review of the Lower East Side Tenement Museum for the *Journal of American History,* Charles Hardy III noted, "By crossing the boundaries of ethnicity and class, public and private, past and present, the museum has the potential, as Gary Kulik wrote in his 1992 report to the American Association of Museums, 'to be not just another museum, but to be part of a watershed moment in the history of museums.'" The museum's active role in its community makes it a model site not just for interpreting diversity but also as an advocate for social action. The Lower East Side Tenement Museum is one of the best examples of how social history has influenced historic preservation and provided a method for depicting historic houses as complex places where race, ethnicity, class, and gender intersect.[40]

The evolution of historic house museums functioning from shrines to sites of social relevance has not been a linear progression. As Eichstedt and Small found during their visits to plantation museums, the tendency to hold on to less complicated stories that valorize "great men" and whiteness still exists, even now that the "new social history" is no longer so new. Historic house museum staff members are finding that the need to provide unique and engaging visitor experiences may require change in their organizations. The Lower East Side Tenement Museum is a unique institution, but its commitment to relevance may be adopted by any historic house museum. For many sites, the stories of domestic servants have allowed them to provide new experiences and relevance to a broader audience.

Interpretation of Domestic Service at Post–Civil War House Museums

In 1986, Patricia West, a curator at Lindenwald, President Martin Van Buren's home in upstate New York, published the initial "charge" for house museums to begin investigating their domestic servants and presenting their stories in educational programs. Over twenty years later, many museum professionals have echoed her recommendation and followed through with research on domestic servants, new tours, and special programs. In 2003, I conducted a nationwide mail survey to find out how significant domestic service has become in house museum interpretation and to what extent the new social history had influenced the content of tour material. I found that domestic service has become a more regular part of the standard guided tour, but the information I gathered from my respondents suggests that greater complexity and more nuanced interpretations are still needed.

At Lindenwald, Patricia West explained, "we have introduced the house servants, young Irish women, into our interpretive program. This raises the issues of ethnicity, gender, class, and work, which we consider to be significant interpretative material illustrating the incorporation of 'the new social history' into a house museum." She and other staff members have published articles describing the servants who worked at the site, and explaining their approach to interpreting them. The first, written by West in 1986, introduces the idea of incorporating social history into house museum interpretation. The bulk of the article is dedicated to describing how sites can conduct research to illuminate the lives of servants, ranging from site-related archival material to public documents such as the census. Other general primary sources such as household manuals illustrate the way work was to be done or suggest the proper relationship between servants and employers. West did not explain how Lindenwald staff has coped with the challenge of sensitive issues such as gender, race, and ethnicity, something that would have provided readers with useful advice on a difficult subject.[1]

In 1992 West published a more detailed article about domestic servants at Lindenwald. Her article puts the site and its household staff in their historical contexts. She draws from two significant social histories, Faye Dudden's *Serving Women* and Daniel Sutherland's *Americans and Their Servants,* to describe the duties of servants at Lindenwald and in domestic service generally. She also includes the names and ages of the site's predominantly Irish servant staff. Instead of providing advice for the house museum looking for ways to reinterpret its site, this essay introduces the servants at Lindenwald and their world. In doing so, it models the results of a successful research endeavor that can be the basis for interpretive programs.[2]

Five years later, Jim McKay and Gregg Berninger, rangers at Lindenwald, concisely described the visitor's experience of domestic service in the NPS publication *Cultural Resource Management.* Their article provides a walk-through of five areas directly related to servants (although the authors acknowledge that most rangers make reference to servants throughout the house): the servants' dining room, kitchen, laundry room, cook's bedroom, and servants' staircase. In some of these areas, the focus is on specific tasks: putting a hand in the oven to gauge the temperature or using the Italian ruffle iron to maintain President Van Buren's fancy clothing. In the servants' dining room, rangers introduce the Irish servants and the impact of the potato famine on American immigration. They use the architecture of the servants' areas to discuss working and living conditions. They point out the proximity of the cook's bedroom to the kitchen, and the challenges created by the eighty-eight-step spiral staircase, which female servants wearing long skirts used many times a day to move items throughout the house. The authors do not indicate in this brief article whether they discuss the way servants interacted with one another or their employers.[3]

The example set by Lindenwald likely spurred the growing and steady interest in domestic service interpretation. Publications on house museum management and tours began advocating for interpreting both sides of the household. Sherry Butcher-Younghans's *Historic House Museums* (1993), a comprehensive reference for house museum care, preservation, interpretation, and management, advises to avoid "presenting a romanticized view of the house and events surrounding it, or elevating the former residents to the stature of 'great men and women.'" Butcher-Younghans recommends that interpretation be broad and include servants, slaves, gardeners, and chauffeurs, among others. The authors of recent interpretation manuals for historic house museums, *Great Tours!* (2001) and *Interpreting Historic House Museums* (2002), call attention to the importance of servants and enslaved people in house tours. Each offers practical advice about starting new interpretive programs, and recommendations for training guides to address controversial topics. An NPS bulletin, "Telling the Stories" (2000), instructs interpretation planners to embrace controversy by noting that "interpretation that avoids difficult subjects presents an unrealistic and ultimately uninteresting view of the past." Two recent essay collections focusing on preserving and interpreting women's history include articles that specifically address ways that domestics can be integrated into tours and special programs. Clearly, the interpretation of domestic service has gained many advocates, and their voices have become even louder over the past fifteen years.[4]

In October 1994, the National Trust for Historic Preservation presented a one-day conference for historic site staff entitled "The View from the Kitchen." The session attracted historical society and house museum personnel from across the country. Lectures by historians of domestic service provided the necessary context for understanding household work between the mid-1800s and mid-1900s. Barbara Carson, a historian and material culture specialist, addressed how the history of domestic service can figure in the presentation of objects typically associated only with the owner families, a technique she calls "perspectivist interpretation." Speakers gave advice on how to research domestic servants, warning that museum professionals need to get used to working with "fragmentary evidence." Conference participants divided into smaller groups later in the day to work with museum professionals, including Christy S. Coleman, then director of African-American Interpretation and Presentation at Colonial Williamsburg; Meggett Lavin, curator of education and research at Drayton Hall in Charleston, South Carolina; and Sandra Mackenzie Lloyd, the curator of education at Cliveden in Philadelphia. These group leaders presented examples of first- and third-person interpretation and new approaches that better acknowledge the presence and activities of servants. The day's final event was the screening of *Freedom Bags,* a documentary produced by Elizabeth Clark-Lewis, whose oral histories of former black domestics in Washington, D.C., became the core of the film and her book *Living In, Living Out.* Participants received an annotated bibliography of domestic service scholarship and copies of information sheets completed by attendees describing how their sites interpreted domestic service. Those who could not attend had the opportunity to order audio tapes of the lectures from the National Trust. Articles about the workshop in the National Trust's periodical, *[Historic] Preservation,* and the AASLH's *History News* summarized the proceedings of the event, further raising the profile of the subject matter. By providing an overview of the history of domestic service and practical suggestions from other colleagues, "The View from the Kitchen" was not only a rich resource for sites anxious to incorporate the stories of servants, but an indication of the growing importance of the topic to house museum professionals.[5]

Interest in the subject also seems to have penetrated museum studies on the graduate level. Patricia Chambers Walker's master's thesis, "A More Complete History: Interpreting Domestic Servants at Historic House Museums," investigated whether servants are interpreted at house museums, how the site is used in such interpretations, whether domestic servants are interpreted separately or in conjunction with the house owners, to what extent servant life is discussed beyond their work, and the difficulties of developing and implementing this type of interpretation. She based her conclusions on the results of a nationwide mail survey of house museums interpreting all periods, and visits and interviews with personnel at the National Trust sites. She found that although 81.8 percent of sites capable of interpreting servants do include information about domestic staff in their tours, the amount of material varies. At some sites, servants are discussed only anecdotally; at others, they inspire a major interpretive theme. Most fall somewhere in between. She also assessed the depth of servant interpretation according to the inclusion of work and living conditions and personal aspects of servant life, such as family life, leisure activities, or conflict with employers or other servants. Based on these criteria, she found that 68.4 percent of sites interpreting domestic service did so "in-depth." Of those sites classified as such, sites interpreting slavery were more than twice as likely to interpret conflict between servants and their employers or other servants. They also provided more information about leisure activities and family life than did their counterparts at sites interpreting free servants. Based on Walker's survey, slave sites seem to have been doing a better job of putting the world of enslaved people into a broader context by defining them outside of their work roles. At sites interpreting free domestic workers, interpretation seemed to relate primarily to workers as laborers and generally avoided discussing ethnicity and related prejudices. Walker's research identified several factors that hinder the interpretation of servants, such as lack of documentary evidence and/ or artifacts, inadequate finances and staff to conduct research, or servants' rooms that are closed to the public or are no longer extant. Walker found that most sites experienced little resistance to interpreting domestic servants from staff, board members, guides, or visitors. Her research clearly established that house museum staff are generally aware of the need to research and interpret domestic servants, that the amount of attention the subject receives is variable, and that the lack of documentary and artifactual resources is considered a significant challenge to developing new interpretation.[6]

The publications, workshops, and findings of Walker's survey mentioned above illustrate that efforts to incorporate race, gender, and class into house museum interpretation intensified during the 1990s, and they suggest that including domestic servants in tours has become relatively common. However, these developments raise further questions about how material about servants is presented and received "on the ground." Having worked in the historic house museum field for more than a decade, I know well that programs that sound good on paper and at workshops often perform much differently and usually require revising and retooling before they are effective with visitors. Thus, I also sought to supplement the written ruminations of scholars by soliciting direct testimony about domestic service interpretation from others responsible for developing this material and overseeing its use. To collect information from a broad spectrum of house museums in terms of geography and staff size, like Walker, I conducted a nationwide mail survey of house museums that interpret periods after 1865. I also visited several house museums, generally representing the same interpretive periods, to assess firsthand the influence of the new social history on these institutions. Thus, I assembled a quantitative and qualitative assessment to refine what has commonly been only anecdotal information shared through informal networks.[7]

While Walker's survey included sites interpreting all historical periods, I limited mine to post–Civil War interpretation. In doing so, I created a sample that would share specific historical contexts. My own research on domestic service focuses on the late nineteenth and early twentieth centuries, which motivated the decision to narrow my field according to time period. Some of the issues I selected to address as topics of significance to house museum interpretation are influenced by post–Civil War developments, such as the use of domestic technology, the "servant problem," and ethnicity, which saw regional changes during this period of "new" immigration and the Great Migration.

In addition to building on the social history themes addressed in Walker's study, I also wanted to investigate the presence of artifacts and archival materials related to servants. Walker found that among the most frequently cited reasons for not interpreting domestic service was lack of archival information and artifacts relevant to domestic servants. Anyone familiar with researching a site's domestic servants understands the many gaps in family and public documents. Most families whose homes have been opened to the public did not leave extensive collections of account books or other documents that typically identify servants. Given the transitory nature of domestic service, personal belongings of their employees normally did not remain among their employers' possessions. Furnishings for servants' rooms tended to be simple, inexpensive pieces that the house's owners did not see fit to keep, or that were discarded during the transition from private residence to public site. However, my site visits and personal experience researching Brucemore's servants indicated that some house museums do have access to extraordinary materials, and those that don't may still manage to develop engaging ways to educate visitors about social and class divisions within the household. I hoped my survey would identify interpretive themes that could be adapted by house museums wishing to interpret domestic service. Understanding the materials that are typically available was particularly valuable to this effort.

The data and methodologies of earlier surveys, especially Walker's, and my experiences with interpreting servants at Brucemore led to the big questions of my survey: given that domestic service is increasingly a part of house museum tours, how critically are the concerns of social history, particularly race, class, and gender, presented in this interpretation? Many sites have stated their intentions to create more accurate and diverse interpretations, but how many have been able to follow through with this goal? The potential exists for house museums to present an interpretation of domestic service that is rich in detail despite limited site-specific information. With some notable exceptions, themes focusing on race/ethnicity, class, and gender were not found to be significant themes in house museum tours. Respondents offered many compelling reasons for their absence and recognized the importance of interpreting domestic servants. Given my respondents' perception of a high level of visitor interest in the topic, further refinement of this interpretive theme should be a goal for all house museums, and it may be achieved by developing a more sophisticated approach to interpreting the servants' work that is already a substantial part of most domestic service interpretation.[8]

My survey yielded quality information from sites of all sizes and regions. Many respondents wrote detailed comments; some sent brochures, guide training material, and photographs or biographical information about their servants. In retrospect, I better understand the limitations of the survey and some of its questions. The choices provided for some questions should have included "unknown," a category I created during the coding process, since many wrote it in. Some questions could have been more specific, such as the one that asked respondents to identify the ethnicities of servants. I included as one choice, "We do not know the ethnic backgrounds of any of the servants who worked at our site." As I received completed surveys I realized that using "any" as a qualifier was too limiting. A better alternative would have been, "We do not know the ethnic backgrounds of *all* of the servants who worked at our site." Some respondents crossed out "any" and wrote in "all," and others marked the selection in addition to specific ethnicities. When compiling the data, I distinguished between sites that did not know the ethnicities of any of their servants and those who have some information about them.[9]

At the beginning of the survey, I included the following definitions to clarify my use the terms *standard tour* and *domestic servants* or *servants*. Identifying the meaning of the term *standard tour* seems to have helped, since many respondents did differentiate material about servants that was presented only during special tours or programs. The word *servant*, however, prompted some interesting responses:

> I would say very little is pertinent to our area—no one here would ever have considered themselves "servants"—day laborers, yes—wage earners, yes— "maid"—perhaps; *housekeeper*, yes. However, many old timers today served wealthier residents and retirees.

> "Maids" and "chauffeurs" in our town were not really servants.

> [It] would probably be better to refer to them as workers not servants. They were treated as employees and not in the typical manner of domestic servants at the time. They were helpers of a man with a large house and were not seen as beneath him or his guests.

The term *servant* was problematic during the historical periods in question, and evidently modern guides and visitors still struggle with its connotations. Many American-born women objected to the term and were sensitive to the stigma it carried in society. The word has slightly different baggage in the South. At antebellum plantations, tour guides often refer to slaves euphemistically as servants. Jennifer Eichstedt and Stephen Small identify this practice as a form of symbolic annihilation, but guides defend it as being more historically accurate, because that was the word used by many masters. Eichstedt and Small refute the legitimacy of this claim by explaining that "the euphemism was used in the past because the reality of the situation was too ugly to be directly faced; this does not seem like a good reason to continue its use today." One of Walker's respondents also indicated that former domestic employees were sensitive to use of the term *servant*.[10]

Servant remains a complicated term, and although I would not avoid using it for that reason, perhaps some guides would be more comfortable using it in conjunction with terms they find less demeaning. *Help* and *hired girl* were commonly used. While it is a more appropriate term for early-nineteenth-century domestic workers, in many rural areas or smaller towns, the relationship it suggests persisted longer than in urban areas. *Domestic* is also an appropriate term for the late nineteenth and early twentieth centuries, as are the specific job titles *maid, cook,* etc. For sites that interpret into the mid-twentieth century, *domestic employees* or *domestic staff* may be more appropriate. Guides can also address the semantic issue directly, the approach taken by Maymont House's exhibition "In Service and Beyond: Domestic Work and Life in a Gilded Age Mansion." The gallery guide for the exhibition notes, "In different periods and regions, various terms have been applied to household laborers: 'servants,' 'domestics,' and 'help.' Over time, American domestic workers have generally rejected the title 'servant,' preferring instead specific titles such as 'cook' or 'butler,' or simply to say that they worked 'in service.'"

One phrase that some respondents seemed to have found unfamiliar is the "servant problem." As I will describe in more detail in later chapters, women frequently used this phrase to describe their difficulty hiring and keeping good servants. This item had the highest number of "no answer" responses in the section of rated topics. If the phrase had been defined, it might have been skipped less often and generated some written comments.

I organized the survey to gather four categories of information: the makeup of the site's current personnel, its servants (number, positions, ethnic background), the interpretation of servants, and reasons for not interpreting domestic servants. The first section, "Your Site," was to collect basic information about house museum staff size and employment status (full- or part-time, paid or volunteer), age of institutions, and interpretive themes. The information I received provides a rich overview of the sample's basic resources.

One piece of information I endeavored to collect was the year that the site opened to the public. Writing about interpreting servants at Lindenwald, Patricia West in 1986 stated that because it was a new institution, its curators began with a blank slate. A 1989 AAM survey, "Museums Count," indicated significant growth in the number of historic sites and history museums in the second half of the twentieth century, with 60 percent of the former being established since 1960. Over one-fourth (27.7%) of house museums responding to this question in my survey opened between 1970 and 1979, the most frequently cited year being 1976 (thirteen opened that year). Over half (56.3%) opened in the post–Civil Rights era (1970 and after). It is reasonable to assume that many of these institutions would be more sensitive to more diverse approaches to interpretation, and their staff more likely to have been exposed to social history as college students. However, given that the greatest number opened during the bicentennial decade, it is equally probable that many founders had celebratory goals in mind. A later question that addresses when sites began interpreting domestic service indicates that the most significant periods for the integration of servants' stories were the 1980s and 1990s.[11]

Staff size is frequently cited as a hindrance to including more information about domestic service. Most sites have few paid or volunteer staff with the time to devote to the requisite research. A survey of historic house museums conducted by Peggy Coats in 1989 found that 72 percent of institutions had on average fewer than two full-time staff. Respondents to my survey reported a range from zero to 250 full-time employees; 17.9 percent indicated they had no full-time paid staff. The median full-time staff size was two, and the most frequent responses were one and two (each with fifty-eight). More than one-third (38.9%) of all sites have one to two full-time staff; nearly another third (30.4%) have between three and ten full-time staff, which suggests that average staff size increased slightly since Coats's survey. Two hundred fifty-six respondents reported the size of their part-time staff, which ranged from zero to 200, with a median size of two and the most frequent response being one. Seventy-two percent of all respondents had four or fewer part-time staff. Thus, the average house museum has a total of one to four employees, full- and part-time. Even for a small site, this level of professional staffing is severely limiting, particularly during lean economic times when finding potential sources of income becomes even more crucial, and more effort must be put into securing funding. The lack of adequate staff is among the concerns behind the current sustainability discussion.[12]

Volunteers have played a critical role since the beginning of the preservation movement. Like Ann Pamela Cunningham, many women and men fought to save landmark residences of local and national significance. Volunteers tend to be heavily involved with these house museums after they open to the public, either as paid or volunteer staff or as tour guides (interpreters). It is not an exaggeration to claim that without the work of volunteers, most house museums would have to close their doors or would not have opened them in the first place.

Respondents highlighted the importance of volunteers as a labor source and reported a range of involvement, either full- or part-time. Over two-thirds (69%) have no full-time volunteers, and 19 percent have one or two working in this capacity. A site run fully by volunteer workers has many challenges, the least pressing of which might be gathering information about domestic service. One respondent noted that their site "is managed by volunteers and we lack the necessary guidance to present an interesting interpretation of domestic service."

Part-time volunteers are often the backbone of historic house museums. Half of my respondents (50.3%) have twenty or fewer part-time volunteers, ranging from one to over a thousand. Sites with part-time volunteer staffs in the hundreds are not unusual, and they tend to have bigger and more specialized professional staffs and gardens or large grounds, and/or they host large special events or rentals. The number of hours put in by a volunteer can also vary greatly. Some are "regulars" who work a specific shift weekly; others do only seasonal work or particular tasks a handful of times a year. Of all staff and volunteer categories, more sites were likely to have at least one part-time volunteer than any other position. These large numbers of volunteers suggest a need for free labor, but also indicate public interest in these museums.[13]

Guiding tours is one of the most common volunteer jobs. Whether to use paid or volunteer guides has long been a subject of debate in house museum circles (some use both). Paid guide positions are usually low-wage and are likely to draw college students (the seasonality of house museum visitation is convenient for students needing summer jobs), middle-class individuals looking to supplement their household income, and retirees. In their manual *Great Tours! Thematic Tours and Guide Training for Historic Sites,* Levy, Lloyd, and Schreiber highlight the advantages of paid guide staff. For example, they tend to work more regular and frequent hours than volunteers, which gives them more opportunities to hone their skills, connect with professional staff, and stay apprised of the latest site research. Paid guides are also more accountable, especially when changes are made to the interpretation. One disadvantage the authors did not mention is that sites who hire guides for seasonal help may not be able to retain them for the next season. Since volunteers are not paid and typically have long-standing relationships with the institution, it can be easier to keep them involved throughout the year.[14]

Volunteer guides sometimes require more supervision and training, but they can also be very effective. They are more likely to be retirees and available during the workday; those with full-time jobs can take only weekend shifts. Many volunteers enjoy the opportunity to spend their free time in what are usually beautiful places where they are allowed special access. Some have specific interests in history, antiques, or other types of material culture. Their desire to give time and their typically passionate interest in the site can make volunteers successful guides. They are a self-selected group, so they usually enjoy working with the public. Some of the best are retired teachers who carry their classroom experience into their work with the public.

Working with guides, paid or volunteer, can be challenging when the professional staff modifies the interpretive material. While guides trained after the "change" have few problems, the habits of longtime staff or volunteers (some likely to be "charter" volunteers, given the number of house museums that have opened in the past thirty years) are more difficult to influence. Many continue to dwell on the way the house used to be (especially if restoration has occurred since they started guiding) and focus too heavily on how and why it was changed, a problem identified by some critics of Colonial Williamsburg, due to several interpretive overhauls during its seventy-year history. While I agree in principle with this critique made by Handler, Gable, and others, they do not consider that these situations also provide opportunities to educate the public about preservation. Guides should be knowledgeable about specific restoration projects and basic preservation issues to help steer them from the nostalgia to the interpretive benefits of the restoration.

Occasionally, guides are stubborn in their resistance to change. While survey respondents indicated that guides respond very well to including material about servants, one respondent noted "retraining volunteers—next to impossible" as a hindrance to interpretation of domestic service. Another concurred: "We receive no city funding and it is a challenge just to find volunteer docents to keep the house open, much less to require docents to adhere to a specific interpretive plan. Many docents prefer the 'Great Man' approach to the owner's life, others are interested only in the aesthetic house (fine furnishings and architecture)."

A large majority of survey respondents have more volunteer guides than paid. Only one-fourth (26%) have paid guides exclusively, one-third (33.4%) have volunteer guides exclusively, and slightly more than a third (37.7%) have both. Of the last category, 70 percent have more volunteer than paid guides. Historic house museums depend considerably on the work of volunteer guides who provide their primary interpretive product. Only 2.9 percent have no guides, most likely relying on a self-guided tour. Since the guided tour is the essence of most visits to historic house museums, it is important for site staff to understand the strengths and limitations their guide staff may have regarding the interpretation of domestic service or other social history themes.[15]

To close the questionnaire's first section, I asked respondents to share their sites' interpretive themes. Given the wide variety of people, places, and events connected with historic houses, the responses revealed a diverse array of subjects and themes. However, several trends did emerge. Many reflect the traditional or celebratory approaches to historic site interpretation: the lives of the owners or famous residents, arts and architecture, "upper-class" and "well-to-do" lifestyles, and specific periods (most often the Victorian or Gilded ages). Other themes show evidence of social history's influence: local and state history, "everyday life," domestic life (including that of slaves and free servants), women's history/suffrage, and gender roles.

The information provided by respondents in the first section of the survey indicates a growing maturity in the historic house museum field. Personnel resources, although still very small, seem to have grown slightly in the past fifteen years. A large number of new historic house museums opened in the 1970s, and they have become more likely to have staff with advanced history degrees, given the decline in academic jobs. Interpretive themes, while still traditional, are moving, like preservation, from the sacred to the socially relevant.

The questionnaire's second section asked respondents to provide basic information about servants that had worked at their site and whether they had information about them. I also asked about the resources they had available for interpreting domestic service, the significance of specific servant-related themes in the standard tour, and guide and visitor reactions to servant material. Four-fifths (80.1%) of the respondents reported the presence of servants during their interpretive periods. The western and the noncontiguous states had the lowest percentages of house museums where servants had been present, a pattern consistent with the historical distribution of servants. Roughly one-third of respondents reported one to three servants, one-fifth between four and six, one-sixth (14.4%) seven to twenty, and a very small number of sites with more than twenty. That the greatest number had one to three servants reflects servant populations in the nineteenth and early twentieth centuries, when the average household with servants employed only one, and occasionally two. The total percentage of all one-servant households was likely higher circa 1900 than that of my survey sample, since the type of homes traditionally preserved as museums tend to be those of wealthier families with larger servant staffs. The house museums in my survey, though, do represent a full range of sites that would have employed servants, and those with large staffs do not dominate my sample.[16]

In multiple-servant households, each person performed specific duties according to his or her position within the backstairs hierarchy. Responses to question 3 regarding the types of specialized servants at each site continue to illustrate diversity among the responding sites. The most frequently employed servant was the cook, a common addition as middle-class families climbed the social ladder. Gardeners and maids-of-all-work were the second-most common, followed by chauffeurs. Equally noteworthy is the list of "other" workers written in by respondents, which include relatively common servants like laundresses, seamstresses, house-men or handymen, and very specialized employees (not all of which were probably considered "servants"), including tennis professionals, organists, security personnel, and animal caretakers.

Respondents were asked to describe their servants using a list of ethnic backgrounds representing the most common working in domestic service according to the 1900 census. I provided the option of marking "unknown" or writing in other ethnicities. Domestic servant populations differed regionally according to immigration patterns. Although the young Irish woman represented the stereotypical servant girl, this was the reality primarily in the Northeast. African Americans made up the majority of domestic servants in the South, Scandinavians and Germans were common in the Midwest, and Chinese and Japanese men in the Pacific Coast states. In general, immigrants made up the majority of domestics regardless of their ethnic background, but awareness of prejudices against specific ethnicities in certain regions is important for a more accurate depiction of the household's social context.

Nearly three-fourths of the respondents (72.9 percent) reported some interpretation of domestic servants. Modest regional differences did emerge, particularly sites in the midwestern and Plains states being less likely to interpret servants, while northeastern and Pacific Coast states were more likely to do so. Some respondents marking "yes" for question 6 identified their interpretation of servants as limited or very general: "[Yes] but not in great detail, only as a reminder that they were present"; "We discuss slavery and describe the work of the house slaves but we don't focus very much on servants after the Civil War"; "It's not interpreted, but we show a maid's room and lightly mention other aspects. At Christmas it is stressed during a special open house"; "Mention is made of servant areas in the house. No great deal is given on standard tour"; "It is not stressed, but if guests inquire we tell them"; "Minimal—there is mention of where the servants' quarters were, the kitchen is part of the tour and mention is made of the floor and wall-mounted buzzers that rang in the servants' quarters."

These and other comments illustrate very incidental discussions of servants, namely, that they are "mentioned." Of the above comments, the most interesting specifies additional emphasis on servants during a Christmas open house, although the respondent did not indicate what this entailed. Another site includes a first-person interpretation of the Gilded Age housekeeper during Christmas programs. One might assume that if the material is available for a special program, it could also be incorporated into the everyday tour. The question the Christmas open house raises is whether the servants depicted during that event are used to create a more realistic depiction of holiday celebrations or if they are playing primarily decorative roles.

This section established the basic characteristics of the sites that participated in my survey and shows that the servants who worked in these homes were similar to what has been determined to be "typical" in the period following the Civil War. The survey allowed me to collect data from a sample that represents domestic situations in a variety of socioeconomic levels. The positions for which families hired help were typical based on the small sizes of servant staffs in the middle- and upper-middle-class homes. Cooks and gardeners supplemented maids-of-all-work as families climbed the social ladder. The ethnic backgrounds of servants represent the regional differences based on immigration and settlement patterns. For the majority of survey participants, these servants were now present in the sites' interpretive tours.

The questionnaire's section entitled "Interpretation of Servants at Your Site" offered respondents the opportunity to provide detailed information about their approach to interpreting domestic servants. My goal was to learn more about the resources available at historic house museums, the extent to which specific social history themes are present in their interpretation, the reactions of guides and visitors to this material, and the nature of special programs that offer visitors an in-depth examination of domestic servants.[17]

Respondents overwhelmingly identified third-person interpretation as the technique used at their site, which underscores the significance of the guided tour in most visitors' experience of house museums. Several indicated the use of first-person interpretation, most often for special programs only, many of which feature servants as main characters: "Educator does living history presentation of a maid with [the] maid's real life daughter to groups (also used as a school program)"; "We did a 1st person program once—it was well received—we interpreted maids, chauffeur, cook"; "1st person interpretation of butler, seamstress, cook, maid (also done for school groups)"; "1st person program called 'Tales of a Chauffeur' offered a few times during the season."

Such first-person interpretations have been used both to portray the lives of actual servants—the most innovative being the first example, which involved a descendant of one of the site's domestic workers—and "generic" servant types. The latter are usually easier characters to develop. In some cases, interpreters use the name and biographical information of an actual servant and extrapolate his or her work and behavior from period sources. Handler and Gable's discussion of conjecture and authenticity also applies to "generic" servant characters: emphasizing that the characterizations of the servants are based on speculation, and those of the family on "facts," tends to undermine the credibility of the former. If a servant is interpreted in first person alongside the lady of the house, visitors should be reminded that both characters may be based on specific "facts," but each incorporates some amount of conjecture.

Although servants may be interpreted in any room of a house museum, most often it occurs in their own work and living areas. Thus, the ability of visitors to enter or view these rooms makes a significant impact on the amount of information they receive about domestic servants. Five-sixths (84.8%) of respondents that interpret domestic service as part of the standard tour have servant rooms open to the public; of these, three-fourths (76.5%) indicated that some or all are period rooms. These rooms include: the kitchen, servants' bedrooms, butler's pantries, general pantries and other storage areas, laundry rooms, and servants' halls and stairs. Rooms in the servants' wing are typically low-priority on restoration schedules, but as house museums complete critical projects, such as stabilizing the structure and significant restorations, the increased interest in servant interpretation, kitchens, laundries, and servants' bedrooms encourages sites to pay more attention to formerly neglected spaces. My survey research revealed that at that time, for each category of servant room, the majority had been restored to reflect their use by servants.

The servants' room visitors most commonly see is the kitchen, mentioned by nearly 150 of the 190 sites interpreting servants; nearly half are presented as period rooms. Responses to other questions about artifact collections and the interpretation of work and technology explain the prominence of the kitchen as a location for discussing domestic service. The kitchen provides excellent opportunities for interactive and first-person interpretation programs and demonstrations, which tend to be very popular with visitors. Cooking tools, equipment, and historical packaging from food and household products often can be acquired at auctions and antique stores, making kitchens ideal candidates for restoration.

The order in which visitors see the family and servant rooms also has a significant impact on the experience of the site. Tour flow at most historic sites privileges the owner families. Visitors are greeted at the main entrance as a guest would have been during the interpretive period. Guides show rooms on the family side first, which can diminish the tour of the servants' area, particularly if there is little time left by the time the group reaches it. This is the predominant visitor experience, but some respondents indicated a willingness to try different approaches. One site noted that they had recently reversed their tour flow to create a different visitor experience: "Our tour was changed in the last few years from entering the house through the front formal entrance to entering from the corn barn to the back working porch/stoop (where slaves & servants worked & etc.) to the kitchen where this theme continues." Several sites have created traffic patterns that make it either difficult or impossible to avoid the domestic side of their story before seeing the opulent side of the house.

While servants who worked in the main house are likely the most frequently discussed, other opportunities exist for interpreting the labor of outdoor workers. Historic houses that were originally part of large country estates often included carriage houses, recreation buildings, barns, servant housing, and guest cottages. The expense of maintaining elaborate estates increased in the twentieth century, and most have been dismantled. Although these homes were once well outside the city limits, residential development has consumed much of their real estate, incorporating what were once quiet retreats into the urban landscape. While few historic estates have retained their full acreage, support buildings have survived at some. By interpreting these additional buildings, house museum staff can address the activities of gardeners, coachmen, chauffeurs, and other outdoor help, most of whom were men. Thus, gender separation in work comes to the forefront as a topic of discussion. While I did not investigate interpretation of these buildings in detail, I did want to survey their prevalence and whether visitors were able to access them. Some 43.7 percent of sites that interpret domestic servants have support buildings that are accessible to visitors. Many sites adapt these structures to serve modern uses; primarily visitor services such as exhibition and orientation areas, gift shops, and restrooms. Some sites have carriage or automobile collections open for public browsing. These buildings offer additional opportunities for interpreting the variety of duties and people performing them and should be considered in interpretive planning.

The lack of servant-related artifacts and documentary material is regularly cited as a challenge for sites desiring to interpret their domestic servants. My survey indicates that while such valuable interpretive materials are rare, they do exist. At 60.2 percent of sites with domestic service interpretation there are small artifact collections relevant to servants. By far the most common are tools and other work-related equipment. Some respondents noted that these objects were not always the actual ones used at their site, but period objects substituted for the originals. The tools represent a crosssection of the duties performed by servants and other hired workers. Kitchen tools, vacuum cleaners and other household appliances, laundry equipment, and sewing machines represent the work of house servants. Several sites own original furniture from the servants' rooms. Others noted gardening, farm, and stable equipment, which provide evidence of the jobs performed by outdoor workers. Several museums are lucky to have livery in their collection, which adds much to the interpretation of domestic service by illustrating the division uniforms created between the servers and the served.

One respondent rightly identified another way of interpreting servants through artifacts: "anything the [family] owned would have been cleaned by servants," a reminder that any house museum has some potential to describe the less glamorous aspects of life, regardless of the lack of personal objects owned by servants. Interpreting objects located in the owner family's rooms from both perspectives also takes into consideration the power of objects. When a collection includes only objects related to the owner family, the lack of such items connected to the servants may make them seem less "real" unless the artifacts are interpreted from the point of view of all who had associations with them.

A handful of sites are fortunate to have a personal item or two that had belonged to a servant. Personal artifacts like prayer books, cards, and books formerly owned by servants can be found in some house museum collections. Two respondents provided information about servant-related artifacts that are unique or significant to the interpretation. One noted, "Items in house purchased by servants for owners on periodic trips to China—vases, dishes, embroidered hangings, bronze statues, etc."; the second, that

> We have a c. 1940 red wool Santa Claus suit worn by the chauffeur when the homeowner gave X-mas parties for village children; a small chair (extremely poor condition—not on view) returned to museum by descendant of a maid who was given it by homeowner when she left service; two chairs (in excellent condition, restored and on view) given to museum by a descendant of

friend of chauffeur who was given them by homeowner. These two chairs had been used in the main house whereas the other chair mentioned above (the one in poor condition) had been in the maid's own bedroom.

These examples illustrate the often circuitous paths that artifacts take on their way back to their original location, but more importantly, they can be used to interpret relationships between servants and their employers. The first shows servants acting in an uncommon role, as the means for procuring luxury items for their employers. It is unclear whether these were gifts for their employers given upon returning from visits to their native land, or purchases made at their request. Either situation can illustrate affection and trust between servants and employers. The materials and utility of the luxury items could also be juxtaposed with other servant-related artifacts mentioned by this respondent: "wooden yoke for carrying buckets, cleavers, rice sacks, chopping blocks, etc."[18]

Archival references to the servants of specific households are also scarce, but respondents to my survey provided examples of extant materials. Archival collections were slightly less common than those of artifacts, with 52.4 percent of sites interpreting domestic service reporting them. Photographs were mentioned most often, and references in letters, correspondence to and from servants, account books and records of servants' wages, and oral histories are also well represented. Few respondents indicated the presence of particularly unusual documents in their collections. Only one provided a detailed list of items: "Letters between servants and owners, letters written to servants by their family abroad, photos of servants and family members by themselves and with owners, WWII ration books in servants' names, Chinese books, etc." Most examples of servants' presence in the archives are from the employer's perspective. The few instances in which letters and other writings by servants have survived should be examined carefully, especially in the case of correspondence with their employers. The relationship between employer and servant may also be suggested by how employers addressed their servants and vice versa.

Oral histories of domestic servants have a significant presence in historic house museum interpretation. They were mentioned frequently, both as part of archival collections and off-site research. Since many American house museums interpret relatively recent history (within the past hundred years or so), site staff and volunteers have been able to take advantage of having people who remembered the house as a residence or workplace (or their descendants) share their stories. It was my experience at Brucemore that regardless of the connection, whether the visitor was a servant, a factory employee, or the person who mowed the lawn or delivered the paper on occasion, people usually wanted to share their connection to this historic place. My conversations with other house museum personnel suggest that this is a common phenomenon that has resulted in more complete information about servants. However, much of this material needs to be used carefully, as the memories of some interviewees may have acquired a nostalgic patina.

Since most sites have limited materials in their own collections, off-site research at libraries and historical societies is a common way of finding additional site-specific material about servants. More than half (56.5) percent of respondents have conducted such research on their domestic staffs. Many respondents cited the census and city directories as useful sources, in addition to tax records, cemetery records, and collections of family papers located off-site.

General resources, such as period etiquette manuals and women's magazines, histories of domestic service, and period newspaper articles, give site-specific material richness and texture by extrapolating how servants may have worked and lived in particular households. As Handler and Gable observed at Colonial Williamsburg, some interpreters equated enslaved African Americans with conjectural information and used it as a reason not to discuss them. However, similar educated assumptions are usually used when interpreting the owner family's story, and that fact does not diminish its impact.

The percentage of respondents that use such general information is equal to that of those who do not (48.7%). Speaking in favor of this material, one respondent explained how the complexities of domestic service could be illustrated in general terms when specific information does not exist: "[This was] a New England mill town, and we talk about the fact that given a choice, young women usually preferred the higher wages, higher status, and greater independence of working in the mills instead of working as domestic help. But we can't answer with certainty the basic questions of who, what, when, where, and why domestic service was (or was not) part of our sites." For most regions, the distribution of sites that do or do not use such material was relatively even, with the exception of the Pacific, in which 82.8 percent of sites do not use general information. One reason may be that scholarship on domestic service is heavily weighted in favor of regions east of the Mississippi.

Of five categories of general information provided, "histories of domestic service" was marked most, followed by "period etiquette" and "household manuals." Since the 1980s, social historians have published several solid histories of domestic service, covering the colonial era to the late twentieth century. Etiquette and household manuals proliferated in the Gilded Age and the Progressive Era, some featuring just one chapter or section about managing domestic servants, others book-length discussions of the issue. Regional history collections and period newspapers are less frequently consulted. The "help wanted" sections in newspapers provide a good overview of the demand for servants in specific cities, since they usually indicate the type of servant desired ("girl for general housework," cook, butler, etc.) and, occasionally, ethnic preferences. Period magazines are utilized the least, according to this group of respondents, but as I will demonstrate in later chapters, they can and should be used more extensively to address the popular image of domestic servants and the expectations of the women hiring them. Overwhelmingly (65.6%), respondents indicated that they use this information to supplement their site-specific material. Just under 20 percent indicated that general information is their primary resource for interpreting domestic servants.[19]

The fact that so many house museums do include domestic servants in their interpretation is an encouraging sign that interest in social history has made some impact on the way sites present their stories. However, simply mentioning the presence of women, minorities, and workers is only a small first step. Once sites have decided to include domestics in their interpretation, they should continually look for ways to improve the depth and sophistication of the information and its presentation.

To get a better sense of the thematic content of servant interpretation, I asked respondents to rate a series of servant-related topics in terms of their significance to their interpretation on a scale of five (5) to one (1), five indicating "very significant" and one "not significant." The intention was to include a variety of common issues, not all of which centered on the "negative" aspects of domestic service.

Given that defining servants by their duties and interpreting them in their work spaces is common, it is somewhat surprising that the difficulty of their work is not given more attention. Less than one-tenth (8.4%) rated this topic as very significant, although more (19.9%) rated it fairly significant (4). One-quarter (24.1%) indicated that this topic was not significant to their interpretation of servants. Perhaps the simplest and least controversial way of describing the duties of servants is to refer to the difficulty of the work, not necessarily in terms of skills but in its intensity and the long hours.

Unless sites have task lists in their archives, it may be difficult to provide specific examples of an average workday for the domestic staff. One respondent noted the presence of "recipes, pictures, notes to housekeeper as to what is required to set up the house in the morning" in their collection, but such documents are rare. However, one can speculate about the servants' workload by considering the size of the house, the number of residents, the number of servants and their "specialties," and the equipment available at the time. Household manuals and magazine articles provided guidelines for how to schedule the servants' workdays. While one must bear in mind that readers did not always follow this advice to the letter, these examples do provide insight into the type of workday that many women expected their servants to follow. Published reports of experiences in domestic service also support interpretation of difficulty of servants' work, both its physical and emotional impacts.[20]

Since kitchens are the most frequently included and restored servants' rooms on house tours, food preparation often plays an important part in interpreting the difficulty of servants' work. Kitchen programs are included in tours of many sites to demonstrate the preparation of period cuisine. Interpreting the difficulty of servants' work should also be a conscious effort to reveal more than the process of completing tasks or the nostalgia of the "olden days." Several issues could be explored: the number of steps required in the production of a specific dish, the physical and mental fatigue, or misunderstandings due to language barriers. A typical multicourse bill of fare from the period (or one from the site's archives, if one exists) suggests the amount of time a cook needed to prepare all the items being served and the large amount of china, silver, and crystal required to serve the meal, all of which had to be cleaned and put away before a servant could retire for the night.[21]

Several respondents elaborated on their interpretation of work and its meaning for visitors. One noted that their site was "currently in the process of revamping [a] tour which may include stronger descriptions of staff's duties." Another indicated that description of servants' work was not isolated from other information on the tour but is "interwoven with the general commentary and history." Visitor interest in servants' work manifests itself in many questions: "Visitors want to know how much labor and how many people it took to run a household with a 32 room mansion"; "We have found that such interpretation rounds out our site [interpretation] as a whole—answers many visitor questions: Who kept this place clean? Did Mrs. K do the cooking? Who took care of the gardens, etc." One respondent provided a specifically strong endorsement by visitors: "Our visitors are fascinated with the servants' work and the whole 'upstairs/downstairs' concept."

Many respondents suggested that visitor interest in the servants' work is due to their ability to relate to these duties in their own lives. Comments such as, "People can relate better to servants/working class than to wealthy," were common responses in the survey and have been made by museum professionals in various personal communications during the course of my research. The comparison is definitely a legitimate one in modern society, where most people are responsible for doing their own household labor, often in addition to demanding paid work.

Since equipment and tools were the most frequently mentioned servant-related artifacts at house museums, it follows that respondents rated "Use of domestic appliances and technology" as among the most significant topics. Close to one-fifth (18.3%) identified it as "very significant," and one-fourth (24.6%) rated it of at least average significance (3). Nearly twice as many respondents gave appliances and technology the highest rating compared to the related topic of difficulty of servants' work, which may suggest that the interpretation of appliances and/or technology focuses more on the object than on the meaning it had to those who used it.

This particular theme is more dependent on the presence of physical artifacts than others in this survey. Often, the original residents, and in some cases the early administrators of historic sites, did not find house-hold appliances or tools worth saving. While they can be described in the context of modern versions of the technology (for example, how the early electric washing machine differed from the modern version), having the physical object facilitates a more concrete interpretation. If there is evidence that the servants used vacuums, electric irons, washing machines, and other technology, it is not necessary to have *the* vacuum, iron, or washing machine (account books and bills from stores often provide such documentation) to make interpretation credible. As Spencer Crew and James Sims have suggested, use of "generic" objects is more acceptable in interpretations of nineteenth- and twentieth-century life because mass production made products accessible nationally. Such equipment is available if one has the time and is willing to look, particularly at antique stores and auctions (both in person and online), which some respondents have found to be useful sources for period objects. Volunteers and staff members interested in antiques may be willing to get involved in the search. These items are also common in the collections of county and state historical societies, whose staff might be willing to negotiate a loan in addition to joint programming or cross-promotion.[22]

The interpretation of household technology as it related to servants should take into consideration the place of servants and new appliances in the home. One can easily juxtapose the machine and the servant, with interesting results. The purchase of household appliances was often a response to the shrinking servant labor pool, either as a complete replace-ment of the human servant or as a supplement to increase productivity by reducing, not eliminating, servants. Industrial machines and Frederick

Winslow Taylor's theories of scientific management served as models for the efficiently managed home. Perhaps most significant to the machine metaphor is that women often described their servants as similarly inanimate objects, to the extent that writers in women's magazines frequently reminded their readers that servants were, in fact, human beings. When interpreting change, it is also important to ask visitors to consider what the change meant in its historical context as opposed to taking the presentist approach of "Isn't life so much better today" or encouraging nostalgia for an era of seemingly greater simplicity. From the present-day perspective, an early-twentieth-century vacuum cleaner looks like a futile tool, but in its own day, housekeepers may have found it an improvement over previous methods. Interpretations of technology should also consider the argument of Ruth Schwartz Cowan's book *More Work for Mother: The Ironies of Household Technology from the Open Hearth to the Microwave* (1983) that household technology reduced drudgery but raised expectations of cleanliness, which meant that some cleaning tasks occurred more frequently and hence did not reduce the total hours of work.[23]

The potential for historic house museums to address immigration and ethnicity is a key way for these institutions to incorporate social history into their interpretation. They provide a tangible locus for exploring the activities and relationships that immigrants participated in as they negotiated life in a new country. Only a very small number of respondents indicated that this information was completely unknown. While few sites have complete information about their servants' ethnic backgrounds, most have some, usually derived from research in census records.

Despite the availability and apparent possession of such information, as a theme it is of medium-to-low significance, according to my respondents. Just over one-tenth (12.0%) indicated that the ethnic backgrounds of servants was very significant to their interpretation, compared to nearly one-fifth (18.8%) who rated it of medium importance, and almost one-third (28.8%) who rated the theme as not significant. Information on ethnic backgrounds, if included at all, most likely is presented simply as a "fact," without any contextual background. Several respondents distinguished between the urban immigrant domestic servant and local hired girls (typically white and native-born): "In this region [New England], long before the arrival of Irish domestics, it was common to have household servants who were daughters from inland farm families"; "[W]e compare rural setting with city expectations of domestic help." The urban/rural divide is useful context for describing rural or small-town households, where the older traditions of "help" persisted longer than in the cities.[24]

Some referred to specific ethnic groups. Most first-person characters with identified ethnic backgrounds are Irish. One site indicated that a program on Irish servants was in development; another indicated that it already has a successful Halloween program interpreting the role of Irish servants in bringing this celebration to the United States. A California respondent described how the site incorporates the presence of immigrant servants into local and regional history: "We use what little we know of the Chinese servant at our site to interpret the larger concept of the history of the small Chinatown in our city and the general history of the Chinese immigration to the West." Two sites related stories about Japanese servants that illustrate acceptance and prejudice. In one, the servant came to the United States with $1 and died a millionaire; the second tells of a Japanese couple who went back to Japan to avoid internment during World War II.

The interpretation of race and ethnicity presents some challenges at sites interpreting free domestic servants. A Virginia site offers a focus tour on domestic service that addresses the difficulties of African Americans during the Jim Crow era. The difficulties of interpreting race prompted a thoughtful comment about the interaction of guides and visitors: "It is a rather sensitive issue. I personally have a harder time discussing the servants' roles with African-American visitors—not because I don't think I should—but because I want to be sensitive to their feelings on the subject." Addressing the lower status of immigrant servants can also be tricky. At many homes with large servant staffs, the ethnicity of servants influenced backstairs hierarchies. British butlers and French ladies' maids were important symbols of status both upstairs and downstairs, while others, particularly servants who arrived as part of the "new immigration," had low social positions even among their peers. In communities where a specific ethnic identity is predominant, guides might find the interpretation of hierarchy and prejudice among immigrant servants more difficult.[25]

Overall, answers to this particular question and one later in the survey concerning special programs seem to indicate that while information about ethnic backgrounds of servants might have a limited place on a standard house tour, special focus tours and programs investigate this issue in greater depth. For some house museum professionals, the desire to address immigration is serious, but there is little opportunity for follow-through: "I studied immigration history in grad school concentrating on domestic service so if there were a way to include it—I would!"

Working conditions were rated slightly higher in significance than the work itself, with nearly one-third (32.4%) indicating it very significant (5) or fairly significant (4) (23.0%). This broad category incorporates work spaces and equipment in addition to the ways employers treated their staff. It may also be more fully treated than work itself because it relies less on object collections. A house with a relatively intact servants' wing usually has enough architectural information to assess the nature of physical working conditions. The size of kitchens, laundries, and workrooms, their location (e.g., attic, main level, or basement), and the number of windows and amount of natural light can indicate the basic amenities employers provided for servants' work. Sites that still have original equipment such as stoves, drying racks, indoor plumbing, and convenient cold storage can address working conditions on a deeper level in conjunction with the emergence of new technology.

The servants' stairs are also a powerful physical experience. These narrow, steep staircases tend to make profound impressions on visitors and their ability to consider some very basic factors of servant working conditions. While allowing visitors to use these stairways is the ideal experience, when this is not possible (because of accessibility or safety) being able to look up or down these staircases can suffice. Wear patterns on stair treads and banisters are also evocative. At Historic New England's Phillips House in Salem, Massachusetts, the site manager once drew my attention to the presence of black marks along the bottom of the door connecting the second-floor servants' stair landing and the family side of the house. These appear to have been made by shoes kicking the door open, presumably because one's arms were full. Simple observations like this one help visitors imagine the activities that took place in now-quiet servants' wings.[26]

Respondents rated living conditions as slightly more significant than working conditions; 12.8 percent rated this theme very significant, and 24.6 percent rated it fairly significant. Living conditions can be interpreted in much the same way as working conditions by examining architectural spaces such as servants' bedrooms, dining rooms, and other amenities. These areas can be good illustrations of living conditions regardless of whether the rooms are empty or restored, because they can suggest the servants' quality of life. Even if these areas are not open to visitors, a floor plan can be used to show they are present. The amenities a family could provide its servants are usually easy to determine. The number of bedrooms compared to the number of servants can suggest the level of privacy they experienced. If a family was known to have four live-in servants, but there are only two servants' bedrooms, how might this have affected their living conditions? The presence of a common area, such as a servants' dining room, indicates that the family was sensitive to their needs to have a place to eat their own meals and to gather or invite visitors, or that the employer followed the latest advice regarding how to retain servants.

Bathroom facilities are also an important issue, since servants who had to share with their employers could face difficulties with basic hygiene. Evidence of wages and time off are important indicators of the employers' attitudes toward servants. Scanning the census for households with servants in the site's neighborhood can illustrate how it compared to peers and whether other servants lived in close proximity. The home's location can also suggest servants' access to social activities and the degree to which they were isolated from people outside of their workplace. Homes in the country, although beautiful retreats for their owners, were often shunned by servants who disliked the distance from friends and family, services like markets, and their churches.[27]

The social stigma of domestic service, a subject frequently discussed by servants and their employers in the late nineteenth and early twentieth centuries, is a relatively insignificant topic in historic house museum tours. Nearly half (45.5%) gave it the lowest rating, and only a small fraction (2.6%) gave it the highest rating. Like the term *servants,* this topic also elicited some comments from respondents: "'Stigma?' Working at our site was considered prestigious and jobs were coveted according to servant documents"; "You are making assumptions. The 'servants' were paid employees, just as the cowboys, carpenters, and hay crews. They were more known and respected within the household, but they were not an 'issue.'"

Even more than the term *servant, stigma* has a degrading connotation. However, as I will demonstrate, it was the term used in conversations about the servant problem and one reason young women avoided domestic service in favor of factory work. For Lillian Pettengill, a college graduate who worked undercover as a servant to learn why women avoided taking this job, one manifestation of this stigma was the fact that the lady of the house would not be seen in public with her servant. As an example, she relates a conversation she had with one mistress regarding whether they could walk down the street together:

> 'Why, yes, Eliza [Pettengill's servant pseudonym], of course I could walk down the street with you the same as any one else. . . . I could, only I mustn't on account of what the neighbors would say if they should see me go out with the girl. Our standards of respectability appear to be the same, and if I had met you anywhere outside, not knowing your work, I should have been glad to follow up the meeting to a closer acquaintance, if that were convenient and proved agreeable. But instead of that you come to work in my kitchen, so I can't know you outside of it. It's wrong, and foolish (of the neighbours, of society), but we have to conform, or where are we?'

Servants also found that other working girls avoided associating with their sisters in service.[28]

Some twentieth-century sites may find discussing such topics with visitors uncomfortable or even impossible if family connections to the site remain. One respondent noted: "Because we interpret fairly recent history, in an area still rural in character, we have to tread lightly. Local visitors and school children are frequently the children and grandchildren of individuals who interacted with the [owner family], including employees." Sites where descendants of the owner families are still significantly involved as trustees may also find difficulties with suggestions that their family members treated or viewed their employees as different than any other person. Interpretation of stigma also needs to be balanced with the fact that for some this position offered the means of survival in a new country. While native-born women generally avoided domestic service because of its stigma, obviously many people took these positions and performed their duties with dignity and with the hope that their children would be able to have more socially respectable jobs.

The quality of relationships between servants and employers is difficult to generalize. As one northeastern respondent explained, "Former servants gave 'mixed' reviews of their experiences. This is likely due to the level of their service and their job performance." Nevertheless, stories about interactions between server and served are key elements to satisfying site interpretation. These were complex relationships that have few modern equivalents. The employment of regular housekeepers, nannies, and maid services does provide a reference point for visitors, but it is hard for most to imagine what it would be like to live with their employer in the same house where their subordinate status is clearly visible because of their dress, access to certain spaces, living conditions, and so on.

Rather than asking respondents to rate the overall significance of "relationships between servants and employers," I used two questions to distinguish the positive from the negative. The significance of friendships rated as considerably more important than conflicts. Respondents shared some extraordinary stories about servant–employer relationships at their sites. Many noted the long tenures of particular servants and emphasized loyalty, bequests in wills, and other courtesies. One site clarified that friendships applied only to relationships between the employer and the butler, an echo of the hierarchy within the servant wing and a more accurate statement of the complexity of such social relations. Another example of the hierarchy belowstairs is evident at one site where "most top servants received a bequest from the estate owner at death. This money they invested wisely and made millions themselves." Others related stories that were less specific about the particular servants' position in the household but provided more details about the people themselves. One respondent described the employer and his Asian servant as "lifelong companions"; when the employer died, his provided his employee with life tenancy on the estate. Another noted, "Our situation is unique. The last resident of the house, a widow, engaged the services of a young African-American girl. This was part of a program administered by the County government in the early 20th century. This girl became like a daughter to the widow and remained with her until the widow's death (42 years!). She is buried in the family plot of the widow." Most of these stories indicated a close relationship between an employer and a servant in which the friendship transcended differences in race and ethnicity. Only one of my respondents specifically mentioned that servants were like "family," a statement frequently used by house museum guides to describe the intimacy of servant–employer relationships.[29]

That some servants and their employers had long-term loyalties to each other is an important point that guides can use as a starting point to address the complexities of such relationships, which are probably less evident than the surface details. Although servants working for wealthy families more often received better treatment, higher wages, and ample amenities compared to those working in middle-class homes, they were still employees relegated to separate living spaces and lower social status. As one commentator noted in 1913, "If those employed in the home were part of the family it would defeat the very purpose for which they are employed. They are employed in order to free the family for outside interests." I have no doubt that servants and their mistresses could and did experience mutually affectionate relationships. At the same time, it was not a friendship of equals. Some mistresses did take maternal interests in their servants, especially the young girls, which is a position of kindness but also power. In the conclusion of her book on domestic service at Maymont House in Richmond, Virginia, Elizabeth O'Leary astutely observes, "No matter the potential moments of understanding or possible protestations that Georgia, James, Frances, or William was 'like one of the family,' the power always remained squarely with the employer." Based on responses from this survey, experiences during site visits, and my own work experiences, stories about "positive" relationships with employers seem more likely to survive than those with a "negative" cast. I suspect this is due to the fact that stories, documents, and artifacts connected with "favorite" servants (who may have lived with and worked for the family many years) have a greater sentimental value than those of servants who came and went or who didn't have the benefit of personal interaction with their employers. Like furnishings and objects within a historic house, the stories that survive are the finest or most treasured.[30]

Conflict between servants and employers had the second-highest total ratings of "not significant" across all regions. One likely reason that this topic has not become an important part of interpretation is due to a lack of information; two respondents specifically mentioned that they did not know of any instances of conflict. If documentation of conflict exists, it often comes from references to discordant relationships with servants in the employer's letters and diaries, or it may be inferred from frequent changes of staff. At Historic New England's Codman Estate, the regular turnover of domestic staff, especially cooks, is well documented in the diaries of the lady of the house, Sarah Bradlee Codman, and in family account books. The fact that the Codmans had a hard time finding a satisfactory cook is discussed honestly when tours visit the dining room.

Unfortunately, reports from the servants' perspective are harder to find. General sources such as these written by servants or reformers working as servants (like Pettengill) suggest how they may have viewed conflicts and disagreements with their employers. These examples can be useful references to illustrate that although servant–employer relationships appear to have been amiable in that particular household, conflict was also possible. The fact that many historic house museums are former residences of the wealthy who typically had more than one servant may explain some absence of conflict. In very large households, lower servants may have had extremely limited contact with their employers, who typically communicated orders via the butler or head housekeeper. These servants probably rarely saw their mistress after the initial interview, if she was even present on that occasion.

However, relationships between servants and mistresses are not the only ones idealized at historic houses. Family relationships are typically presented with a distinct lack of everyday domestic conflict. Thomas Schlereth, professor of American Studies at Notre Dame and regular commentator on public history, has observed,

> House museums, where their histories demand it, might also reveal the marital conflicts of their former occupants such as suggested by one spouse's insistence on separate bedrooms. . . . If we know there to have been child or spouse mistreatment, alcohol or drug abuse (more widespread among 19th-century middle-class Americans than we once realized) or prolonged illness that, in turn, strongly affected life as lived in the historic house, we need to explore how best to interpret such manifestations of what social historian Gary Nash calls "the private side of American history."[31]

Schlereth's comments are now twenty years old, and for the most part there has been no widespread progress made in the interpretation of complex family relationships. Most house museum staff members probably feel uncomfortable discussing such private matters even if conflicts are documented. There may also be an aversion to appealing to the public's interest in scandals. These are both legitimate concerns, and clearly such issues need to be handled with care. When addressed in an honest but sensitive way, family difficulties can provide compelling stories for house museum interpretation.

At Castle Tucker, a Historic New England property in Wiscasset, Maine, guides describe the challenges faced by the home's owners as the Tuckers' finances declined. Richard and Mollie Tucker were well-to-do when they purchased the large Federal era "castle" in 1858, but over time their finances slowly diminished, due in part to Richard's unsuccessful business ventures and costly experiments in steam-propelled ships and to coastal Maine's changing economy. The family's extensive collection of correspondence documents conflict and complex emotional responses to the struggle to maintain the family home. One result of their economic challenges was the preservation of a nearly intact collection of Victorian furnishings and finishes, which serves as a backdrop for this story of survival. Visitors have responded positively to the Tuckers' story, perhaps because one may so easily relate to it. Ultimately, family relationships should be interpreted more candidly to contextualize the discussion of servant–employer interaction. If the only conflicts discussed on the house museum tour involve servants, visitors may come away with the idea that household discord was caused only by the servant problem.

The topic of ethnic or racial prejudice rated slightly higher than conflict overall, despite both having a high percentage of low ratings. Lack of information about or discomfort with the topic may influence the extent to which these issues are discussed. Some ethnic or racial prejudices are well known to historians, such as anti-Irish sentiment, racism based on skin color, and fear of eastern and southern European immigrants. Sites that interpret the early twentieth century should also consider the presence of nativism and its impact on society. Two regions with the most respondents rating this topic a five or a four were the southern North Atlantic states and the southern South Atlantic States, which tended to have large servant populations of Irish and African American servants, respectively.

Some respondents commented specifically on the site's interpretation of ethnic or racial prejudice, often to state that the site's servants received good treatment: "Touched on if questioned about prejudices. Servants at this house were well treated"; "*Class* prejudice too. Adult tour emphasizes the family members maintained strict social hierarchy with their help. More emphasis on *class* differences." The second comment is one of the strongest and most direct statements I received concerning the interpretation of the social structure of households with servants. Although the respondent highlighted class differences, since these were often connected with race or ethnicity it is possible that both are addressed. The first comment is probably typical of many sites in that guides are willing to broach the issue if asked but otherwise may not offer the information.

Respondents rated the earlier question regarding the ethnic backgrounds of servants much more significant than the interpretation of racial or ethnic prejudices. This suggests that although interpreters are comfortable telling visitors that servants were immigrants and divulging their country of origin, they probably say little more. If sites have information on the ethnic or racial backgrounds on some of the servants—and most evidence I collected suggested they do—then to avoid interpreting the significance of their heritage regionally and nationally eliminates an important dimension of the servants' lives. The interpretation of prejudice may be somewhat trickier in the case of white foreign-born servants, like the Irish, whose descendants have since assimilated into American culture.

As with the topic of social stigma, guides should discuss ways to approach prejudice strongly but sensitively. Again, the interpretation of slavery offers some excellent models. *Great Tours!* includes the reading "Interpreting Slavery at Historic Sites: Tips for Guides," which offers suggestions that are useful for sites seeking to address differences of any kind. The authors advise guides to present a balanced view, to find ways to emphasize the individuals who endured slavery and their personal responses to slavery. They encourage guides to "face race" and work incrementally to increase their comfort level and to embrace the complexity of the story.[32]

The final suggestion to embrace complexity is the key to interpreting any potentially controversial issues associated with domestic service, whether stigma, conflict, or prejudice. All rely on understanding the social context of the period one is interpreting and are not necessarily revealed in site-specific materials. Guides may also find it more comfortable to address these issues in the form of questions posed to their audience, not for them to answer together, but to give them something to think about after they leave the site. Freeman Tilden, whose *Interpreting Our Heritage* is a classic handbook for historic sites, suggests this approach in one of his six principles of interpretation: "The chief aim of Interpretation is not instruction, but provocation." He further states that the purpose of interpretation is "to stimulate the reader or hearer toward a desire to widen his horizon of interests and knowledge, and to gain an understanding of the greater truths behind any statement of fact." While a lofty goal, it is an excellent statement of what house museums need to do, and may be particularly effective when discussing controversial issues: be direct about the actions of people in the past, but also leave room for visitors to absorb and think through the controversy on their own. [33]

Since domestic servants were most often women, several scholars have recommended that their stories provide a way to incorporate gender into historic site interpretation. Survey respondents indicated that gender plays a moderately significant role in their interpretation. Although the majority rated the topic as not significant (29.3%), most of the remaining two-thirds rated it of average significance or higher. Discussing gender and domestic servants needs to go beyond simply adding female perspectives in the domestic realm and should address the general status of women during the period. Only one respondent, the childhood home of a famous woman, addressed the role of gender in the interpretation of domestic servants: "It fits in with the lifestyle information to form a story of [her] childhood. It is important for the development of an atmosphere during her childhood years and her feeling toward 'what women should do.'" Most of the servants that respondents mentioned in their comments were women, except for the Chinese and Japanese men present at West Coast sites. However, none of the respondents offered specific insight into how gender issues are interpreted during their tours.[34]

The "servant problem," while an important issue during its time, is for the most part absent in house museum tours. Over half of the respondents (51.8) identified the theme as "not significant." This topic was one of the more frequently skipped, which may indicate that respondents had little information about the issue or that a definition might have clarified the question. The "servant problem" was a hot topic in the period represented by many sites in my survey population. It is a broad issue that is relevant to a wide variety of sites, which I will return to later to address how it may be effectively used as an interpretive theme.

"Benefits" of domestic service is another topic that might have been well served by additional explanation. Although domestic service had many disadvantages that repelled women from this work, even some domestics argued that the position had some advantages. Despite her negative assessment of domestic service overall, Lillian Pettengill acknowledged that she did benefit from her experience, which gave her better health, greater strength, an appreciation of domestic tasks, and the ability to save money. For women who were new arrivals to the United States, domestic service provided practically immediate employment with room and board.

With few expenses to take care of, servants were able to save money easily, and many sent a substantial portion of their earnings to their families in Europe to help them emigrate. A balanced approach to interpreting domestic service can include the argument made by many women of the period (especially mistresses and reformers hoping to encourage American women to enter this line of work) that domestic service was a worthwhile pursuit. Survey respondents did not see this topic as very significant to their interpretation of domestic service; more than one-third (39.8%) gave it the lowest rating, and about one-fifth (23.6%) identified it as having medium significance.[35]

Respondents rated the topic of servants' uniforms the least significant of the thirteen. Since most sites lack photographs of their servants, some may find it too conjectural to discuss the particulars of the subject without specific evidence. The few sites that have actual livery in their collections are extremely fortunate in their ability to present a concrete example.

Livery is, however, an important issue in a thorough interpretation of domestic service. Uniforms were a divisive issue between servants and their employers. As a visual indicator of status, or lack thereof, livery drew a clear line of distinction between the mistress and her servant, regardless of how close their relationship may have been. Given the abundance of general primary source materials that feature images of uniformed servants, it is a relatively easy topic to use to interpret the social climate of the household.

Several sites indicated the use of first-person interpretation of domestic servants, so clearly some have begun to approach the issue of livery through costuming their guides. However, respondents did not indicate to what extent the interpreter incorporates the uniform's meaning into their presentation. Dressing as a servant may be a way to distinguish one character from another, as seen in historical advertisements. Since there appears to be no objection to staff interpreting in the servant's uniform, the next step is to mine its significance and use it as a tool to bring social history alive.

To get an overall impression of the significance of these thirteen topics, I calculated the average rating according to region and question. There are no clear regional trends when the data are considered as a whole; most regions' overall ratings (average for all thirteen topics) fell in the vicinity of 2.4. All but one region rated at least one topic lower than 2, which was balanced by the fact that all but one region also rated at least one topic above 3. Since all regions rated the agglomerated topics below modest significance, as a whole the majority of sites could benefit by enhancing more aspects of their domestic service interpretation. Given the difficulty of covering a lot of material on what is usually a forty-five- or sixty-minute tour, realistically, most guides will not be able to address *all* of these themes in depth on *every* tour. However, if guides learned to touch briefly on a greater variety of themes, it would result in a more nuanced interpretation of the subject matter. Many respondents indicated that there is a great interest in improving interpretation of domestic servants, and I think that as sites continue to mature, the significance of many of the lower-rated topics may increase.[36]

In terms of individual topics, those with the highest ratings concerned the use of domestic appliances and technology and living conditions (followed closely by working conditions). Both topics are easy to relate to tangible objects, which respond to the general visitor's interest in "real things." The architectural spaces can be used as support for interpreting living conditions. Uniforms, the "servant problem," and conflict between servants and employers received the lowest average ratings. While some of the lack of interest in these topics may be explained by wanting to avoid controversial issues, I think much of the problem is the lack of evidence, both physical and documentary, of their presence in the lives of the owner families. History museums and historic sites have long approached their artifact collections from an object-based, formalist perspective; the interest in the idea-based, analytical method is relatively new. However, even lack of such collections doesn't mean that potentially controversial topics can't be addressed, because there are many period sources that present this information and can be used as context. Guides who might be uncomfortable with this material may be receptive to general information about these topics as opposed to specifically attaching the issues to the owner family.

Considering the controversies that surrounded a number of high-profile museum exhibitions during the 1990s, I initially expected some respondents to mention resistance to the subject either by guides or by visitors. On the contrary, both guides and visitors have responded positively to the interpretation of domestic servants. Over three-quarters of the respondents (76.5%) indicated that guide reactions to interpreting domestic service were "enthusiastic" or "favorable." Since the survey shows a tendency to avoid the more controversial issues (prejudice and stigma, for example) in their interpretation of domestic service, it seems natural that resistance is uncommon. Sites should use the enthusiasm the topic of domestic service evokes to build their confidence and as an incentive to make the interpretation of domestic servants more intellectually challenging.

Respondents frequently commented on the reactions of guides to the material, which reveal their curiosity about domestic servants. The sites' lack of information qualified some of their responses, as one respondent noted, "Tour guides still feel relatively uninformed on this topic." Several made comments similar to one respondent's: "If information were included, I'm sure they would be very enthusiastic."

The number of sites that indicated their guides are indifferent or resistant to interpreting domestic service is low, but several respondents clarified these positions. These comments are indicative of the traditional approach to house museums that emphasizes the family, the house, and its contents: "We simply acknowledge it. They were meant to be not seen but had good relationships to the family"; and "If asked, they discuss." Other comments suggested that interest in and focus on domestic service interpretation largely depends on who the guide is, which is typical for most historic house museums: "Some are very accepting and want to know more and some are uncomfortable and want to tell only happy stories"; "A couple of volunteer guides have expressed concern about future emphasis on servants overwhelming the story of the owners. Most are positive about *expanding* interpretation"; "They like naming them and describing duties but no macro-content is provided"; "I think that most are drawn more to the comfortable and luxurious existence of the family. A number of the guides, though, are very enthusiastic about the kitchen/cook interpretation."

The comments of some respondents indicated that including information on domestic servants has generated a great deal of interest and curiosity among guides, and that over time the material becomes well integrated into their understanding of the site. "It is fascinating to our volunteer guides"; "Some began with much hesitation and anxiety, but now it seems to them that without this interpretation the tour would be incomplete"; "Our volunteers want to know more—they are willing to present the material"; "We have always included the servants' quarters and kitchen in our tours. There has really not been a reaction as it is accepted."

Several respondents added that the extent to which guides interpret domestic service also depends on the interest of visitors. For most sites, admission is a major part of their income, and the fear of alienating visitors or losing patrons can drive some decisions about interpretation and educational programs. Visitor studies has emerged as an interest among several museum professionals and most museum conferences now feature several sessions about surveying visitors and identifying audiences. This practice has been slowly adopted in the house museum field and replaces informal information gathering like talking to visitors after tours or programs and occasional unsolicited calls and letters from visitors.

Respondents to my survey suggest that visitor reactions to domestic service interpretation are overwhelmingly positive. Nearly one-fifth of respondents (18.8%) identified their visitors as enthusiastic about the subject, and over half (61.2%) found their reactions favorable. The majority of comments related to visitor responses indicate a great deal of interest: "People sometimes comment that it is good to talk about workers, not just family"; "The kitchen at our museum was converted years ago into an administration area, very often visitors ask where it was and what it was like. They clearly want to see and experience more of the domestic side of the story"; "Often questions about servant areas and why they can't see more. Public interest is very high"; "The first time we offered 'servants' tours' 1,000 people showed up for sixty-four tickets"; "Visitors seem glad to hear about the servants and slaves because there are still many places that do not interpret such topics. Some come with not much knowledge and others who are considerably well read and educated in the areas"; "[O]ur docents receive 99 percent approval ratings from visitors for their tours which cover the Jim Crow era and the civil rights movement that resulted from it." Clearly, visitors have the desire to learn more about the working side of household.

Like plantations that offer African American focus tours, some house museums have started offering tours and programs that address the lives of domestic servants or life at the site from the servant's perspective either for adults or school groups. Few respondents to my survey indicated the presence of such programs for adults at their sites, although I have had the opportunity to learn about some programs through site visits. The events mentioned for the adult audience were primarily living history events, open houses, and tours of servant areas that are not part of the standard tour. The number of sites that offer programs for school groups is also small, but more reported offerings for children than for adults.

The youth audience is an important one at house museums, as it likely is for general history museums and other historic sites. Programs for school groups are not usually financially lucrative in and of themselves but provide opportunities to give children a positive connection to the site at a young age. More importantly, the variety of innovative and engaging school programs highlights the value of house museums as teaching tools, and of all the information I collected, these programs seem to have the most solid grounding in social history. School programs have become much more than field trips and vacation days for students; most teachers use these visits as opportunities to apply classroom learning to "the real thing." As a result, museum educators have become very sensitive to teachers' needs and develop their programs to complement the local curriculum and state or national social studies standards, which often highlight the study of race, ethnicity, class, and gender.

The school programs that respondents described in their surveys fell into several categories. These include comparison activities that pair family and servant, interpretation from the servant's point of view (often using a first-person interpreter), role playing and hands-on activities, and discussions of the duties of servants. Programs that compare the lives of servants and family members often stress relationships, such as the descriptions offered by two respondents: "Both programs [Elderhostel and school groups] focus on a day in the life of the family beginning with the servants preparing food, horses, etc. and includes relationships of family to servants, background of servants, typical day for servants"; "viewing and analyzing social history from a family and servant point of view; first-person narrative—interaction and interdependence of servants and family." These remarks do not indicate what kinds of relationships the guide and students discuss (friendship, conflict, or both), but the focus on this topic is an excellent way to give equal emphasis to both parties, and it offers the opportunity to address sensitive issues inherent in these relationships.

Two other sites reported on programs that use comparison in slightly different ways. One midwestern site's program asks students to evaluate private family and servants' living spaces "in terms of gender, ethnicity, and social class." Defining the lives of servants according to living spaces as opposed to the more frequently interpreted work spaces provides the opportunity for students to understand servants as people and not solely as workers. A New York site's program addresses the differences between the lives of family and servants but also compares how the nineteenth-century servant staff cared for the mansion and how its current stewards take care of the house and its history today.

Some respondents also mentioned offering outreach programs or special school tours that focus on the servant's point of view. These programs often feature staff portraying servants, either during classroom visits or for on-site tours. Some sites provide lessons that focus on specific documented servants, as one respondent described: "We offer a segment of an outreach program which deals with [a] woman of Irish background who worked as a servant and cook in the late 19th and early 20th century (most info from an oral history interview, c. 1975)."

Programs that involve role playing and/or hands-on activities for the students address domestic service in varying levels of detail. Some highlight housekeeping, cooking, and other domestic duties and give students a taste of the physical demands these tasks made on servants. Respondents did not indicate whether the interpretation and performance of this work by the students involved more than the tasks themselves, so it is difficult to determine the extent to which the work was linked to the issues of race, ethnicity, class, or gender. A respondent from Colorado offered a more detailed example of how the site uses role playing by describing a program in which the "children are costumed as family members, servants, and others connected to the house. When we get to the room on the tour where we talk about their character, the children do a hands-on activity their character would have done." Each student receives a biography card with their character's photograph on one side along with their name, position, age, birth and death dates, and a short first-person description on the other. Four servants are part of this program: a chauffeur, maid, cook, and laundress, a group that illustrates a good variety of duties within the household. Several colleagues have mentioned developing similar programs through which students are encouraged to see the site through someone else's eyes. Some have cited the Holocaust Museum's identification cards as the inspiration for this approach.

The most direct approach to school programs with an emphasis on domestic service addresses the servants' duties. One respondent described two specific tours that highlight work: "A cook's duties—life before supermarkets—level of knowledge the cooks needed to have. Also we focus on a 'technology tour' for school students that focuses on labor-saving devices used by staff and family." Both tours offer insight into important aspects of the servant's qualifications and workday, but again, it is difficult to know whether these issues are discussed in their social contexts.

These examples of school programs illustrate that it is possible to provide experiences that have a solid grounding in social history at historic house museums. However, currently, the audience seems limited to schoolchildren, which may be explained in several ways. Many programs such as those described also involve pre-visit activities, some of which are supplied by the site and include facsimiles of archival materials. Curriculum-based programs are also likely to have concrete ties to classroom lessons. In these cases, young visitors are learning about the site before their arrival, and most likely have a debriefing session after they return to the classroom. Guides can skip the introductory information and launch right into specific, in-depth discussions with the students. In my own experience, I have had some of my best tour discussions with middle-school students who were well prepared to address some of the finer points of social history because they have the background material fresh in their minds. Since the background knowledge possessed by adult visitors is usually unknown, it can be difficult to cover much more than the surface issues during the time constraints of the regular tour. However, the programs developed for school groups could, and should, be modified for adult audiences, given the apparent interest that visitors have in servant life.

School programs are not foolproof, however. One respondent noted that some teachers don't use the pre-visit materials, so "students come unprepared and chaperones treat tour as a vacation." Another indicated that their site had offered servant-related school programs, but no teachers showed interest. Despite the difficulties that school programs sometimes create, the examples of success illustrate that some of the best learning taking place at house museums is the result of these efforts.

Respondents to my survey tended to mark multiple reasons why they do not interpret domestic service, but the most frequently marked was "This site lacks the necessary artifacts and archives to address this issue as we would like." Many respondents commented further on the difficulty of documenting domestic servants due to lack of records, scant evidence, or vague archival sources. One remark describes problems faced by most sites nationwide: "The museum archives contain a few photographs of African Americans who appear to be servants or farm hands. Hard facts concerning any details of their roles is either unavailable or inconclusive." The consensus among respondents whose sites do not interpret domestic service is that the lack of documented information is a significant reason behind their decision.

The recurring references to the need for site-specific documentation are similar to those experienced by Richard Handler and Eric Gable during their fieldwork at Colonial Williamsburg. Even though many of my respondents indicated a willingness to use general information to supplement their interpretation of domestic service, there does seem to be a stigma attached to it. For some, the use of conjecture undermines the institution's authority, as suggested by one respondent: "We simply do not know enough about domestic arrangements to say anything definite. As a university-affiliated museum, we are taken as 'gospel' and we have to be really sure of our facts before we can include anything in our tour."

The ability to find the documented information to build these tours upon is dictated by the availability of personnel and financial resources, both of which are limited at most house museums. Many respondents commented on their desire to include domestic service in their interpretation or to improve existing programs, and that their lack of resources prohibited it. Several indicated that the help of unpaid workers would be needed to jump-start research and interest in the theme: "If one docent would take the lead and incorporate servants, the rest would likely join in. We are extremely short-handed all around, so an enthusiastic docent could change things for the better"; "I think the inclusion of domestic servants is an interesting idea, but realistically it probably won't happen here unless it becomes a volunteer's 'project'"; "The household help—only a cook that we know of—is *very* poorly documented. We need either a graduate student or academic to look at two questions: the use of Chinese as domestics in California and, more specifically, how were they employed *and* who were they?" The first section of my survey documents the chronic problem of house museums being shorthanded, in that the paid staff tends to be lean and volunteers must fill in the gaps. With the baby boom generation entering retirement, historic house museums should consider how members of this group might be able to contribute to their research needs. In their article "A Golden Age for Historic Properties," John Durel and Anita Nowery Durel claim that this active group seeks ways to deepen their knowledge, and historic sites have collections and archives that may interest them. Research projects related to servants may have appeal to talented retirees willing to volunteer their time.[37]

The presence of domestic servants in house museum interpretation continues to increase, although for many sites they continue to be background characters. The inclusion of domestic servants is a nod to the new social history's emphasis on race, class, and gender; however, much house museum interpretation does not significantly address many of the complex issues a more nuanced representation of domestic life would require. While there is evidence that some aspects of discussing domestic service create resistance in interpreters or visitors, lack of resources seems to be a much greater hindrance to developing these programs. Even staff members with advanced degrees in history do not guarantee that tours will be able to incorporate a full and complex view of a house's social dynamics. At sites with small staffs, keeping the doors open and the structures stable are the most important parts of their jobs. The most successful and thorough domestic service interpretations, thus far, have been developed at larger sites. They have also taken shape over substantial periods of time.

Many respondents who identified themselves as already interpreting domestic servants indicated their desire to improve their programs as personnel and financial resources become available. The general feeling of survey participants was that domestic service is an important and worthwhile subject that can provide their visitors with a more well-rounded, informative, and relevant experience of the site. While many of their responses indicated that the presence of social-history-related subject matter is still superficial, the development of well-researched school programs and a general enthusiasm for the topic bodes well. As one respondent put it, "Would love to do more interpretation on the subject in the future. Social history is the main interpretive focus of our site and domestic service interpretation would fit perfectly into our current tours and special events."

The interpretation of domestic service has made significant progress in the past two decades, but it can be even better. For most sites, the barriers are primarily a lack of money and time, a problem faced by a large number of house museums, and given the current crises many institutions find themselves in, making this change in their tour may continue to be a low priority. However, as house museum professionals look for new ways to remain relevant, tours and programs that highlight servants and their worlds can meet those needs. The chapters that follow are designed to assist house museum staff in recovering, interpreting, and amplifying some of the voices from the back stairs.

The Ideal, the Real, and the Servant Problem

My survey respondents may not have rated the "servant problem" as a significant theme, but it was an issue that women who employed servants discussed at length. In 1881, Harriet Prescott Spofford published a book with the provocative title *The Servant Girl Question*. This book-length treatment was but one of many ruminations on the "problem" or "question" that preoccupied many white, middle- and upper-class women during the late nineteenth and early twentieth centuries, an era when changes in American society and culture made its answer elusive. According to Spofford, "If two matrons meet in the street, one cannot fail to catch the names of Bridget or Nora in their colloquy, for it is not beneath their dignity to sympathize upon a thing that has grown into an overpowering shadow upon domestic life; if they make each other a morning visit, it would seem to be for the sole purpose of talking over the merits and demerits of these individuals." The changing composition of European immigration, the northern migration of African Americans, increasing employment and educational opportunities for native-born women, industrialization, electrification, and the subsequent development of household technology were but a few changes that complicated the hiring of domestic servants.[1]

Although women in earlier eras struggled with servant problems, the issue seems to have crested between 1880 and 1925, when writings on this subject filled books and women's magazines. It was also dramatized in many visual and literary sources. Today, this period is frequently the backdrop for the interpretation of historic houses and the lives of families who became nationally or regionally prominent during the Gilded Age. Because it touches on so many aspects related to the difficulty of hiring and managing servants, the servant problem has excellent potential for house museum interpreters. The impact of industrialization and technology on domestic life, class and race relationships, immigration history, and gender issues may all be addressed through a theme based on the servant problem. As more house museums expand their relevance beyond the exploits of the "great men" and their families who lived in them, servants and the problems their employers associated with them provide opportunities to contribute to the now well-established "new social history."

When museum professionals and historians turn to general period sources to reconstruct the lives of servants in the early twentieth century, they find a vast amount of material, much of it concerning the servant problem from the employer's perspective. Simply stated, the problem was the difficulty of finding "good" servants and keeping them. The definition of the "good" servant contributed to the issue. Housewives often had unrealistic ideas about the characteristics of the perfect servant, which were exacerbated by images they found in magazines such as the *Ladies' Home Journal* and *Good Housekeeping,* to which they turned for guidance in the training and management of good servants. Advertisers in such publications appealed to their consumers by featuring well-groomed, idealized maids, creating unreal expectations among employers. Women found themselves bombarded by images of ideal servants in conflict-free scenarios, which the reality rarely matched.

On the other side, servants had fewer outlets to voice their perspectives on the problems of domestic service. Servants' accounts sometimes include hints of the ideal, but they also describe difficulties of their work and their relationships with their employers. Their stories further complicate the modern understanding of the relationships between housewives and their help. For the house museum, including these descriptions of life "belowstairs" creates a more realistic and revealing picture of the entire household.

The tension between the real and the ideal that existed in images and print materials of the early twentieth century parallels the interpretive problems of house museums in the early twenty-first century. As some of my survey data suggest, stories told about servants at some historic house museums can be as sanitized as the images found in early-twentieth-century fine and popular art. Employers' relations with servants were always proximate, often intimate, and sometimes affectionate, but were also inflected by conspicuous markers of class difference. H museums struggle to develop nuanced narratives of servant life that ir porate this variety of experiences.[2]

Acquainting visitors with examples of the real and the ideal aids the interpretation of servants at house museums by illustrating the complexity of the servant problem and reminding interpreters and visitors that things are not always what they seem. Obviously, the actual details of domestic life and work (as far as they are known) are essential to the interpretive tour. These "authentic" stories are important parts of a house museum's authority and are parts of the experience that tend to resonate with visitors. However, it is enlightening to discuss the depiction of the "ideal" servant in early-twentieth-century culture, contrasting what housekeepers wanted and what they typically found. Visual and written depictions of ideal servants reflected the desires and fears of women seeking to hire help. These feelings ultimately affected the relationship between a mistress and her servants and can be a powerful plot from which to weave a story of servant life.

The new social history raised the status of public records such as the census and household inventories, materials that can be invaluable in the search for information about servants. The most common sources of demographic information about domestic servants are public records, of which the federal and state censuses are the most revealing. While these data constitute a snapshot, they can show how many servants a family employed, as well as their ethnic backgrounds, ages, and positions within the household. Collecting information from several censuses can provide a basis for extrapolating the ongoing makeup of a home's servant staff and for determining whether the family experienced considerable turnover. Census records are not infallible, however. For example, if a family owned more than one home, their household may have been enumerated in their city home, whereas their country home is the one open to the public. The increasing availability of census and other genealogical information online in more easily searchable databases has made the research much easier and worth pursuing as a first step.

For an overall impression of domestic service nationwide or in a specific state, the aggregate statistics compiled for each federal or state census are useful. These statistics can be good indicators of the servant population for a given year; however, it is often difficult to compare data from different censuses, due to different methods of counting or changes in categories.

It may be more useful to use one year of census data from the year closest to the interpretive period as a snapshot. For example, the 1900 census, the basis of the government report *Statistics of Women at Work*, reports that 20.6 percent of women sixteen years of age or older were gainfully employed, with 24.1 percent of these as servants or waitresses, more than in any other occupation. However, the number of women entering domestic service had started dropping. There was only a 6 percent increase in the number of servants in 1900, which represented very small growth compared with that of other occupations, such as the 305 percent increase for stenographers and typists, and the 203.8 percent increase for packers and shippers. The two previous decades had experienced larger increases in the percentage of domestic servants in the workforce, an 11 percent increase between 1870 and 1880, and a 25.4 percent increase between 1880 and 1890. At the turn of the century, domestic service continued showing signs of change that started in the early years of the industrial age. The 1900 census provides a revealing snapshot of the servant population as the occupation crested before its more significant declines in the 1910s and 1920s.[3]

Servants, like most working women, tended to be young city-dwellers and either African American, foreign-born, or first-generation Americans. In 1900, the census described 27 percent of servants as "African American/Indian/Mongolian"; 27.6 percent were white foreign-born women; 19.2 percent were native-born of foreign or mixed parentage; and 26.2 percent were white native-born women of native-born parentage. While white native-born women constituted more than one-fourth of those in service, this occupation ranked as the thirty-ninth most common occupation for those of native-born parentage, and thirty-eighth for those of foreign or mixed parentage (compared with fourth for African Americans and eighth for foreign-born white). More than half of servants were born in the United States, but native whites of foreign parentage were still considered immigrants. Servants under the age of twenty-five constituted 53.4 percent, and 76.7 percent of servants were single. For many young women, domestic service was a temporary stage in their lives, and they moved on to other jobs or marriage as soon as they were able. Servants were more common in large cities than in smaller ones and in the country. They were also predominantly female; only 1.1 percent of male wage earners were servants. Typically, only wealthy families could afford to hire men, and they paid them higher wages and put them in more visible positions. Thorstein Veblen noted, "Men, especially lusty, personable fellows, such as footmen and other menials should be, are obviously more expensive than women. They are better suited for this work, as showing a larger waste of time and human energy." Describing the duties of servants in wealthy households in 1903, Mary Elizabeth Carter concurred: "The more liveried *men* in evidence, the better, . . . It is a well-known fact that they *do less* and are *paid more* than any woman about a house."[4]

Statistically, the average servant in 1900 was likely to be female, white, an immigrant or first-generation American, under twenty-five, and single. This generalization matches many of the servants described in women's magazines. Regionally, however, the situation could be quite different, which is illustrated in the *Statistics of Women at Work* report by a chart that breaks down the number of servants according to race and nativity by state and region. Foreign-born servants were dominant mainly in New England and the southern North Atlantic states, where they made up 59 percent and 43.4 percent of servants, respectively. But in the southern states African Americans far outnumbered other groups in service. Some 87.1 percent of servants in the South Atlantic states (North Carolina, South Carolina, Georgia, and Florida) were African American. In the Midwest and western states, where the populations of African Americans were small, the ethnic background of servants was distributed fairly evenly among the native-born, people of mixed parentage, and the foreign-born. In six states (Maine, Vermont, West Virginia, Kansas, Oklahoma, and New Mexico), white native-born women of native-born parentage made up the majority of servants. These regional differences often clash with the national images of the ideal in magazines.[5]

Between 1900 and 1920, the characteristics of the servant population changed dramatically. As World War I and immigration restrictions limited the supply of foreign-born women available for hire as servants, American housewives had to look elsewhere for help. The northern migration of African American women filled some of the positions formerly held by foreign-born servants. Domestic service was one of the few occupations open to African American women in the North. Elizabeth Clark-Lewis's excellent book *Living In, Living Out: African American Domestics in Washington, D.C., 1910–1940* (1994) describes in detail the migration process and the way young African American women negotiated relationships with their employers. Although some African American servants did live with their employers as had been the tradition in the North (especially immediately after migration), they were more likely to be older, married, and day workers, which had been more common in the South.[6]

After 1900, the supply of servants continued to diminish relative to demand for them. To cope with smaller numbers seeking full-time or live-in domestic employment, housewives embraced newly available household appliances that took advantage of electrification. Electric irons, vacuum cleaners, and washing machines were relatively inexpensive and promised to relieve the lady of the house of the servant problem. Producers of these machines frequently touted this advantage in advertising by making direct connections between servants and their products. This practice seems to have been particularly popular for selling washing machines. In 1909, Maytag produced one of its first washing machines, dubbed the Hired Girl; a 1919 ad for the Thor washing machine proclaims, "A Servant for 3 cents a week!" and a 1920 advertisement for the Coffield Motor Washer Co. (disguised as editorial material) describes how these machines are "Solving the Servant Problem." Household technology addressed the servant problem by making the lady of the house responsible for doing her own work. Although these appliances promised to save time by making work easier, ultimately they created more work by raising expectations of cleanliness. Middle-class women eventually stopped hiring live-in servants, but the practice continued in upper-class families well after 1920.[7]

While detailed statistics are not available to describe the employers of domestic servants as a group, their characteristics may be inferred through period materials. Nearly all wealthy families employed servants, usually a staff of specialized workers that could number from five to even one hundred, depending on the size of their house and grounds. These large staffs were modeled on those found at European estates and could include butlers, housekeepers, cooks, chauffeurs, gardeners, and various categories of maids, footmen, and valets. Architects designed mansions with separate servants' wings with relatively private working and living spaces to accommodate the household staff and to separate them from their employers.

However, having servants was not solely an upper-class luxury. As industry created more white-collar jobs, more families achieved middle-class status and had disposable income to hire servants. The cult of domesticity encouraged middle-class women to pursue gentility by turning over the household's dirty work to servants. Thus, having a servant became a symbol of middle-class status. According to Veblen, "the chief use of servants is the evidence they afford of the master's ability to pay." As families indulged in conspicuous leisure (e.g., social calls, sewing circles, charity organizations, and the like), they required servants to clean their homes, increasingly filled with objects of conspicuous consumption: "the apparatus of living has grown so elaborate and cumbrous, in the way of dwellings, furniture, bric-a-brac, wardrobe and meals, that the consumers of these things cannot make way with them in the required manner without help." Since wealthy households with large domestic staffs tend to be over-represented as historic house museums, it is important for visitors to understand that servants also worked for middle-class families and that working and living conditions varied from home to home. Doing so provides a broader context for understanding domestic service and offers a different point of view from which to examine the elite.[8]

Unlike wealthy families who hired staffs of specialized servants, middle-class families typically found this help in the "maid-of-all-work." The more a household earned, the more likely it would be to hire additional servants, but having just one "girl" was the most common situation. The maid-of-all-work was responsible for all housework, from cooking to cleaning to personal service. If she was lucky, her mistress hired a laundress to relieve her of the physically demanding work of doing the wash. The "general housework girl" was the most difficult to hang on to—her hours were long, her mistress often unreasonably demanding, and her social opportunities virtually nonexistent. Thus, it was the middle-class mistress who felt the heaviest burden of the servant problem. While the wealthy were not immune, they had their homes built with amenities, such as private servants' dining rooms and spacious bedrooms, to prevent frequent turnover of staff.[9]

In the mid-nineteenth century and beyond, the servant problem was widely discussed by scholars, mistresses, and servants themselves. Each group had its own thoughts about its causes and possible solutions. Words and images from this era reveal much about how employers and servants negotiated the real and the ideal and their impact on these domestic relationships.

If the frequency of articles about domestic servants in early-twentieth-century periodicals is any indication, there was a great deal to be said about their place in the household. Between 1905 and 1921, the *Reader's Guide to Periodical Literature* indexed over 200 articles about domestic servants. As more families entered the middle class and sought servants as marks of their status, housewives who had little previous experience with servants needed advice regarding these new additions to their households. Suggestions for training, outfitting, and pleasing one's servant were abundant, and women were eager to share their personal experiences and their expectations of domestics. In addition to women's magazines, the lady of the house could consult a variety of cookbooks and household or etiquette manuals. Most of these publications describe the ideal mistress–servant relationship. Whether women followed these recommendations in practice is unknown, but they provide a goal to which households aspired.[10]

Women most likely had in mind their own personal ideas of the perfect servant. In 1904 Frances Kellor conducted a field study of intelligence offices [employment agencies for servants]. She investigated the quality of these establishments, and in the process learned a little about the expectations of both employers and prospective servants. One employer stated,

"I want a waitress—just an ordinary one," which she followed with the additional qualifications of "honest, neat, strong, quick, capable, earnest, willing, trained, good-tempered, nice-looking, not impertinent, sober, willing to resign all the attentions of men, religious, and willing to wear a cap." A second employer defined a good servant as one who "carries out her employers' wishes and is faithful to their interests, and will not neglect them for her own affairs—no matter how important." In addition to these desired personal characteristics, employers wanted to find women who were willing to work long hours with few opportunities for vacation and social interaction. Even when employers were able to hire servants that fit such ideals, personality differences could still make a servant unsuitable, as one mistress indicated: "Our 'ways' didn't suit her she said; we were too sudden. Well neither did her 'ways' suit us; she was too pre-meditative. I do not say she was not a good servant. She was, but not for us. So she went."[11]

The ability to tolerate hard work and long hours was often mentioned as a trait of the "good" servant; however, race and ethnic background were often important, if often unspoken. In *Americans and Their Servants*, historian Daniel Sutherland claims that a "*good* servant meant more than being efficient; it implied a specific race, nationality, religion, and personality." Employers could be particular, and their desires were likely exacerbated by the many images of ideal servants that surrounded them in the print media. Although there was not one composite ideal, many northern women focused their desire on the white American servant of native parentage. The issue of a servant's ethnic background became problematic in the mid-nineteenth century and continued to be so into the first quarter of the twentieth. In 1900, the majority of servants were either immigrants or children of immigrants, but a century earlier this had not been the case. In the pre-industrial era, young, native-born, white female domestic workers, known as "help," were very common. "Help" was not just a euphemism for domestic service but described the focus on assisting the woman of the house with chores that were far too labor-intensive to handle on her own, as well as farm chores or other production activities. Help or "hired girls" often lived in the neighborhood or were relatives who came to work on a casual, usually temporary basis.[12]

The emergence of industrial capitalism and urbanization changed the job and the relationship between housewife and helper. Help came to be known as domestic servants, or "domestics." Native-born women who had worked as help began taking jobs created by industry, leaving immigrants and African Americans, who had fewer job opportunities due to prejudice or a lack of skills, to fill most servant positions. Instead of recruiting neighborhood girls, housewives found servants by using intelligence offices, through newspaper advertising, and on occasion by "stealing" servants from other households. The relationship between mistress and servant was based on the former supervising the latter, rather than the shared burden of the housework that characterized the earlier situation. Domestics were more likely to be strangers in the family's home, and they brought different languages, customs, religions, and skin colors into these intimate spaces. They were usually separated from the family by distinct eating, working, and sleeping quarters. Servants were commonly described as being "in the household but not of it." One servant reported to Lucy Maynard Salmon, a history professor at Vassar who conducted the first academic study of the servant problem, "Ladies wonder how their girls can complain of loneliness in a house full of people, but oh! it is the worst kind of loneliness—their share is but the work of the house, they do not share in the pleasures and delights of a home." The shift from help to domestics was the result of the change from a production-based to a consumer-based economy. The household no longer produced its own soap, candles, textiles, and other goods for trade but gradually began to rely on consumption of goods and services. The servant no longer contributed to production but abetted consumption.[13]

Some authors in national publications recognized this change and lamented the lack of American-born girls desiring paid household work. In her 1905 article "Put Yourself in Her Place," Jane Seymour Klink notes: "The social aspect of domestic service has been changed by the fact that, since 1860, succeeding tides of immigration from various countries have swept over the United States, and the foreigners who replaced the 'help' of New England had been fitted neither by birth nor environment for the social equality which had been granted to their predecessors as a matter of course." Klink was among many northern women who held on to a memory of a mythical "golden age" of socially equal, native-born American servants.[14]

However, exactly when the North had experienced this era was never identified, especially since the shift from help to domestics was gradual and regional. In the South, women defined their golden age as the antebellum era, but in the North there was a general longing for the time of the "old family retainer," like the one their mothers hired. In effect, any earlier era or region had it better. Salmon noted that "there is in every clime the tradition of a time when household helpers were abundant, competent, and cheap—a golden age, when harmony reigned in the household and domestic discord was unknown." As a result, some women believed that one solution to the servant problem was to make the work more appealing to American girls and lure them back into these positions:

"Any girl coming to this country, and willing to take a place as a cook or waitress, can find work three times over the moment she steps on land. We must look for other sources of supply. We must train and educate our own American girls to fill these places, classifying these girls as part of the great labor problem which here demands and should engage concerted effort in its solution."[15]

What was lost in the glow of this nostalgia was that not all earlier women had positive experiences with help. Faye Dudden cites the diary of an 1820s New York farm woman named Phebe Orvis Eastman and her experiences with Mary Ann Heath, a "good girl" from the neighborhood. Although Mary Ann could satisfactorily spin and mind the children, her difficulty with other domestic work frustrated Mrs. Eastman: "'I have more to do than I had before I hired a girl,' she wrote. Two days later she reported 'learning Mary Ann to wash, not tractable.' In February she confessed herself 'almost tired out and sick of hiring help,' and a few days later she dismissed Mary Ann. 'I find I can keep my house more decent without a hired girl than with one,' she wrote."[16]

Middle-class women hoped to recruit native-born American girls back into domestic service to end the servant problem. However, this was a hard sell, as factory and department store work became the employment of choice for young native-born women. Their potential mistresses could not fathom why they would choose factory work over working in the home, and cited the latter's advantages: better pay, healthier work, and better preparation for running their own homes. Nevertheless, young women continued to value their liberty over the benefits they might reap while living under their employer's thumb. When asked, working girls were quite clear about the advantages of other employment: "'If conditions were right, I would rather do housework than anything else, but I would not have a woman say *my servant* referring to me.' . . . 'I came to the restaurant after doing housework thirteen years. I like this much better, for my time is my own and my room; if I wish to have my friends in and serve a cup of tea I can do it.' . . . 'Work is heavy, customers are hard to please; but when the store closes I am *free!*'"[17]

Not only did American-born girls shun service, but some commentators argued that once assimilated, immigrants would follow them from the back stairs to the factory: "Jenny's American forefathers had fought for a different idea. Jenny's mother may have been a hired girl, but she was a respected member of a farm household. No; Jenny will never become a servant. She goes into a factory. Selma, as soon as she learns English, follows her there. . . . For after a foreigner has been a while in America she, too, refuses to be a servant."[18]

Although nationally, native-born women were less likely to work as servants than were their foreign-born counterparts, they did not avoid domestic service completely. As cited earlier, in some regions of the United States, native-born servants were relatively common. Rural states in particular, where industrialization was lighter, and where populations of immigrants and African Americans were smaller, were home to more American-born servants. This point is often missed when focusing solely on the period literature, which primarily reflects labor conditions in the Northeast.

If one were to speculate on the backgrounds of domestic servants simply based on their appearances in fine art and popular women's magazines at the turn of the century, it might be assumed that women were successful in their endeavors to hire more American girls. Although artistic depictions included servants with different shapes, skin colors, and ethnicities, they disproportionately represented those conforming to the Anglo-American stereotype. These images reflected the servant problem by emphasizing the rarely obtainable ideal in terms of competency, refined appearance, and "American-ness."

Many images of servants also employed the stereotype of the "American Girl," who dominated popular imagery between 1880 and 1920. In *The Girl on the Magazine Cover: The Origins of Visual Stereotypes in American Mass Media* (2001), Carolyn Kitch argues that media stereotypes of women originated in the popular mass publications of the first three decades of the twentieth century. In particular, illustrator Charles Dana Gibson's "Girl" was seen almost everywhere and transcended class, age, and regional boundaries. This fictional glamour girl dominated standards of beauty from the 1890s to World War I. Gibson's illustrations were published in *Life, Collier's,* and *Scribner's,* and sold individually as prints, and on a variety of products, including wallpaper. Other illustrators such as Harrison Fisher and Howard Chandler Christy further promoted the image of the American Girl. Each had a slightly different visual style but they all depicted the same basic type. Kitch notes, "By searching for beauty standards specifically in the small world of the native-born, white upper class, the press created a selective view that paralleled President Theodore Roosevelt's public worry about 'race suicide.' . . . Physical beauty was a measure of fitness, character, and Americanness."[19]

How, then, was one to tell the difference between the servant and her mistress? In virtually all fine and popular images, white female servants are dressed in the typical servant livery. Some mistresses required uniforms to emphasize the difference between servant and mistress or to reinforce the maid's role as a household ornament. Employers also imposed livery to control the attire of servants on the job; since room and board were part of their compensation, servants saved money more easily, which some used to buy copies of the finery worn by their mistresses. Household manuals often advised on the appropriate attire for servants, and the long black dress and white apron were standard recommendations for the afternoon livery of chamber and parlormaids and waitresses, as illustrated in *Mrs. Seely's Cookbook*. Uniforms also served a decorative purpose in the home, which many fine artists explored in their representations of domestic scenes.[20]

Servants strongly disliked livery, as did some commentators on the servant problem. Salmon felt that the "cap and apron sometimes indicate the rise of the employer in social scale rather than the professional advance of the employee. The wider the separation in any community between employer and employee, the greater is the tendency to insist on the cap and apron." In white households with African American servants, even though skin color clearly distinguished between the server and the served, uniforms were still commonly required. African American servants interviewed by Elizabeth Clark-Lewis looked upon them as symbols of ownership: "[T]hem uniforms just seemed to make them know you was theirs. Some say you wore them to show different jobs you was doing. Time in grey. Other times serving in black. But mostly showing you was always at their beck and call. Really that's all them things means!" In domestic scenes with white servants, the uniform usually served as the only indicator of who was the mistress and who was the maid.[21]

Images of domestic servants appear in both fine and popular art, but more often in the latter. As Elizabeth O'Leary has thoroughly demonstrated in *At Beck and Call: The Representation of Domestic Servants in Nineteenth-Century American Painting* (1996), painters who included servants in their scenes rarely used them as vehicles for social commentary. Rather, domestics appeared primarily as ornaments. They infrequently occupied the center of the image and usually played supporting roles in the domestic scene. Despite the fact that servants were a common feature in many households, particularly the wealthy ones traditionally featured in fine art, their relative invisibility in paintings seems to correspond to their actual roles behind the scenes.[22]

Domestic servants were featured more regularly in popular sources. Articles in the *Ladies' Home Journal* and other national magazines depicted them as looking much like their middle-class mistresses. They were overwhelmingly white, thin, healthy, and young, with little or no traces of ethnicity or heavy physical labor. Popular magazines addressed the ornamental aspects of having domestic servants, often very directly. Some articles illustrated how mistresses could outfit their maids in more stylish aprons and dresses, using depictions of young white women as the models. For example, in the March 1910 issue of the *Ladies' Home Journal*, a one-page article titled "The Correct Apron for Maids" illustrates a call to the mistress's aspiration to good taste. The brief text reminds her that the appearance of her maid reflects directly on her management of the house and that she should provide appropriate aprons for different household situations. Illustrations of seven maids decorate the top register of the page. Each wears a long dark dress and a differently designed apron and cap. One holds a serving tray, another pushes a cart with a tea service, and another appears to be sweeping. Some are turned away from the viewer to model the backs of their aprons. All are elegantly posed with pleasant faces and carefully arranged hair. They have physical features similar to those used to depict the lady of the house in other parts of the magazine. The article truly gives the reader a standard of decor to which to aspire.[23]

Both the editorial material created for women's magazines and the many advertisements surrounding it were calculated attempts at portraying ideal domestic worlds, with the goal of spurring consumption of goods. It is difficult to know to what extent women bought into these ideals. Some scholars have suggested that women were "trained" to notice and read advertisements through contests and other techniques. In early magazines, the advertisements were located at the back of each issue; thus, publishers needed ways to convince advertisers that their ads would be read. For example, *Good Housekeeping* featured rebuses and puzzles using product brand names. Women considered such publications the "trade journals" of the home and trusted sources of information about products.[24]

Roland Marchand argues that advertising offers less an image of reality than of fantasy. Since the sale of a product was the purpose, advertisers illustrated what the readers wanted to be rather than what they were. Such an emphasis on social fantasy is borne out by the factitious representations in these early-twentieth-century illustrations, a period when actual servants were considerably more likely to be African Americans. Marchand notes that, of 186 advertising illustrations of maids he recorded in advertising tableaux of the 1920s and early 1930s, 158 depict them with physical appearances very similar to the "leading ladies" (an additional thirteen show some difference but retain the characteristics of being "young, white, and slender"); fifteen advertisements depict servants who are "black, plump, or noticeably older than the mistress."[25]

The phenotypical similarity of servants and mistresses is evident in many advertisements, only some of which might be directed to a particular class. Ads for luxury items such as silver platters and trays seem like a natural place to include a liveried servant, as in a Gorham silver ad that appeared in a 1920 issue of *Country Life*, a magazine with a leisure-class audience. The illustration features two women, one who serves and one being served, both with nearly identical physical characteristics. The ad copy describes a woman's love of silverware, its tradition, and its beauty. However, most owners of such a fine silver service were able to admire its beauty because they had servants to polish it for them.

Uniformed servants also appear in ads for more common, everyday household products. A Welch's grape juice ad in the March 1914 issue of the *Ladies' Home Journal* features a pleasant, happy maid serving bottles of grape juice to a crowd at a children's party. Advertisements for vacuum cleaners and other household appliances depicted servants using these products, even though in many cases the lady of the house purchased such items to make it possible to dismiss her servants. Personal care items like soap and deodorant also regularly featured images of domestics, in some cases suggesting the highly intimate spheres in which such women worked. In nearly all cases, the servants are depicted as attractive white women in traditional servant livery.

Since statistical evidence reveals that the majority of domestic servants from the late nineteenth century to 1920 were most often immigrants or people of color, to what can one attribute the many illustrations of idealized white maids with no traces of ethnicity or hard labor? One interpretation of these images is that they played into the social fantasy of hiring and retaining native-born help. The trim, elegant maids pictured in most images and advertising represented the people northern housewives most wanted to hire. These were the "quality" girls, who in fact avoided service in favor of jobs with more freedom. Perhaps the boldest statement of this desire was written by Harriet Spofford:

> We owe a great debt to our foreign help; yet, for all that, it is only natural that we should prefer our own people in our own homes when we can have them there. Mutual forbearance goes a great way between mistress and maid, native and foreigner, Catholic and Protestant; but where the elements are naturally so antagonistic, and the interests so utterly apart, union is hardly possible; there is always something foreign in the household, and there is disintegration at the very foundation of home; but with servants of our own race, religion, and habits, the family is complete.

Other women stated frankly that they wished to hire servants who were like themselves: "This is what constitutes a good servant—the likeness to her mistress!" While some may have been referring to sharing a similar temperament, their desire for similarity probably went much deeper.[26]

Based on such comments, some women evidently had conflicted feelings about hiring immigrant or African American servants. While ethnic differences could make it easier to keep servants subordinate, they could also create anxiety in the household. When advertising for servants, some employers specified desired races, ethnicities, or religious backgrounds. For example, the "help wanted" ads in a 1919 issue of the *Chicago Tribune* featured several requests for white help and Protestants, and a handful specified German, Swedish, or French help. Spofford was one of the few that spoke frankly about the desire for servants of specific ethnicities, as well as about the fickleness of employers: "It is not upon nationality nor upon religion that the trouble hinges altogether, though these things have very much to do with it. You may think, for instance, that nothing could be worse than your Irish girl, till you get an African one; the Swede who takes the latter's place is only good while she is fresh . . . the sprightliness of the French maid is as aggravating in its own way, and the stolidity of the German makes you long for the blarneying tongue of Bridget once again."[27]

Household manuals also indicated the preference of certain backgrounds for particular jobs in the household. Mary Elizabeth Carter advised readers of her book *Millionaire Households and Their Domestic Economy* (1903) that French lady's maids, British butlers, and French chefs were the most desired for households of status. Families who could not afford such a pedigreed staff might take the advice of Mary Sherwood's *Manners and Social Usages* (1918) and look to hire English parlormaids or, if those were unavailable, Irish or Swedes who had been in the United States for some time. "Green girls," or new immigrants just starting in domestic service, could be shaped according to a mistress's wishes, but immigrants who had acculturated to American ways were usually more desirable.[28]

As immigration patterns changed, so did the feelings about certain immigrant groups in service. Irish servants initially took the brunt of the ridicule, especially in the Northeast, where their presence was practically ubiquitous. A high percentage of Irish immigrants were female, and these women were willing to take menial positions that others wouldn't. Being the first white immigrant group to dominate domestic service, they became a focal point for complaints about the servant problem, as Spofford noted in *The Servant Girl Question*:

> Who, for example, at the time, would have supposed that the great potato famine of Ireland should send its influence into our closets and drawers, among our dusters, mops, and dishes, in disorganizing the old system of domestic service in America and inaugurating a fresh one, bringing about new ways, new faces, new customs, acquainting mistresses with new natures

and new demands, driving the old 'help' into mills and workshops and behind counters, and abolishing the whole manner of the colonial life, as it had descended, so far as the kitchen and its appanage were concerned?

"Bridget" or "Biddy" became the servant stereotype and frequently the subject of jokes about domestics. She was depicted as being a bad cook, having little concern for hygiene, and working as a papal spy.[29]

In the late nineteenth century, Irish and western European immigration gave way to waves of southern and eastern Europeans who took their places in the lower rungs of society. Many of the newly arrived immigrant groups shunned domestic service, and Americans' fear of these new and different people made the formerly disdained Irish more attractive. In 1925, Christine Frederick explained, "Fewer servants are recruited each year, and the good Irish and German stock which entered service twenty years ago is being replaced largely by the southern European, Bohemian, and Slav girls, who are much harder to train into our American ideals." Fifty years earlier, few would have referred to Bridget as good Irish stock.[30]

Many images of immigrant servants suggested ethnic stereotypes in their attempt to depict the ideal as it applied to this category of domestic help. In a 1912 article in *Good Housekeeping*, "The 'Girl' Problem," Izola Forrester laments that there weren't enough quality women entering domestic service. She identifies a number of reasons for the problem, including the social stigma attached to service and the fact that many immigrant women scatter after landing in the United States and end up in the "white slave trade" rather than service.[31]

Illustration was the preferred medium for depicting the ideal, since it was most easily manipulated, but Forrester's article shows that photos were subject to similar treatment. Lewis Hine photographs and small cartoons illustrate her article. The photos primarily depict immigrant women, wearing scarves or other ethnic clothing. Their ethnicities are identified in the brief captions. Very few photographs clearly identify servants without requiring captions; one that does is of women standing in front of an intelligence office. In the rest, everything but the women's heads is deleted and juxtaposed with captions that evoke stereotypes. While Hine usually wrote descriptive captions, those in this article are probably not his. For example, one on the title page says, "Two jolly girls from Finland who are specialists in laundry work and are doing quite well in this country, thank you." Another caption juxtaposed with a disembodied head reads, "Housework is natural and easy for the hardy women of the Northern European countries." Hine took many photographs exposing poor labor conditions at the time of this article, but this article employs his photographs of immigrants to serve different aims. At least one is from his Ellis Island series, which was not taken in the context of a study of domestic service. The captions turn what were sympathetic portraits into depictions of ethnic stereotypes.

Identifiably foreign servants were uncommon in advertising, which makes the use of Joseph J. Gould's illustration *One Touch of Melody Makes the Whole World Kin* an interesting choice for an Edison phonograph advertisement in a 1908 issue of the *Ladies' Home Journal*. In the image, an elegantly dressed lady and gentleman stand next to a table with their phonograph. On the opposite side of the scene stand four uniformed servants, two men and two women, who seem delighted by the sounds coming from the machine. The two groups are segregated spatially and by their different styles of dress. The servant group includes an African American man (depicting the "Uncle" stereotype), and three others whose physiognomies suggest differing European backgrounds. The line of text below emphasizes the visual separation: "One touch of melody makes the whole world kin." Although the statement claims the Edison phonograph has the potential to bring these two groups together, all the visual evidence contradicts it. In this image, the servants are from another world: they are different physically and, presumably, culturally. Their employers, despite their best efforts to elevate the cultural knowledge of their staff, have succeeded only in amazing them. The illustration further suggests that servants are simple-minded and childlike.[32]

By the late nineteenth and early twentieth centuries, images of assimilated immigrants also existed. Bridget and her backstairs peers continued to be a source for visual humor and ridicule, but she could occasionally be portrayed in a more favorable light in fine art and popular illustration. Charles Dana Gibson took a more sensitive approach to depicting Bridget and domestic servants in general, either through using particular physical types or by placing servants in positions of agency. His illustrations came to be well known across class divides, since copies of *Life* in particular, although written primarily for the "smart set," were passed on through multiple readers. Gibson's illustrations earned a following among domestic servants, who apparently appreciated the fact that he gave them the upper hand in many scenes. In *An Imitation of the Lady of the House*, a group of servants (male and female) relax in the servants' hall, while one maid parodies the mincing mannerisms of their mistress as the rest of the group laughs heartily. The majority of servants in this and other Gibson illustrations featuring servants do not share the same physical attributes of the "Gibson Girl," although some are close. They represent different physiognomies and body types, but their differences are not played up for humor's sake.[33]

Foreign-born servants created a complicated situation for housewives looking for help. While employers sometimes feared the differences that foreigners brought into their homes, they also relied upon them to staff their households. When World War I and subsequent immigration restrictions reduced the number of immigrants in the servant labor pool, the "servant problem" took on another meaning. By the 1920s, domestic service in the North had changed. Fewer women relied on live-in help in favor of day workers and household appliances. African Americans who had migrated north became a more common fixture in northern households.

For the southern housewife, the ideal servant had long been an African American. The history of slavery in the South and the continued prevalence of black servants following the Civil War meant that most families were comfortable managing and being served by black servants; African American servants there far outnumbered those from other ethnic groups. Virginian Orra Langhore explained, "When a Southerner speaks of servants, negroes are always understood. Irish Biddy, English Mary Ann, German Gretchen, and Scandinavian maids are yet unknown factors in our problem. Black Dinah holds the fort."[34]

As in the North, the servant problem was created by scarcity and the loss of an "ideal," but the relatively recent emancipation of slaves played an important role in these conditions. Southern women complained that supply was not equal to demand, due primarily to the migration of African Americans to northern cities, which was accelerated by World War I. Some intelligence offices in the North "specialized" in African American servants and "imported" them from the South, thus further depleting the domestic servant pool. Early-twentieth-century southern women also claimed that the current labor pool was inferior, as they looked back with nostalgia to the obedient slaves their parents' generation had supervised.[35]

As African Americans migrated during the early twentieth century and immigration restrictions limited the number of foreign-born servants, they became more common in northern households. Clark-Lewis's series of interviews with black domestics in Washington, D.C., reveals that these women were well aware of their limited job opportunities. Nettie Bass recalled the employment situation for white and black women before World War I:

> Where brother and his second wife took me there was nothing but colored people. Some people had whites in other places, but they'd be too old to do better. Young ones? They'd only stay 'til a better job would come along—a store, factory, or office—somewhere would take them. Plus them people had to pay whites more. A butler made the best money. And a white maid—my

God they made ten times or more what we did. But we [African Americans] knew we'd always do housework, and had to take any little bit we got. If not, what? They [employers] know'd you was never getting store, factory, or government work. You was there for life.

African American women working as domestics in the North typically "lived out" in their own homes rather than with their employers, reflecting the traditions of southern slavery, in which they were housed in separate quarters.[36]

In the North or the South, African American servants were depicted using a specific visual language that appropriated the culture of the "Old South." Fine artists and popular illustrators typically employed the stereotypes of "Uncle," "Mammy," or "Dinah" in their depiction of African American servants. Uncle had a fringe of white hair. Mammy's physical traits included being heavy and sexless, and she was depicted wearing a kerchief on her head; although stubborn and independent, she was kind, loyal, and devoted to the white children that were her responsibility. Dinah inhabited the kitchen and was often portrayed as more bold and domineering. While white servants were visually identified by the black dress, white apron, and cap, black female servants were depicted wearing aprons and headwraps. The headwrap in particular became a signifier of Dinah or Mammy. This article of clothing was thus transformed from a symbol of African origins and pride into a mark of servility. These stereotypical images reflect a different "ideal," the slaves of the antebellum era, when servants were loyal and willing to serve.[37]

African Americans appear infrequently in women's magazine advertisements, and when they do, they are servants or spokespeople for household brands (such as Rastus the Cream of Wheat chef or Aunt Jemima). The advertising copy usually invokes nostalgia for the antebellum era and its perceived romance. Aunt Jemima is the best-known advertising icon to utilize the mammy stereotype in its appeals. She debuted as the spokeswoman for a brand of pancake mix in 1893 at the Chicago's World's Columbian Exposition, where Nancy Green portrayed the character in a booth shaped like a giant flour barrel. The Aunt Jemima campaign was particularly successful in the 1920s, due in part to the work of the J. Walter Thompson advertising agency, but perhaps also because Aunt Jemima personified the ideal servant at a time when immigration restrictions increased the severity of the servant problem. She also blurs real and the ideal, because advertising and promotions like those of the 1893 World's Fair were ambiguous about the true existence of the character. One 1929 advertisement's copy includes an example of the myth created for the product: "Years ago these same cakes were famous up and down the Mississippi River. The news of Aunt Jemima's tender cakes with their wonderful flavor was carried from plantation to plantation. But in those days only her master and guests could have them. While her master lived, Aunt Jemima closely guarded her recipe." Aunt Jemima's popularity led to related promotions such as dolls and cookie jars, which further ingrained the image of the southern mammy.[38]

As a general source of visual material for interpreting domestic servants, advertisements are a common resource. Often they stand in for the dearth of images of real servants; in other cases they serve as complementary contextual material. These are, however, complex images that should be unpacked for visitors, or visitors should be provided with the tools to analyze them. These ideal images can be effectively used to address the high expectations of mistresses, the function of livery, and ideas of the perfect household in the late nineteenth and early twentieth centuries.

When one turns to the rare images and writings of actual servants, new issues and stories come to light. These scarce sources provide valuable insight into the lives of servants that both counter and augment the idealized depictions. Photographs are particularly valuable resources for discussing domestic servants, since they make visible parts of the household that were invisible on a normal basis. However, such images are often shaped by the ideal. Posed photographs of household staffs document the presence of servants in a home, thereby elevating a family's status. A photograph taken by Charles Van Schaick of Norwegian laundresses, cooks, parlor maids, and scullery girls in Black River Falls, Wisconsin, circa 1890 includes seven women, some in aprons, posed with items that presumably symbolize their roles within the household. The children's nurse holds a child, the scullery maid peels a vegetable over a bowl, the parlor maid carries a broom and dustpan, and so on. The photo has not been linked to a particular family. Such a large and specialized staff working for one family would be an important symbol of status, which might inspire an employer to this kind of documentation. However, pride apparently did not require that the photograph be taken in the employer's home. Careful study of the image reveals that the group of women is posed in front of a backdrop depicting a parlor. The edges of the "set" are visible, and other Van Schaick photographs use this same setting. The documentary nature of this image is overwhelmed by the anonymity of the subjects and their setting. The women's names have not been recorded (they are identified only as "Norwegian"), and their employer is not identified. They essentially become generic representations of servants, or the specialties revealed by their props. The anonymous nature of the photo has affected its modern use as a general image of domestic servants.

It has appeared regularly in scholarship on servants, but without specific discussion of the image itself. In fact, the edges are occasionally cropped, thereby eliminating the ambiguity of the setting.[39]

Even photographs of servants that can be linked to specific families are usually shrouded by varying levels of vagueness, making the servants more like objects than people. A group photograph of servants at the Codman Estate in Lincoln, Massachusetts, is similar to the Van Schaick image, but a little less staged, and attributable to a specific family. Several house museums possess similar images in which certain idealized characteristics from fine art and popular culture are retained. The servants are well groomed and wear clean, pressed clothing. They are not disheveled from the hard work they undoubtedly endured. They are posed, and although their positions are not alluded to by the presence of household items, they are not shown actively at work. In most cases, the subjects of these images have also lost their identity due to poor documentation or very generalized identification ("the cook," "the maid," etc.). Identification of some servants in the Codman image has survived; the three women on the left are identified by first name only, while the two on the right, Marie Reine Lucas and Watson Tyler, who were employed for long periods by the Codman family and were photographed multiple times, are better known. Such photographs can also indicate the use of livery in a household. In the Codman image, a variety of types of livery are worn, while Ms. Lucas, as the children's nurse, wears regular clothes, and Mr. Tyler wears a suit. The motive behind such portraits is lost to contemporary viewers. Were these purely documentary images, or do they indicate a sentimental connection? Without knowing more about who took them and why, these photographs remain enigmatic but valuable documents.[40]

The depiction of servants both in and out of uniform complicates the interpretation of livery as an essential part of domestic service. While uniforms were important indicators of difference and status in fine and popular images, they are not always present in the few images of actual servants that have survived. At Brucemore, only one member of the household staff besides Ella McDannel was photographed in uniform. A snapshot of Henrietta Abadie, a maid for the Douglases in 1907, wearing typical servant livery was preserved and labeled in a family scrapbook. The photograph suggests the use of livery in the Douglas household, but this one image represents only a single moment in time.

Of all servants, governesses and children's nurses seem to be the most frequently photographed, due to their closeness to the children. These staff members, regardless of race or ethnicity, are also typically the most fondly remembered, and they had more intimate relationships with their employers than other servants experienced. They also were less regularly photographed in uniform, since prescribed attire for nurses was less common. The Douglas scrapbooks include many photographs of Ella McDannel both in and out of uniform. A double portrait of McDannel holding an infant Barbara Douglas shows her wearing a uniform, although it is that of a trained nurse rather than typical black-and-white livery. A snapshot taken on the beach in Santa Barbara is typical of most images of McDannel with the Douglas children in that she does not wear a recognizable uniform. Images of servants out of uniform call into question whether livery was as ubiquitous as fine art and popular images suggest it to have been. The servant in uniform may also have been primarily a signifier of the "ideal" servant that was most signifi-cant in the context of images that were to be seen by others. In the case of candid snapshots, such as that of Ella McDannel with the Douglas children on the beach, the private audience of the Douglas family did not require reminders of the status their nanny indicated. These photos of servants out of livery also serve as reminders that servants were people who had at least a limited life outside of their work.

While images of actual servants provide more trustworthy documenta-tion of the history of domestic work, clearly they may also be manipulated to reflect the ideal. These images are problematic, especially when they were not taken by servants themselves but by photographers who posed them in visually attractive compositions. Although few servants left behind written evidence, that which does survive presents yet another means by which historians can try to understand their work and daily lives. These sources include magazine articles and books written from the servant's point of view. The published accounts of life "belowstairs" are complicated, to say the least, since they are most likely to be modified by editors or completely ghostwritten. While diaries and personal letters are more immediate and trustworthy primary sources, they are a rare treasure. In the absence of such resources, period writings by servants can be care-fully employed as firsthand accounts from back stairs.

In some cases, middle-class women posed as servants and wrote about their experiences to expose the poor working conditions that existed in many American homes and to investigate the causes of the servant problem. Two of the best-known examples are Inez Godman's article "Ten Weeks in a Kitchen," published in the *Independent* in 1901, and Lillian Pettengill's book *Toilers of the Home* (1905). Godman's investigation was inspired by her reading of the "Woman's Page," which featured nothing but "growls and groans over servants." She endeavored to find out who was to blame for the friction between maids and mistresses by shedding her middle-class life and working briefly as a domestic herself. [41]

Godman's article is chiefly concerned with the physical demands of domestic service. Of less interest to her are living conditions ("My room was small, but well furnished and heated"), the required uniform the lady provided, her wages, or the low social status of her position, all of which were repeatedly cited by commentators as major causes of the servant problem. She notes that when doing housework in her own home, she was saved by the ability to take frequent breaks, but as a servant the strain was constant. Ironing was a particularly strenuous job. She eventually learned some shortcuts, but did not find that she got tougher; rather, each week she weakened. Instead of asking her mistress to lighten her thirteen-hour day, she left her position in domestic service.[42]

Even after her grueling experience, Godman admits that if she were forced to earn her living, she would still work in domestic service. She might have lighter work as a second maid, but she would have to room with another girl and would have less control over her environment. The difference between the author's experience and that of any full-time servant is that Godman was able to give up service when her position became too much trouble or in some way undesirable. Most women did not have this choice. Although her brief experience as a maid taught her to require her own maid to retire at 9:00, after only a ten-hour day, the author does not appear to have gained any awareness of the inferior social position in which she placed her maids. Her experience does, however, illustrate the physical demands of working in service.[43]

Perhaps the best-known account of the "undercover reformers" is that of Lillian Pettengill, whose 400-page work describes her experiences as "Eliza" in the homes of five different employers over a year spent in service. She documented her experiences in great detail, including re-created dialogues with her employers and fellow servants. Her goals were similar to Ms. Godman's:

> I have observed, heard, read and believed that the respectable American girls who work will cheerfully starve and suffocate in a mill, factory or big department store, or live almost any other kind of life, rather than grow healthy, fat and opulent in domestic service; and this when the housekeepers do all but stand on the street corners as they pass, beseeching them to come in and help. How can my countrywomen, with their own living to make, be so blind to the butter side of their bread?

She had heard much about the servant problem from her housekeeping friends, but little from the perspective of the servant. Therefore, she decided to put herself in the place of a servant with the name "Eliza" and capture her experiences in words.[44]

Presumably because she was a native-born American girl, Pettengill's experiences may have been different from those of the average immigrant servant. She received many compliments on her fine appearance, and some employers treated her better than other servants. Her encounter with a potential employer in the intelligence office taught her how it feels to be treated like a commodity when "having considered me from top to toe, [Mrs. Alexander] remarked with much enthusiasm and for all the world as if I were a prize cow up for sale, 'you are a very nice *looking* girl; yes, a *very* nice looking girl.'" Although few written sources explicitly note the desire for an attractive maid, Mrs. Alexander's comment suggests that she saw in Pettengill the traits of the ideal maid so prominent in popular media. However, she decides not to hire Pettengill, because she doesn't think she is physically capable of the work. A later employer, Mrs. Kinderlieber, thinks that Pettengill reminds her of her recently deceased daughter because she is "so nice and refined looking and delicate."[45]

"Eliza's" refined appearance seems to make her employers more comfortable with inviting her to share their table. Her first employers, the Barrys, invited her to eat in the dining room with the family (although James, the African American coachman, ate alone in the kitchen). Their invitation made Pettengill uneasy, as she already felt her place: "I felt my isolation, alone in a big house full of people, with whom, though kindly and friendly, I could not feel one, for I was not of them." Mrs. Kinderlieber also invited her to eat at her table (when there was no company), something she never allowed other "girls" to do, but Pettengill's refinement made her more acceptable. Still uncomfortable with the situation, she found herself wishing that she were "a rough Irish girl" allowed to eat alone in the kitchen. These employers treated her more like the "help" of earlier years, presumably because she had more in common with them than the immigrants they usually employed.[46]

Pettengill found her first three mistresses, although occasionally moody, relatively decent to work for. She met her greatest challenge in the Scharff household, which consisted of a couple and their daughter. They employed Pettengill as their chambermaid and waitress, to share the household work with Frieda, the German cook. Pettengill's chief complaints with this position were the attitudes and demeanor of her mistress. Mrs. Scharff's general rule was that she expected a full day's work, even if she must provide busywork. She expected her help to have their days off when it was most convenient for her, rather than follow the originally agreed-upon schedule. In the end, Pettengill reflects that "Mrs. Scharff has worked me harder than she had any right. But that I wouldn't mind if she would take the trouble to be decent. She nags when she's pleasant, and when she's not pleasant—well, I never before worked for a woman with a bigger temper or less control of it; and I never will again." Her final employers, the Hollises, although more reasonable, expected a girl used to hard work, and Pettengill experienced swollen feet from being on them so much.[47]

Pettengill's experiences with fellow servants were as varied as those with employers. While working for the Scharffs was unpleasant, her conditions were favorable in that Frieda, the family's German cook, was affable and helpful. She found the opposite situation at the Hollises, whose servants gave her a very cold reception and did little to help her adjust to her new place. Tilly, the cook, was particularly difficult. She constantly compared Pettengill to her predecessor, whom she liked very much, and she withheld information, which restricted Pettengill's ability to do her job well. The one member of the servant staff of whom Pettengill speaks well is Timothy, the African American coachman, who managed to maintain a sense of calm during periods of strife among the servants.[48]

At the conclusion of her experiment in domestic service, Pettengill understands the working girl's aversion to this occupation. She offers several reasons why she no longer considers domestic service a good job: a lack of professional pride, unreasonable mistresses, unrelenting work, and the social stigma that prevented her from associating with her employers or people of their class outside of the kitchen. Although she admits that the job provides some benefits and that she does like doing domestic tasks, she would not choose to be a servant for any length of time.[49]

Women who were not as fortunate to come and go from domestic service as Godman and Pettengill also had opportunities to tell their stories. Between 1902 and 1912, the *Independent* published eighty-two autobiographical essays by "undistinguished Americans." Editor Hamilton Holt sought to "typify the life of the average worker in some particular vocation, and to make each story the genuine experience of a real person." These essays featured many types of employment, from sweatshop work to higher education, and the subjects included men and women from diverse ethnic backgrounds. Some wrote their own essays; those unable to do so had their stories written by an interviewer, which were approved by the subject. Six essays focused on the lives of servants. The variety of servants featured (cook, nurse, washerwoman, and butler) illustrate the more specialized positions as opposed to the portraits of the maid-of-all-work created by Godman and Pettengill. The servants depicted in the *Independent*'s "lifelets" represented a group that was more likely to work as part of a staff in an upper-class household. These servants were African American, Japanese, Irish, German, and French, plus one unknown (probably native-born). These vignettes from behind the scenes provide some of the few examples of first-person servant stories and reveal that although there are many common threads, experiences of servants could be quite varied.[50]

Two lifelets depict a relatively positive picture of domestic service in the early twentieth century. "The Story of an Irish Cook" (1905) is perhaps the most upbeat and reads as a standard rags-to-riches story. An immigrant family comes to America, starts out working in domestic service, and through dedication is able to move into more socially respectable jobs. The children fare even better. The Irish cook, the essay's narrator, and her sister Tilly both start in the United States doing general housework. They stayed with their employers for extraordinary lengths of time; the narrator worked for one family twenty-two years; her sister, eighteen. The author credits her success to the fact that "me and Tilly was clean in our work and we was decent, and, of course, we was honest. Nobody living can say that one of the McNabbs ever wronged him of a cent. Mrs. Carr's interests was my interests. I took better care of her things than she did herself, and I loved the [children] as if they was my own." Overall, the Irish cook feels that she has done well by her move to America and her employment as a domestic. She also represents the opposite of the stereotypical Irish servant as discussed above. The Irish cook had become an ideal servant through being dependable and loyal.[51]

"The True Life Story of a Nurse Girl" (1903) also presents a relatively pleasant picture of servant life and shows an immigrant leading what she considers to be a successful life. Frustrated with low wages in her native Germany, Agnes looks forward to a better life in America: "I heard about how easy it was to make money in America and became very anxious to go there."[52] Two of her siblings had already migrated to the United States and were earning decent wages working as servants in wealthy households.

When she finally came to America, Agnes found a string of positions where she earned good wages and received time off. Although she left two positions she found unsatisfactory, she has no negative feelings about domestic service. On the contrary, she finds many advantages working for a wealthy family. As part of a staff of twelve, among which social distinctions also existed, she "dined with the housekeeper and butler, of course—because we had to draw the line." At this position she earned twenty-five dollars a month and got two afternoons off per week. She spent summers at Newport and Long Island and felt well provided for: "A girl working as I was working does not need to spend much. I seldom had to buy a thing, there was so much that came to me just the least bit worn." She also compares the benefits of domestic work in the United States to that in Germany, noting, "Wherever I have been employed here the food has always been excellent; in fact, precisely the same as that furnished to the employer's families. In Germany it is not so. Servants are all put on an allowance, and their food is very different from that given to their masters." Like the Irish cook, the nurse girl is pleased with her achievements. Not only has she found decent work, she is given time off, which allows her to enjoy outings with friends to her favorite place in New York, Coney Island.[53]

A Frenchman, author of "A Butler's Life Story" (1910) has mixed feelings about the life of servants. Before coming to the United States the author had several jobs in his native France and then went to England and got work as a butler. He learned English at his first jobs and eventually left to take other positions with decent employers. He talks about a butler's work with a sense of pride: "Butler is soul of domestic establishment. He stand in middle responsible for all order. He is between servants and masters, and it depend on him that things are to go well." Despite his contentment with working in this capacity, one of his employers had trouble keeping cooks, so he began preparing meals.[54]

After being cheated while trying to buy a restaurant in France, he said to himself, "Why you not to America, the land of millionaires and bad cooking." He has little good or bad to say about his first experiences working in America, and remains proud of his work: "Now I am great chef. All the millionaires know my cooking and some say, 'There is none like him—no not in all America." Despite his reputation, the author is displeased with the treatment of chefs in this country: "The rich people here they do not know that chef has a soul, that he is an artist, as a poet or a painter. They look upon chef as only animal, cattle." He decided to go back to being a butler and is for the most part satisfied with the life he has earned in America, although he believes the new rich "live like a pig in a palace." Englishmen are true gentlemen to work for, but in America the wages are better.[55]

The cook, nurse, and butler describe the benefits of domestic service that were possible if one found a good place. They identify the ideal from their perspectives: good wages, time off, and reasonable employers. Other lifelets illustrate that not all servants were so fortunate. They show the difficulties of taking stigmatized positions that required long hours of menial work. Of the four authors known to be immigrants, the writer of "The Confession of a Japanese Servant" (1905) is the only one unhappy with the life he found in America. Japanese and Chinese men were commonly found in the households of families on the West Coast. He came to get an American education (which he was able to do) but learned more about the stigma of domestic service and its adverse effects on the intellect.

As a slightly built Japanese boy of seventeen, he had difficulty finding any positions outside of domestic service. The work was hard, since he was new to housework. Over the course of his employment, he worked in a boarding house, in private homes, and on a steam yacht. Unlike the French butler, the Japanese servant has no pride in his position: "I am distinctly felt I am a servant, as the mistress artificially created the wide gap between her and me. . . . I know I am servant full well, yet I wished to be treated as a man." Not only do his employers look down on him, but more well-off Japanese families and fellow students will not talk to him. The German nurse feels well fed and cared for, but the Japanese servant has different experiences. The servants in one household were not allowed to laugh and talk aloud and were given meat fit only for the soup or for dogs. Ultimately, he concludes that being a servant is detrimental to the mind: "To be a successful servant is to make yourself a fool. This habitual submission will bring a lamentable effect to the one's brain function. Day after day throughout the years confined into the kitchen and dining-room, physically tired, unable to refresh yourself in the way of mental reciprocity, even the bright head will suffer if stay too long as a servant."[56]

The story told by "A Washerwoman" (1904) illustrates the difficult hours and stigma experienced by servants doing general housework and explains why some women chose the physically demanding work of laundry over that of the maid-of-all-work. The washerwoman does not divulge her ethnic background, although one might assume she is native-born, since she entered the workplace due to a poor state of finances after her father's death, rather than as the result of emigrating to a new country. She tried department store work first, but she disliked it and found the wages impossible to live on. When she decided to look for a servant position, she deliberately sought a job as a maid-of-all-work, because she did not want to share a room. She was able to choose between seven places but did not settle until finding "what seemed ideal—a clean, tidy, little house with a family of two—mother and son."[57]

However, she feels a stigma attached to her work, both as a housemaid and as a washerwoman. While working in general housework, she confided to a friend, "'I can't see any of my friends. I'm ashamed to tell them where I am.' Now, this is the worst of it. I had many dear friends from whom I was drifting because I could not receive them in my kitchen." Despite considerable improvements in her living conditions as a washerwoman, she continues to feel shame working in the housework trades. A fellow boarder noted that she didn't work weekends and asked her if she was a teacher. The washerwoman replied in the affirmative: "Why not let her think I taught? If she knew what I was doing she would be greatly grieved."[58]

The author of "More Slavery at the South: A Negro Nurse" (1912) presents the African American perspective of domestic service. Since age ten,
the nurse had done domestic work in a variety of positions—as "house-
girl," chambermaid, cook, and finally, a nurse. In thirty years, she had
worked for only four families, unlike servants in the previous life stories
who changed jobs more frequently. She establishes her credibility at the
beginning of her story:

> Belonging to the servant class, which is the majority class among my race at
> the South, and associating only with servants, I have been able to become
> intimately acquainted not only with the lives of hundreds of household ser-
> vants, but also with the lives of their employers. I can, therefore, speak with
> authority on the so-called servant question; and what I say is said out of an
> experience which covers many years.[59]

Some of the Negro nurse's experiences were common among servants
of all colors and ethnicities. She worked fourteen to sixteen hours a day for
little pay and had few opportunities to spend time with her own children:
"You might as well say that I'm on duty all the time—from sunrise to
sunset, every day in the week. I am the slave, body and soul, of this family.
And what do I get for this work—this lifetime bondage? The pitiful sum of
ten dollars a month!" She laments the lack of unions and other organizations that could fight for higher wages.[60]

Race also affected the Negro nurse's experiences. She states that two-
thirds of African Americans in her town are servants of some kind, and
she sees the conditions of servants as being only a little better than slavery. Like slaves, she and other black female servants are placed in danger
because their masters do not respect the virtues of black women. Servants
who are sexually abused are powerless against their attackers; if a woman
takes them to court, she is sure to lose; if she succumbs, she might get
better treatment. Sexual exploitation of servants by masters affected
women of all colors and backgrounds. Servants were vulnerable due the
power relationships of the household, their isolation, and the intimacy
they experienced in the execution of their duties. However, the southern
caste system made it a more common experience for black servants.[61]

These brief autobiographies provide several views of domestic service from the servant's perspective. Some felt that their lives had been
improved through the position; others suffered from the stigma associated with it or, in the case of African American servants, continued to be
exploited as if they were enslaved. The diversity of opinions expressed
in the writings of mistresses and servants provides a model for the way

house museums should interpret domestic service. Since there was no single experience that applies to all houses, tours can reflect what it meant to work in domestic service during the period they interpret through a variety of perspectives.

Awareness of the depiction of the ideal and the real servants emphasizes the complexity of the servant problem and the resources available to understand it. House museums have the opportunity to challenge their visitors to think critically about the way servants were perceived in the past and how they should be understood in our own time. This awareness also should discourage the tendency to focus primarily on the ideal aspects of the servants' lives at a given historic site. It is important to remind visitors that they are seeing but one example of life "belowstairs."

Photo Essay I

The Servant Problem Illustrated

■ Beginning in the mid-nineteenth century, women could consult a growing number of cookbooks and domestic manuals for advice on managing servants. *Mrs. Seely's Cook Book* offered detailed descriptions of duties and illustrated appropriate livery for each member of a specialized servant staff.

Waitress, in Morning Livery and Afternoon Livery. Illustration opposite p. 17 of *Mrs. Seely's Cook Book: A Manual of French and American Cookery with Chapters on Domestic Servants, Their Rights and Duties and Many Other Details of Household Management.* New York: Macmillan, 1914. Courtesy of The Schlesinger Library, Radcliffe Institute, Harvard University.

■ Advertisements for silver and other finery that feature servants remind visitors that although people of means purchased these objects, their use and care involved domestic workers.

Country Life, May 1920, 53. Courtesy of The University of Iowa Libraries

Advertisement for Ridgways Genuine Orange Pekoe Tea, from *Town & Country* magazine, December 1922. Courtesy of Historic New England

■ Many advertisements that included the lady of the house and a servant depicted them looking virtually the same. The only difference was typically the servant's black-and-white uniform.

■ Servants were often featured in advertisements for domestic appliances such as refrigerators, washing machines, and vacuum cleaners. These objects lightened the drudgery of servants' work and in some cases reduced or eliminated the need to hire domestic help.

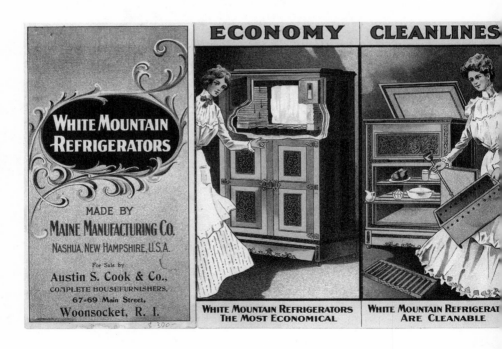

Advertising brochure for White Mountain Refrigerators, Maine Manufacturing Company, Nashua, New Hampshire. Courtesy of Historic New England

HOW BIDDY SERVED THE TOMATOES UNDRESSED.
"Indade, Ma'am, an I'll not take off another stitch, if I lose me place."

"How Biddy Served the Tomatoes Undressed," trade card for Kirchberg & Keenan, Detroit, Michigan, ca. 1880. Courtesy of Historic New England

■ American attitudes about Irish servants were complicated at best. "Bridget" and "Biddy" were frequently the source of jokes and the subject of frustration in discussions of the "servant problem."

■ The illustration used in this
Edison Phonograph advertisement
is a rare depiction of a group
of servants in which race and
ethnicity are depicted, despite the
presence of stereotypes.

The Ladies' Home Journal for June 1908

*"One touch of melody makes
the whole world kin."*

THE Phonograph would never have become the great popular entertainer it is but for Edison. He made it desirable by making it good; he made it popular by making it inexpensive.

The EDISON PHONOGRAPH

has brought within reach of all, entertainment which formerly only people of means could afford. It has even displaced more expensive amusements in homes where expense is not considered.

THE NEW RECORDS FOR JUNE

are the work of artists of reputation. Each is perfect of its kind and many of your kind are included. You can hear them at any Edison store May 25th. Get of your dealer, or of us, THE SUPPLEMENTAL CATALOGUE, listing all the new June Records, THE PHONOGRAM, describing each Record in detail, and the COMPLETE CATALOGUE, which lists all Records now obtainable for the Phonograph.

Thomas A. Edison. NATIONAL PHONOGRAPH CO., 73 Lakeside Avenue, Orange, N. J.

Advertisement for the Edison Phonograph, *Ladies' Home Journal,* June 1908, 50. Courtesy of The University of Iowa Libraries

■ Charles Dana Gibson was
best known for his illustrations
of Anglo-American beauties,
but he also created sensitive
illustrations of domestic workers.
His lighthearted lampoons of
the moneyed classes suggest the
servants' perspective of upper-
class life.

Copyright, 1905, by Life Publishing Co.

STUDIES IN EXPRESSION.

AN IMITATION OF THE LADY OF THE HOUSE.

Charles Dana Gibson, "Studies in Expression: An Imitation of the Lady of the House," *Life*, January 23, 1902, 70–71. Courtesy of the Library of Congress

■ This remarkable posed portrait suggests the roles of specialized servants within a large or wealthy household. Their anonymity is one challenge of working with images of domestic servants.

Charles Van Schaick: Norwegian laundresses, cooks, parlormaids, and scullery girls, Black River Falls, Wisconsin, ca. 1890. Courtesy of the Wisconsin Historical Society, image number WHi-1919

Servants of the Codman Family: Ellen, Nelly, Mary, Reine, Watson, with the dog, Rover. Codman Estate, Lincoln, Massachusetts. Codman Family Manuscript Collection. Courtesy of Historic New England

■ Several historic house museum collections include group portraits of servants that document the size of the family's servant staff and the use of livery. This is one of four snapshots of a group of servants at the Codman Estate that were preserved in a family photograph album. In this case, all the servants were identified by at least their first name.

■ This snapshot, pasted in one of the George Bruce Douglas family's scrapbooks, is the only known image of one of their servants wearing livery. This image served as the model for creating a maid's costume for "living history" interpretation at Brucemore.

Maid in uniform ("Henrietta"). Courtesy of Brucemore Archives, Cedar Rapids, Iowa; National Trust for Historic Preservation

■ Ella McDannel, the Douglas children's nurse, was photographed in uniform with her youngest charge, Barbara, in 1909. Later images of Miss McDannel depict her wearing typical early-twentieth-century clothing.

Ella McDannel and Barbara Douglas, ca. 1909. Courtesy of Brucemore Archives, Cedar Rapids, Iowa; National Trust for Historic Preservation

■ Although many depictions of African American servants in popular images featured stereotypical images of cooks wearing headwraps, in reality, African American domestics often wore traditional black-and-white livery.

Mr. and Mrs. Montague and their servant. Courtesy of the Cook Collection, Valentine Richmond History Center

Using the Servant Problem to Interpret Domestic Life

For sites just beginning to explore the possibilities of addressing domestic service in tours, or for those who want to enhance a current program, this chapter offers suggestions for building an interpretive tour based on the "servant problem." Using the servant problem as an interpretive theme supplies information about the lives of servants, promotes a narrative approach to domestic service, and addresses it from multiple perspectives, thereby providing context that makes a site's history more well rounded and meaningful for tour visitors. This approach also emphasizes the complex relationship between mistress and servant and neglects neither the presence of conflict nor class or ethnic differences.

Before launching a new site interpretation, a considerable amount of planning and research is required. Current opinion in the house museum community suggests that all sites could benefit from taking a step back and assessing where their programs and interpretations are headed and how they might improve. The process of implementing new interpretations, like those highlighting domestic servants, can provide a breath of fresh air and give house museums opportunities to shed their roles as shrines and become socially relevant sites. Involving community members in the planning process should benefit both parties: the house museum staff learns which stories and techniques will engage visitors, and community members have an opportunity to take a more active role in shaping the institution to better meet local needs and interests. Although most house museum personnel responding to my survey reported that the inclusion of domestic servants in their interpretation has been well received by staff and visitors, change in itself creates the potential for resistance and can be lessened by engaging stakeholders in the process.[1]

House museum professionals are just beginning to evaluate the needs and interests of their visitors, and in order for sites to continue to grow and remain relevant to their communities, visitor surveying must become a more common practice. In *Interpreting Historic House Museums*, Jessica Foy Donnelly states, "To be effective places to learn something about history, house museums must reflect in their interpretations not only knowledge of historical facts, but also knowledge of their audiences—who visits, what they expect, why they come, how they learn, what they think about their experience, and who doesn't come and why." Researching audiences, however, has not been regularly undertaken at historic house museums. Such work requires more than collecting zip codes: one must take time to talk one-to-one with visitors, members, volunteers, trustees, and members of the community who have not visited the site. For example, some museums have begun to use focus groups to gather information and have found the process useful in launching new programs or interpretations. The American Association for State and Local History (AASLH) has also launched a performance management program for historic house museums to help these institutions evaluate tours and programs and use limited resources to the best of their abilities.[2]

Through audience research, site personnel might be encouraged by the public's willingness to learn about controversial issues at museums. Audience research for the City Museum in Washington, D.C., revealed that constituents expected the institution to address race and slavery, among other difficult topics. Visitor surveys, focus groups, or community forums can help site staff determine hot-button issues, so they may decide on ways that exhibits and programs can foster productive discussions about difficult issues. These conversations not only further the process of making museum material socially relevant but also foster goodwill between the museum and its constituents.[3]

House museum professionals and staff at historic sites within the same region can also provide support, advice, and the potential for cooperative programming. Thanks to the Internet, they have greater access to their colleagues. Annual and regional conferences and meetings of organizations such as AAM and AASLH still provide wonderful opportunities for contact and professional development, but museum and house-museum-specific discussion lists create the potential of a virtual conference every day. The topics discussed on the AASLH moderated historic house museums Listserv range from practical curatorial and housekeeping issues to philosophical discussions about whether there are too many house museums. Weblogs, or "blogs," are also becoming common forums for discussing museum issues; some professionals have established personal blogs, and museums and historic sites are also using them to communicate with their audiences. Such resources are free, easily accessible, and provide a useful sounding board for new ideas.[4]

Cooperation can make a big difference for institutions that have limited personnel and resources. House museums and historic sites within a particular region have successfully worked together to generate new ideas for interpreting race and gender. In "'Raising Our Sites': Integrating Women's History into Museums," Kim Moon describes a three-year project funded by the National Endowment for the Humanities that introduced new findings in women's history into the interpretation of fourteen historic sites across the state of Pennsylvania. Each site worked with an assigned scholar from a nearby college or university with expertise in a needed area. These scholars conducted research in libraries and archives and supervised the research of site volunteers. The relationships developed between the scholars and museum professionals also rejuvenated the latter's pursuit of scholarship, which often ebbed when the site's daily operations become their priority. The project also included meetings of all participants and created a valuable network for the site staff, who are often isolated from resources outside of their immediate communities. Moon noted that the program "provided a way for participating sites to share their successes and challenges with others across the state, take a leadership role in a particular aspect of programming—archival usage, audience development, or educational outreach—and exchange resource information and expertise with other sites that were attempting similar work." The result of the "Raising Our Sites" project included expanded interpretation of women at several sites, and the next phase had plans to focus on laborers and servants, religious and ethnic groups, African Americans and Native Americans.[5]

The National Trust for Historic Preservation coordinated a similar project to assist six of its house museums with their interpretations of slavery. Between September 1999 and February 2000, two or more staff members from the six sites met for day-long workshops, which rotated among the museums to familiarize the group with one another's resources and to provide case studies. Two history professors also facilitated discussions at these sessions. Between meetings, participants read contextual sources, conducted site-specific research, and developed new interpretive themes and programs for their sites. Susan Schreiber, then director of Interpretation and Education at the National Trust, found that the experience strengthened the resources of all staff and provided access to the perspectives and expertise of outside scholars. As a result, "participants have begun to focus on the stories of individuals; even when the information is sketchy, there is a real person there, not just a group, and that makes a difference—and will make a difference to visitors."[6]

These two programs provide excellent examples of ways that museums and historic sites, which typically have limited financial and personnel resources, can work together to improve their interpretation and reach more diverse audiences. They provide the support and community that are needed to take bold new steps. "Raising Our Sites" also demonstrated the value of cooperation between historic sites and academics who can bring new scholarly perspectives to bear. Citywide collaboration can also provide energy for programs. House museums and local history institutions can pool their resources to present joint exhibits and programs related to work and domestic service. For instance, the county historical society loaned period examples of household technology for Brucemore's temporary exhibition about domestic servants, filling a gap that the house museum's collection could not. The old saw "Many hands make light work" couldn't be truer for the small to medium-sized institutions that benefit from collaborative efforts among museums, scholars, and community members.

Interaction and collaboration with other sites and constituents during the planning process can provide support for house museums as they move toward implementing research conducted on their former domestic servant staffs. For most sites, which must rely on general information about servants to create a more vivid picture, the servant problem is a topic that is rich enough to provide historical context, yet narrow enough that guides can stay focused on a theme. The previous chapter illustrated that the servant problem was represented in a wide variety of primary sources, both visual and textual; however, respondents to my survey revealed that these materials are not widely known by house museum interpreters. Preparing a binder with copies of primary resources about domestic service and its problems during the site's era and in its region is an excellent project for interns or volunteers, especially those with access to a good university library or the Internet. This collection of materials can be the foundation for interpretation and a tool for training guides. While most of these sources described an ideal that was probably not attained by most households, they illustrate what female employers (especially middle-class ones) aspired to. Site staff and guides should discuss the implications of these ideal depictions both for their original and current audiences.[7]

Even general information may be interpreted through the lens of a specific region, state, or city, particularly by using public records and government reports and statistics. Aggregate census data and government labor reports often provide demographic information about domestic servants. One might consider these data in conjunction with industrial factors, since factories attracted many young women away from domestic service. The city's industrial development during the site's interpretive period might shed some light on the potential servant labor pool.

Immigration patterns affected the supply of servants in some states and regions. When providing general information about how immigration related to domestic service in the area, sites should be sensitive to specific regional immigration patterns. National publications such as the *Ladies' Home Journal* frequently mentioned Irish domestics, who were practically ubiquitous in the Northeast, but not in the Midwest or South. Even within regions, differing patterns exist. Also consider that in rural areas where there was less competition with factories for labor, and fewer immigrants or African Americans, native-born women may have made up a larger percentage of the servant population. Tedious but useful tools for gathering information about the servant population of individual cities are the federal and state censuses. For example, I chose one year in which the Douglases' household is recorded in the census, scrolled through all sheets for the city of Cedar Rapids, and kept tallies of the ethnic backgrounds of servants as well as the number of servants living in individual households. While this procedure lacks total precision, it does provide a revealing snapshot of domestic service at a moment in the city's history.[8]

Early-twentieth-century images also reflected attitudes about servants and the servant problem. Servants can be difficult to personify, since they were so often transient and practically invisible in the household. If a site has images of servants who worked there, reproductions of them should be displayed in areas where servants are discussed. When the collection lacks such materials, one might consider using popular images of servants such as advertisements. In either case, but especially in the latter, staff should encourage guides and visitors to observe and note how images can be manipulated to depict situations and relationships that were desired rather than those that existed.[9]

When discussing domestic service on tours, visitors benefit from hearing how the staff researched the domestic servants. If space is available, make copies of primary sources available for browsing. This provides the opportunity to get a firsthand experience of the work of historians. Discussion of historical research techniques gives visitors a "behind the scenes" perspective of the way history is "done." Widespread interest in genealogy has already introduced many visitors to the techniques used in researching domestic servants. Sites should not be hesitant to indicate that information has been gathered from general primary or secondary sources. Part of the reason that general information must be used is due to a lack of documentation of servants, which itself indicates their place in society. Rex M. Ellis, vice president for the historic area at Colonial Williamsburg, emphatically advocates the use of general sources if necessary because "history is a puzzle consisting of a set of pieces that are incomplete because all of the facts are not, and simply cannot be, known. Historical interpretation, therefore, must extrapolate from the known truth." After the site's staff has collected this arsenal of primary resources, they will be ready to determine how to use the evidence as an interpretive theme.[10]

In order to transform shrines into socially relevant institutions, house museum professionals have developed strategies to bring context into their tours and to make them more than just a laundry list of objects. Three museum professionals, Barbara Abramoff Levy, Sandra Mackenzie Lloyd, and Susan P. Schreiber, published *Great Tours! Thematic Tours and Guide Training for Historic Sites* (2001), to support the development of more engaging interpretation. The authors claim that the most effective tours organize information according to storylines and themes, which visitors will find easier to digest and remember than strings of raw data. This technique also encourages guides to be more selective when choosing what to discuss on their tours and to use the site's material resources to their best advantage. The resulting narrative tends to be more engaging for visitors.[11]

The main organizational tool, the storyline, summarizes the site's most historically significant information and is demonstrated by three to five interpretive themes, which illustrate more focused issues that may be anchored by the site's material culture. Some themes may be site-specific, while others address regional or national trends. These three to five points are the ideas the site hopes visitors will remember from their visit. The guides use themes as plots for the house's narrative, which is told through the site's physical evidence, namely artifacts and architecture. *Great Tours!* provides detailed information about how historic site personnel can develop a storyline, themes, a thematic tour outline, and suggestions for training guides to adopt the new method.[12]

As an interpretive theme, the servant problem addresses many social and cultural changes present in the late nineteenth and early twentieth centuries: industrialization, immigration, social class, and gender roles. The size of the domestic staff and their working conditions varied from household to household, but the servant problem had the potential to affect most families. Writers at the turn of the century identified the problem as "one of the burning questions of the day. It colors current literature, and even has its own bibliography. In drawing-rooms, in clubs, on the street, in all the places where men and women meet, it is sure to make its voice heard." While the middle classes were most susceptible, the upper classes were not immune, especially after World War I, when the war and other forces significantly decreased the number of immigrants entering the United States. Historic houses are typically former residences of the wealthy, but they can be used to discuss the general servant problem by looking at the amenities and resources they had that middle-class homes did not. The servant problem also opens opportunities for discussing working conditions, the stigma of domestic service, and local immigration patterns. Finally, the servant problem offers the opportunity to discuss various relationships within the home: those between servants within their own hierarchy, those between servants and their employers, and those between women of different classes and ethnicities (mistress/maid relationship). One might phrase an interpretive theme based on the servant problem as follows: *The "servant problem" affected the way employers and servants viewed and interacted with each other.* This one sentence provides the plot for a basic story about domestic servants at a typical historic site.[13]

To make the servant problem engaging for visitors, guides need to provide visual hooks to hang their story on, such as images, artifacts, and architectural elements. The artifacts found at historic house museums overwhelmingly represent the lifestyle of the owners; however, that fact does not limit their interpretive potential to just the wealthy. "Perspectivistic history" can suggest new ways to look at the possessions of the upper class. For any artifact in the collection, one can ask the following questions: How would a servant have related to this object? Did it require special or frequent cleaning or maintenance? Does it represent an attitude that might have affected the relationship between employers and servants? For example, the Gorham silver advertisement discussed in the previous chapter illustrates that although silver was a luxury item associated with the wealthy, part of the enjoyment of silver came through the fact that the owners had people to clean it. Any object or room can be interpreted through the perspective of different people: the owners, children, guests, or servants. Acknowledging this fact and exploring it makes the interpretation of artifacts rich and engaging. This approach brings the house alive with a variety of personalities and encourages guides to interpret domestic servants throughout the house, not just in the kitchen or other servant-specific rooms.[14]

Granted, the time limits of guided house tours do not to allow for such a richly detailed interpretation of *every* object in the house. However, it is possible to interpret one or two artifacts in each space through multiple perspectives. Most period rooms include one artifact that can serve as the focus for the room's interpretation. Other objects in the room can be simply identified and tied into the theme. At Brucemore, the brass butler's screen in the dining room provides such an opportunity. This screen, a piece original to the interpretive period, allows guides to discuss the room's use as well as relationships between the family and servants. The screen functions primarily as a physical and emotional divider between the domains of the family and servants. The side facing the family is decorated with a series of country and hunting scenes, which might reflect the leisure of country estates like the one the Douglases created in Cedar Rapids. It is shiny and polished like the rest of the family's possessions. The opposite side, which faces the butler's pantry, reveals the screen's construction and is not decorative. This object provides the first example of the stylistic dichotomy of the mansion: the family side is luxurious and decorative, the servants' side is plain and functional. The guide might ask the group of visitors to consider the different feelings family members and servants might have had about the screen.

In addition, the screen's placement and the spatial relationship between the dining room and butler's pantry affected the seating arrangement. Mrs. Douglas sat nearest to the screen, at what most visitors identify as the "head" of the table. Sitting in this position gave her the ability to communicate with the butler, who served the meal. More importantly, the screen removes from the family's view the work necessary to prepare and serve the meal. One can expand the theme of the "hiding" of work and utensils to other objects in the room, such as the sideboard and china cabinets, where additional silver and tableware were stored. The screen can also be used to discuss the relationship between employers and their servants. This very prominent artifact makes a strong statement about the division of the servants from family members. This point can be further extrapolated to discuss the function of servants' uniforms as decorative distinctions between servants and family.

Often the most valuable and unique objects take center stage in historic houses, but small and seemingly insignificant artifacts can be used to make powerful points. Barbara and Cary Carson have suggested how interpreting home security and various kinds of locks can illustrate the division of households. Some sites include cupboards and cabinets whose owners felt must be individually secured to prevent theft by servants. The Carsons note that "a thoughtful interpreter can use something as simple as a lock and key to conjure up a vanished social system of masters and servants, the work routine of staff of (usually female) domestics, and even something as intangible as the ambivalent trusting—yet distrustful relationship between workers and supervisors."[15]

Other objects built into nineteenth- and early-twentieth-century houses speak to the issue of the divided household. Communication devices like call bells and speaking tubes illustrate the separation of the family and servants and the ability to have servants at beck and call through the use of technology. Call bells were one-way communicators—family members used them to indicate where a servant's assistance was requested, but servants could not use them to communicate with their employers.

Kitchens and laundries that retain their original equipment are rich sources of physical evidence, especially in terms of the technology available to the servant staff. Unfortunately, the equipment is often in short supply. Did the family provide the servants with the latest in "labor-saving" devices or technology such as indoor running water, electricity, wood, coal, or gas ranges? If the technology itself is no longer present, evidence of its existence is often found in ledgers, diaries, and other family documents and in the building itself. Many commentators on the servant problem suggested the purchase of household equipment could keep the staff happy. An author in the *Ladies' Home Journal* proclaimed, "I have found every one of my labor savers used and appreciated by the varied workers who have served me. Therefore, I would buy for maids' use quite as many labor savers as for my own use, because with their aid the work is almost invariably so much better done, as well as being easier and quicker." Others claimed it was useless to do so because servants refused to use the machines: "I had the most obstinate general housework girl that ever lived. She was middle-aged and set in her ways. None of my appliances appealed to her. She grumbled and grumbled because I insisted on the use of the breadmixer, Dover egg-beater, sink brush for washing kettles, and other of the commonest conveniences."[16]

One can also consider the sanitary issues related to service areas, particularly in kitchens and laundry rooms. While hygiene and sanitation were matters of great concern to Americans at the turn of the century, surprisingly service areas were sometimes overlooked in this regard. In a 1907 article in *House and Garden*, Erie L. Preston asserts that

> The very places in the establishment where it was easiest for germs to lodge and thrive, owing to the prevalence of dampness, heat and in many cases lack of sunshine, seem to have been the ones last considered in the great movement towards more perfect hygienic and sanitary surroundings . . . .

Open plumbing and modern labor saving and hygienic devices should be installed in every kitchen, pantry and laundry, of any home that is to house a family which lays claim to keeping abreast of the times or to be 'up' in topics of current thought or scientific discoveries.[17]

Interpretive staff should consider whether the kitchen and other service areas would have been easy to keep clean and sanitary. The materials used for covering the floor and walls may provide some clues. The sanitary conditions of the service areas reveal the family's attitude toward their staff as well as the amount of work necessary for servants to complete to keep their work space clean in addition to their other duties. In some cases, the modern cleanliness of restored house museum kitchens creates an interpretive problem, since these rooms were hardly comfortable for servants engaged in work that involved heat and dirt.[18]

Relatively intact laundry rooms can offer the opportunity to describe one of the most hated chores in the household and the way that it liberated some working women. Although laundry was a physically demanding and despised chore, for many erstwhile live-in servants, it provided opportunities for freedom. Laundresses typically did not live with their employers (except those employed in large and very elaborate households); thus, they had more control over their hours and work environment, and freedom from being at their employers' beck and call. The life story of the washerwoman cited in the previous chapter is one example of the somewhat liberated nature of this position. Elizabeth Clark-Lewis found during her interviews with former domestics that laundresses often provided advice about living out. Thus, laundry equipment offers the opportunity to address both live-in and live-out domestic service.[19]

No matter how rich their collection of artifacts and documentary sources, most historic sites also use architecture to interpret working conditions and relationships between servants and employers. The following are questions to consider in terms of interpreting servant areas that are accessible to visitors:

* How are the servant areas separated from the family's? Are there inconspicuous doors to servant areas? What kinds of buffer zones are there between the two parts of the house (e.g., hallways, butler's pantries)?

* What areas of the house does the servant staircase access compared with the family staircase? Are some floors accessible only by a particular stairway? How are the servants' stairs physically different from the family's stairs?

* What building materials are used in the servants' areas compared to the family's? What are the stylistic differences or similarities?

* Did the family provide a special common area for the servants' meals and/or recreation?

* Which cardinal direction do the servants' rooms face?

* Do servants' bedrooms have access to heat? Are fireplaces present in homes with central heat? If so, are they in some servants' rooms, but not in others (suggesting a hierarchy of staff)?

* Where did servants enter the house? Where did family enter?

* Did certain servants within the household have nicer accommodations than others? Are there any architectural cues that suggest hierarchy among the servant staff?

* Did the servants have access to their own bathroom facilities? Would they have had to share facilities with their employer? If so, what issues might this have raised? If the servants had their own bathrooms, how do they compare to those used by family members or guests?

* Are servant work spaces, such as the kitchen, efficiently laid out to minimize the number of steps taken by the cook?[20]

Many of these questions may be addressed as they relate to the servant problem. Amenities such as servants' dining rooms, pleasant bedrooms, and private bathroom facilities made wealthier families less susceptible to the servant problem. Advice to middle-class women instructed them to be considerate of the environment they provided for their servants and made a direct link between living conditions and the servant problem. One author explained the benefits of providing pleasant sleeping quarters for servants:

> This kind of a room, with a spotless maple floor and clean walls painted with oil paint, may be the one thing that will keep your maid servant loyal and true to you when your less thoughtful neighbors are worried with help troubles. . . . Every house ought to have a separate bathroom for the servant near her sleeping-room. . . . A small room off the bedroom, with a plain bathtub, washbowl and toilet will do more toward solving the servant problem than any luxury you can imagine for your maid.[21]

Another concurred: "'How to get and keep our servants' has become a topic of universal interest. Almost every angle of the subject has been touched upon and debated, but it seems to me that the very human side of providing adequately for their personal comfort, so that they may be happy and contented in their daily environment, has been more or less disregarded." At least one article also featured photographs of simple but pleasant servant bedrooms.[22]

The presence of a servants' hall or dining room presents opportunities to interpret the differences between middle- and upper-class households as well as servant life beyond their work. Wealthy families were generally the only group that provided their servants with such an accommodation for their comfort; in middle-class homes, the servant(s) typically ate and entertained visitors in the kitchen. Leisure is not often discussed in the context of servants, since they did not have much free time. This is an important point to make, but visitors should be aware that servants had limited time off (usually Thursday afternoons and every other Sunday) when they could relax, visit friends or family, and attend dances and other amusements. A turn-of-the-century investigation of working women in Massachusetts found that "some of the houseworkers have little or no opportunity for recreation, but some indulge in skating, theatre-going, or dancing, while others spend their free time with relatives or friends. One says that where she was last employed there were 10 or more employés who had a hall to themselves, and that it was 'good as a theatre every night.'" During her undercover work investigating domestic service, Lillian Pettengill joined fellow servants in one home in playing dominoes, checkers, and cards in the evening.[23]

One difficulty with servant spaces is that, except in rare occasions, these rooms have been the most frequently modified following their residential histories. Their furnishings have typically been lost, since they were not seen as important by the families who owned the house, and may have been discarded during the transition from private home to public institution. Rex Ellis notes, "Artifactual evidence is almost always scant for slaves, servants, indentured servants, Native Americans, and other marginal communities. It is shortsighted and irresponsible, however, to allow that lack of evidence to justify silence about those individuals and their roles in the site's history." Some sites interpret these rooms without furniture and focus on what the architecture can reveal about the function of the room, the level of concern that the homeowners had for their servants, or what it might have been like to inhabit these spaces. Using the architecture as the primary evidence has advantages; it gives visitors an exposure to the techniques of "reading" houses but also emphasizes that what is not present is often as telling as what is saved. This approach also takes the focus off of objects and places it on ideas. Therefore, an analysis of a site's servant spaces, equipment, and amenities can be a valuable tool for helping visitors understand the servant problem and may suggest how a particular family may have fared in "keeping" servants.[24]

For example, Brucemore guides interpret one unfurnished servants' bedroom on the standard tour. This room is relatively large and pleasant. However, when one looks closer, it is evident that the Douglases cut some corners in this room. The floor is simple yellow pine; the edges have been painted brown, leaving a bare patch in the middle that has never been protected by anything but a rug. Inexpensive wallpaper was hung in this room, and a tear in the paper reveals that when the room was redecorated, previous layers of paper were not removed but were papered over. The servants' bedrooms are also the only bedrooms in the house without fireplaces, although they did have steam heat. The expense of installing a fireplace was not considered necessary for a room that family and visitors would not see. The overall interpretation of this room is that although the Douglases made this room pleasant for the two or more servants who lived there, it was not a place where they invested considerable financial resources.

If a site decides to reconstruct the furnished appearance of a servants' room, there are resources to turn to for recommendations. Articles in contemporary periodicals and household manuals, such as those cited earlier, describe ways to furnish servants' bedrooms. Furnishing plans produced by National Park Service sites (usually available in the government publications department of most university libraries; many are now available on the National Park Service Web site) can offer suggestions as well. The Historic Furnishings Report for Lindenwald includes relatively detailed descriptions of the furnishings and fixtures either extant or reproduced for their service rooms. Sagamore Hill's report has very detailed descriptions for each room in the servants' wing, which include lists of artifacts and simple renderings of the proposed restoration. While each site faces quite different circumstances in terms of what is documented or saved from these areas, these resources provide basic information to support a restoration of generalized servant spaces.[25]

The authors of *Great Tours!* suggest that house museum administrators provide their guides with short biographies of the main characters in the home's story and that these should include backstairs personalities. While not all sites will be fortunate enough to have names of servants listed in on-site archives, the availability of information from the decennial censuses between 1870 and 1930 can often provide basic demographic information that can be the basis of servant biographies. These portraits can be used to add depth to the story told by guides. Elizabeth O'Leary's recent book on the servants at Maymont House includes a "Biographical Directory of Dooley Employees, 1880–1925," which provides excellent character sketches, of various length and detail, of the people known to have worked at the house.[26]

Biographies will assist guides in presenting information about servants in active-voice versus passive-voice constructions. In *Lies across America,* James Loewen notes his frustration with continually hearing servants discussed using the passive voice, which deprives them of agency. For example, he notes that "guides tell the visitors that 'the right hand wing is where the laundry was done' while 'the left wing' was for the cooking." He found this use of the passive voice at most restored plantations, effectively making the slaves invisible. Jennifer L. Eichstedt and Stephen Small also frequently found use of the passive voice in their extensive investigation of plantations in Virginia, Georgia, and Louisiana. Since the names of servants are often unknown, it can be easier to fall into using the passive construction. While using generic terms such as "the maid, the butler, and the nanny" might be the only option for sites who have yet to uncover the names and backgrounds of servants, these terms can be used to describe the work of servants actively. When they are known, referring to servants by name gives them more of a presence and emphasizes the fact that servants were not invisible but had identities, birthplaces, and families.[27]

It is often difficult to incorporate the biographies of servants into tours when their specific activities were not documented. At Brucemore, I used Alfred Batten, one of the butlers, as an example to paint a picture of what his duties and interactions with his employers might have been. I discussed the fact that Alfred probably answered the door and acted as an intermediary in the custom of "calling" in the great hall and study. Several rooms later, in the dining room, he served the meal and oversaw the care of the china and silver stored in his pantry. The butler's pantry was a symbol of Alfred's position at the top of the servant hierarchy and the trust placed in him by the homeowners. He was one of several men employed by the Douglases, and his presence indicated their social standing. Near the end of the tour, when the group visits the servants' bedroom, I showed a photo of Alfred and Ivy sitting with the children of the head gardener. After hearing about Alfred throughout the tour, the group can finally see him. Another photograph in this room of his brother Bert, the Douglases' chauffeur, illustrates that several members of the Batten family worked at Brucemore either long- or short-term. Brucemore is fortunate enough to be able to give visitors some faces to attach to names, but even sites without visual resources can use names to discuss a servant with the same level of significance as a family member, thus providing a richer and more balanced picture of everyday life.

While some servants may be introduced only by their name and a description of their work, and others are discussed in detail, the key is that the service areas are "peopled" and that visitors get a sense of the community that existed there. Some information may be presented in static displays for visitors to examine either in special exhibition areas or in the house itself. Using exhibit panels as part of the house tour can offer some control over the interpretation of servants, which is frequently inconsistent due to the different interests of the guides or visitors. These materials can also be used to raise issues that guides are less likely to discuss. One concern about this technique is the panels' potential to slow down tours as visitors stop to look and read. Skilled guides usually find ways to deal with such situations. For example, a Brucemore guide explained at a refresher session that he points out the staff chart (repurposed from a former exhibition on domestic service) immediately after visitors enter the room, which gives them some time to look at the information while he speaks. Most Brucemore guides reported that the panels assist their interpretation of servants.

Whenever possible, it is important to address the servant problem from the perspective of the servant. By doing so, the servant problem is depicted as a multifaceted issue that had different meanings for employees and employers. Some house museum collections include diaries and other documents of owner families in which domestic troubles are mentioned. However, to the best of my knowledge, diaries have yet to surface in which servants describe how "servant problems" affected them. The best existing resources are the first-person accounts described in the previous chapter, such as the *Independent* "lifelets" and Pettengill's extensive treatment of the subject. A reference to one of these sources can provide another point of view that broadens the context of specific servant experiences.

Although servants' perspectives were not documented as often as those of their employers, authors in national publications did not ignore the possibility of a "mistress problem." The phrase "servant problem" privileges the owner families, as it identifies the servant as the cause of conflict. It is important to be aware of opportunities to discuss the issue from the other perspective. Many servants as well as general commentators cited causes of the problem as the fault of the mistress. Employers had unreasonable expectations of their servants, often due to their not knowing how to do the work themselves. Pettengill addresses the restatement of "the servant girl problem" in the concluding chapter of her work:

> It was observed, too, that the seven [women who supervised her] were loud and continuous in complaint against the obtainable help, zealous in advertising their own reasonable kindness and the easy lot of a maid in their household.

> By my experience and observation there would seem to be a fixed ratio between the complacency of a woman's speech on this matter, the severity of her criticism upon the workers, her own outrageous management, and her incapacity to direct an underworker. The "Housekeeper's Problem" is a better name for the housekeeper's difficulty, since the housekeepers contribute so largely to its bitterness.[28]

The fact that there were not enough servants to meet demand gave them a certain amount of power. If their present situation or mistress did not suit them, it was usually easy for servants to find another job quickly. For example, in Pettengill's undercover work, she worked for five different families within the span of a year. She is not terribly troubled when something doesn't work out, since there are plenty of jobs to be had. The situation was exasperating for employers, but when looked at from the servants' perspective, this was an important source of power. In such a "seller's market," servants could afford to be somewhat choosy about their employers.

My survey revealed that most historic house museums choose to interpret domestic service using third-person techniques, which are suggested in the recommendations above. As I will illustrate in the case studies, several house museums successfully interpret domestic service by using costumed guides and either first- or third-person living history techniques. Living history is broadly defined as "anything that evokes a link with the past" and thus does not require that interpreters be "in character." Museum professionals are not unified in their enthusiasm for first-person interpretation. However, when done accurately and engagingly, this method can have great appeal to visitors.[29]

One model for first-person servant interpretation is provided by Margaret Lynch-Brennan in "The Servant Slant: Irish Women Domestic Servants and Historic House Museums." She describes ways that house museum staff can find out who the servants were and gives an example of a program based on three themes: the immigration of young, single, Irish women was based on economic and social reasons; the material and social culture of their native land differed significantly from what they found in the United States; and the homes in which they worked as domestics can demonstrate positive and negative aspects of this work. She follows her description of these themes with a walkthrough of a tour entitled "Who Was Biddy? The Irish Servant Girl Tour." This model is based on an interpretive period circa 1867, and while photographs of Lindenwald are included in the article, Lynch-Brennan does not specify this tour as the production of any specific house museum. As Mary Collins, the interpreter (using a credible Irish accent) elaborates on her life and duties as suggested by the above themes, she guides her group through both the family and servant areas of the house. While this model tour is specifically geared toward Irish servants, with some additional research on other ethnic groups on the part of a house museum's staff, it could be adapted.[30]

Lynch-Brennan suggests that house museum staff might also consider offering other kinds of domestic service tours using third-person interpretation similar to those I will describe in the case studies. During my years at Brucemore, the staff experimented with several tours and programs using different techniques, including "living history." The staff was looking for a way to liven up the Wednesday evening holiday tours, and I suggested having someone (who turned out to be me) dress in a servant's costume, bake cookies, and interpret the kitchen from the servants' perspective while the visitors stopped for their treat. This addition to the regular holiday tour turned out to be very successful, with little additional promotion. My uniform consisted of a simple black dress, and an apron and cap that were modeled on those worn by a servant whose photograph was found in one of the Douglases' scrapbooks. On the kitchen table near the tray of cookies, I set up the photo of the servant in uniform and one of a cook named Henry who worked at Brucemore in the 1930s.[31]

I had several goals for my presentation: to describe the technology and amenities of the kitchen as the Douglases' servants would have known it (the advantages of the circa 1927 electric refrigerator helped me interpret this theme), the ethnic backgrounds of the cooks known to have worked at Brucemore, and how servants might have experienced the holiday season. I drew on both specific and general information for my content. I reminded the group that while most people today get Christmas off, this would have been one of the busiest workdays for the Brucemore servants. I used the cookies (snickerdoodles and spritz, both dating at least as far back as the early twentieth century) as part of my interpretation. The Douglas daughters remembered many of their cooks by some of the ethnic dishes they prepared, so it is possible that either the German or Swedish cooks might have made spritz during the holidays. I also provided the names of the cooks and their ethnic backgrounds as part of my presentation.

I found this program to be educational on a variety of levels. The visitors who took these tours responded enthusiastically to the presentation and felt comfortable asking questions about the servants and their duties, so clearly this was an effective means of interpretation for many. The guides who gave tours of the rest of the house told me that they didn't realize how much there was to say about the kitchen until they heard me talk about it. From my perspective, I learned a little about the isolation inherent in the life of a servant. I did not leave the kitchen during the four hours of evening tours, since I was constantly working on cookies, cleaning my utensils, or talking to the tour groups. I had no idea how many people were in the house at any given time and had to rely on other staff members to let me know when a group was coming and how many were in it so I could pour the correct number of cups of cider. I realized that I was fortunate compared to the Douglases' servants, since I did have regular contact and interaction with visitors to the house, as opposed to the cook, who never saw the reactions to her hard work and rarely saw visitors when she was confined to the kitchen. This experiment was successful enough to repeat the program and ultimately led to more living history programs during the holidays that featured interpreters portraying Douglas family members and their servants.[32]

Historic houses can give their visitors an even more direct experience of domestic service by asking them to put themselves in the shoes of a servant through role-playing. This technique generally works best for children, who tend to be less inhibited and more comfortable with imagining themselves as someone else, but a small number of sites have experimented with similar adult programs. The Campbell House in Spokane, Washington, won the National Council on Public History's Student Project Award for their work on a new approach to the site's interpretive tour. Visitors are asked to play a Campbell family member, servant, or friend; they are provided with booklets that explain who their character is and where they fit in the narrative. The tour is in essence a scripted play, which asks the visitors to participate by reading their character's dialogue, printed in the booklets. Three servants are included: the coachman, the cook, and the second-floor maid. The tour takes a unique approach to involving visitors by giving them parts to read, which likely is less intimidating than improvisation.[33]

Ultimately, the goal in interpreting domestic service should be a balanced discussion of what life was like for both parties in the domestic equation. Barbara and Cary Carson have aptly pointed out that a "full cast of characters is needed most importantly, because social history has a higher calling as community history. . . . Social history worth its salt deals with ordinary people *as well as*, not rather than, the elite, and with everyday activities *no less than* world-class events." By offering a broad and inclusive interpretation of everyday life, house museum staff members are more likely to connect with the personal experiences of their audience members.[34]

Illustrating relevance to contemporary issues is another way to provide meaningful visitor experiences, as the Lower East Side Tenement Museum has found with its innovative dialogue-based programming. Karen Lee Davis and James G. Gibb note, "History museums that fail to provide the linkage between the past and the present undermine their role as educators." Today, most visitors can relate to housework—they have become in essence their own maids-of-all-work, but with more sophisticated equipment. When I have described the duties of the general housework "girl" to tour groups, I often get reactions, particularly from women in the group, that suggest that they understand how hard this life could be. The work has simply shifted from servants to the lady of the house. Helping the visitor relate to the work of servants is relatively easy and uncontroversial, which makes it a relatively common topic on a house museum tour.[35]

However, taking the next steps into more difficult terrain can be tricky. Gerald George noted that a historic site "can be a catalyst for debates and dialogues if one has the courage to address difficult issues and fill in the 'gaps in our stories.'" The servant problem raises many difficult issues: interacting on an intimate level with people from different ethnic and economic backgrounds and the subordination of people based on race, ethnicity, class, or gender. These issues are still present in today's society, and not all guides will feel comfortable making this connection with visitors, and not all audience members may appreciate what some might view as political statements.[36]

Helping visitors understand the relationships between mistress and servant is more challenging since the social dynamic of having live-in domestic help is rare in the United States and has been for many years now. However, that isn't to say that no one today hires the labor of strangers to do their housework. Middle-class women in the nineteenth and early twentieth centuries hired servants to free up time to pursue activities that symbolized gentility, such as education, community work, leisure activities, and consumption of goods and services. A parallel situation has arisen since the women's liberation movement. In the early 1970s, Betty Friedan and the National Organization of Women approved hiring out housework to allow women to have time for both careers and families. The trend toward hiring out housework continued into the economically prosperous late 1990s. Between 1995 and 1999, the number of households hiring a cleaner or service at least once a month or more increased 53 percent. At the turn of the twenty-first century, 14 to 18 percent of households employed an outside housecleaner. While this is a relatively small percentage, consider that in a tour group of ten people, at least one or two may have a non-family-member cleaning their home; this is especially likely when you consider that visitors tend to come from the middle class or higher.[37]

One would hope that the conditions for domestic workers have improved since 1900. Many more professions and educational opportunities have opened to women in the past thirty years, yet a startling number must rely on domestic and other service industry jobs to eke out a subsistence lifestyle, and often it takes two jobs to meet the most basic needs. One way that the "servant problem" has been solved in recent years has been the emergence of corporate cleaning services such as Merry Maids and The Maids, International. These companies have eliminated "the peculiar intimacy of the employer–employee relationship." Clients now hire the service instead of the labor of one person (still predominantly female), and the work is typically done in teams. These workers also clean many houses each day, so they may not work for the same clients every day or week.[38]

Although corporate cleaning services have brought a more comfortable impersonality to the hiring of domestic workers, their employees still experience many of the same inequities tolerated by those in their shoes one hundred years ago. By using investigative techniques similar to those employed by Lillian Pettengill circa 1905, Barbara Ehrenreich worked four minimum-wage jobs (including one as a maid) in three cities to determine whether it is possible to make ends meet with such employment. Ehrenreich is careful to note that her experiment had some limitations and that she had some advantages that would not permit a complete replication of the life of the truly impoverished, but her book based on these experiences, *Nickel and Dimed: On (Not) Getting By in America* (2001), suggests that some aspects of working in paid domestic service have not changed.

During the month Ehrenreich spent cleaning houses as an employee of The Maids, International, she experienced many of the same indignities frequently noted by servants of the past. She had to abide by very strict rules imposed by management (which in this case is the company rather than the owners of the houses she cleans): she is not allowed to eat or drink anything while she is in the house working; she is not allowed any breaks (the time spent in the car between jobs is considered her break); and cursing is not allowed at the jobs, in the house, or in the car. Servants of the past also usually lived according to their employers' stringent rules, and during their "breaks" in the afternoon, they were still expected to drop everything to answer the door or answer the mistress's call. Like servants of the early 1900s, Ehrenreich was tested by homeowners. Several servants of the past remarked that their employers often left money lying about to test the servant's impulse to steal. One homeowner serviced by Ehrenreich's "team" placed "little mounds of dirt there just so she can see if they're still there when we're done."[39]

The social stigma of domestic service had been a major deterrent for working women in the early twentieth century, and Ehrenreich's experience suggests that this stigma lingers yet today. Ehrenreich and her coworkers at The Maids wear uniforms, kelly green pants and sunflower-yellow polo shirts. These markers of lower status place them below other minimum-wage workers, as Ehrenreich observes during interactions at convenience stores and supermarkets: "I used to stop [at the supermarket] on my way home from work, but I couldn't take the stares, which are easily translatable into: What are *you* doing here? And, No wonder she's poor, she's got a beer in her shopping cart! True, I don't look so good by the end of the day and probably smell like eau de toilet and sweat, but it's the brilliant green-and-yellow uniform that gives me away, like prison clothes on a fugitive." Ehrenreich's foray into contemporary domestic service illustrates that although a smaller percentage of women work as domestics today, those who do suffer from many of the same injustices of one hundred years ago. In some ways, live-in domestic servants of 1900 were slightly better off in terms of food and shelter, although for many this could not make up for the feudal labor situation they found themselves in.[40]

Cleaning companies also use versions of the "ideal maid" in their marketing that are updated but remarkably similar to the images of the perfect maid in black-and-white livery. A Merry Maids marketing piece from the late 1990s depicted a blond, apparently native-born American woman wearing the company's uniform of a green polo shirt and khakis happily raising her toilet brushes in the air. The text promotes their workers as professionals who, like servants of a hundred years ago, work to make sure their employers maintain their social status: "We love keeping your home—and your reputation—spotless." Most viewers of this ad probably are aware that hiring the Merry Maids will not bring this trim, energetic, blond "maid" to clean their home, yet the marketing executives who designed it are likely playing off the desire for just this sort of household worker.

In terms of ethnic groups in domestic service, the point can be made that even today immigrants often get their first jobs in service industries, as restaurant cooks and waiters, hotel housekeepers, and maids for companies like the one Ehrenreich worked for. A third-grade teacher who brought her class to Brucemore poignantly made this point. The class had eaten lunch and had a tour of a local Chinese restaurant before coming to the estate. When I introduced material about Brucemore's servants, the teacher reminded the class that most of the people working at the restaurant were also immigrants working in similar service industry jobs.

Most guides will not have such a perfect lead-in to discussing the parallels of domestic service a hundred years ago and the contemporary service economy, and they will likely find it easiest to suggest the modern-day relevance of this topic using more subtle methods. A survey of visitors at Colonial Williamsburg found that respondents thought obvious connections to modern-day issues were "an unwelcome attempt at being politically correct." In many cases, an honest treatment of the issues faced by domestic servants will be provocative enough for visitors to consider the connections on their own.[41]

House museums that are just getting started with their interpretation of domestic service may not be ready to dive into the complexity of contemporary relevance. Such discussion is perhaps the next big step once a site has become comfortable with the story it tells about domestic servants. Even if a site is not ready to tackle these issues on every tour, guides should be familiar with them and have given them some thought. In training guides, museum administrators should consider discussing current immigration from the local, regional, or national levels, as well as minimum-wage work. The more fluent that guides are in the links between past and present, the more convincing they will be in showing that history has meaning in modern life.

··· CHAPTER ···

Case Studies in Domestic Service Interpretation

Historic house museums face many challenges when incorporating servants into their interpretation. Yet several sites have created exemplary servant interpretation, special tours, and programs despite limited funding, small staffs, and meager site-specific information about servants. Each house museum has unique circumstances that affect the way domestic service is interpreted. While no "one-size-fits-all" solution to the house museum's "servant problem" exists, a sampling of techniques used by various homes, each with its own strengths and weaknesses, presents a range of resources and styles of interpretation. This chapter outlines the approaches taken by a handful of sites, most from the same region and time period, each with successes and challenges from which to learn.

My case studies are drawn from a series of site visits made primarily between June 2000 and September 2005 but also reflect my experiences since moving to New England in 2006. I selected the museums based on indications that tours addressed domestic service. Several were recommended by colleagues; others reported domestic service as an interpretive theme in the *Directory of Historic House Museums in the United States* (1999). The majority of these sites are located in the Midwest, in part due to their proximity during the primary period of research, but their approaches to interpreting domestic service and the special programs I describe are applicable to any region.[1]

The case study sites are drawn from the same population that participated in my mail survey, those that interpret domestic service in periods after 1865. Viewing sites of roughly the same historical period made it somewhat easier to compare what I experienced at one site with another. Most of my visits were unannounced, so that I would have the greatest possibility of seeing the "typical" tour. My visits followed a course similar to those conducted by Jennifer Eichstedt, Steven Small, and their graduate students while conducting research for the book *Representations of Slavery: Race and Ideology in Southern Plantation Museums* (2002). Eichstedt and Small identify their methodology as participant observation, and their objective to "see what was included in a regular tour" is the approach I took for the majority of my "field research." In addition to taking the guided tour, I also viewed any exhibits at the site, toured the grounds, collected brochures or other complementary materials, and visited the museum store, which frequently is a good indicator of the site's self-image. In most instances I was able to visit only once or twice, so despite my interest in having the standard visitor experience, my visits may not be completely representative. One of the great challenges with house museum interpretation is that it can vary tremendously depending on the guide or the dynamics of the tour group.[2]

I have not included detailed discussions of all my site visits but instead focus on specific types of visitor experiences used to interpret servants from the standard tour to special programs. The additional visits informed my overall impression of domestic service interpretation. I also communicated with several staff members at sites that I have not been able to visit, who provided extensive material about the role of servants in their interpretive programs. The case studies described here represent just a few examples of a growing number of house museums presenting information on servants both in their everyday offerings and in special programs. There are many others that are worthy of inclusion, but I chose to focus on those I have had the time and ability to travel to and see firsthand.[3]

I also include Brucemore as one of my case studies, the site where I worked between 1998 and 2006. While it may be fairly argued that I am less able to be objective about an institution where I was involved in creating interpretation of domestic servants, my experience provides a narrative of the "insider's" view of house museum administration. I attempt to be as impartial as possible and present it as one example of how domestic servants can be incorporated into overall site interpretation when new opportunities arise.

I also had the good fortune to witness the culmination of an impressive domestic service restoration. Maymont, a Gilded Age mansion in

Richmond, Virginia, has been open to the public since the 1920s, but in recent years staff have focused on learning more about the domestic servants and their basement work areas. Their ambitious restoration and detailed interpretation of the downstairs realm opened to the public in 2005. Maymont's significant contribution to the interpretation of domestic service joins a host of other sites nationwide that take this side of their story seriously.

RECLAIMING SERVANTS' SPACES

Space is almost always at a premium at historic house museums. These buildings were built for living rather than for public touring and functions, so most must use some areas in the house for offices, staff and volunteer break rooms, storage of collections not on exhibit, archives, and visitor services. Some historic houses have resident caretakers who live in a small portion of the house. More often than not, the rooms sacrificed for these purposes are servants' rooms. They are ideal for such uses because they tend to be relatively isolated from the main portion of the house toured by visitors. They are plainly decorated utilitarian spaces that were thought to be of little interest to the public.

Over time, many house museums have been able to reclaim these rooms as interpretive spaces. Country estates with outbuildings have the easiest time making this transition by rehabilitating support buildings as visitor centers. Some sites have added modern visitor services buildings that accomplish the same goal. As tenants move out of caretakers' apartments, museum staff often decide to make these former servants' rooms part of the visitor experience. The ability to reclaim spaces and exhibit them either furnished or unfurnished has provided opportunities to tell more balanced stories at Brucemore and several of Historic New England's properties.

Over its more than a quarter-century as a public historic site, Brucemore, a property of the National Trust for Historic Preservation in Cedar Rapids, Iowa, has evolved from an adaptive-use property to a traditional house museum and vibrant community cultural center that has enhanced the interpretation of all its residents. It provides an example of how research on domestic servants can be incorporated into the standard guided tour once servants' spaces that had functioned as offices are reclaimed. Brucemore's advantages include a relatively rich presence of servants in its archives, many accessible servants' rooms, and retention of original country estate features, which provide excellent context for interpreting daily life in its entirety.

Like many house museums, Brucemore was the home of families whose names will not be recognizable to out-of-town visitors, or even to some locals. The mansion was built between 1884 and 1886 for Caroline Sinclair, the widow of Thomas Sinclair, whose meatpacking plant was one of the city's first major industries. The plant also attracted a large number of Bohemian immigrants (now known as Czechs) who settled in Cedar Rapids and worked for Sinclair. Twenty years later, Mrs. Sinclair traded homes with the George Bruce Douglas family. George got his start in his father's oatmeal plant (later to become the Quaker Oats Company) and would go on to own a successful starch processing plant with his brother. The Douglases gave their home the name "Brucemore" (a reference to George's middle name and an allusion to his Scottish heritage), expanded the property from ten to thirty-three acres, and created a country estate, complete with a small farm and recreational facilities.

The eldest daughter, Margaret, inherited the estate upon her mother's death in 1937; she and her husband, Howard Hall, had been living in Brucemore's guest house since their marriage in 1924. The Halls were well-known and respected members of the Cedar Rapids community. Howard's road-building-equipment company, Iowa Manufacturing Company, flourished during World War II, and the couple was extremely active in local philanthropy. Their changes to the Brucemore mansion were mostly cosmetic and included updating the furniture and decor to modern tastes. The most significant change they made to the estate was the decoration of two themed basement recreation rooms, the Tahitian Room and Grizzly Bar. They are also well remembered for their pets. The Halls always kept a pair of German shepherds and for nearly fifteen years shared their home with pet lions, each named Leo.

Margaret bequeathed her home to the National Trust for Historic Preservation and retained life tenancy until her death in 1981. The estate is operated as a co-stewardship property, meaning that the National Trust owns the site and the objects that were part of the original gift, but it is operated by a local nonprofit board of trustees. When the organization initially accepted Brucemore, now a twenty-six-acre estate, complete with the mansion and six outbuildings, it expected that it would become a model adaptive-use property. Instead of functioning as a traditional house museum, Brucemore was to become a home for offices of nonprofit organizations, a rental facility for nonprofits and corporate members, and the host of cultural activities for the community. These needs precipitated the first changes to the mansion's interiors, which were not period room restorations, but the adaptive use of the master bedroom suite, which became a series of meeting rooms. Although the National Trust's initial plans for Brucemore focused less on interpreting the site's history, the public's intense interest in seeing the home led to training tour guides and establishing by-appointment tour hours. The rooms at that time reflected the 1950s and '60s decor of the Hall era.[4]

The first period restorations were undertaken in the mid-1980s, when the mansion's great hall was restored. Wear and tear on the hall's beige shag carpet, installed in 1962, prompted discussion of a period restoration. Instead of replacing the carpet to remain consistent with the Halls' style, Brucemore chose to restore the space to the Douglas era, which was documented by photographic evidence and oral history accounts. By the end of the 1980s, the National Trust had changed Brucemore's designation to "museum property," as a recognition of the site's historic significance. The public continued to show tremendous interest in Brucemore, and tour hours became more regular and frequent.

A Historic Structure Report (1991) provided the springboard for the very productive decade of the 1990s. After examining the physical condition and extant period features of the mansion, the report's authors recommended restoration of the Douglas era interiors, and the board of trustees subsequently established 1915–25 as the site's interpretive period. The Douglases had instigated the most major changes to the mansion, and many of these modifications were still in place. During the 1990s, the restoration of the foundation and slate roof, and the replacement of five massive limestone chimney caps, constituted the major exterior projects. Inside, the dining room, study, and library were returned to their Douglas era appearances. Visitors were able to experience almost the entire main floor as a series of period rooms, which facilitated a more coherent narrative.[5]

Once the major restoration projects were completed, the site had time and finances to revisit site interpretation. The primary changes involved the development of interpretive themes to guide the standard mansion tour. I was hired as an intern in the summer of 1998 to conduct research on the themes, which had been identified by the executive director and assistant director. When I joined the staff in fall of that year, my research evolved into a new training manual for the volunteer guides. The new guide material introduced the themes of art, technology, and the country estate as well as the concept of interpretation through objects. As described in the previous chapter, the goal was to encourage guides to construct a meaningful narrative that placed the Douglas family in historical context. This effort was largely successful, although like all attempts to change interpretive material, some veteran guides were slower to adopt the new material.[6]

Brucemore opened its visitor center in late 1999 in the Douglases' barn, built in 1911. Rehabilitated to include permanent and temporary exhibition spaces, it also houses an expanded museum store and additional public facilities. The permanent exhibition, created jointly by the Brucemore staff and Deaton Museum Services (now Split Rock Studios) of Minneapolis, provided the opportunity to present an "official" interpretation of the estate, focusing on its major interpretive themes. The temporary exhibition space offers room to explore individual topics in depth (such as domestic service, childhood, and vacations) and to display objects and archival materials not normally on display in the mansion. These two spaces give Brucemore interpretive advantages that most house museums do not have.

Staff offices were relocated from the mansion's servants' wing to the barn's former hayloft. In March 2000, the sewing room and one servants' bedroom were added to the standard mansion tour, and the former laundry room and servants' dining room, which previously were open to the public but as the gift shop and an office space, respectively, were reinterpreted as servants' spaces. With these changes, Brucemore has been able to provide a more thorough interpretation of servant life on the daily tour.

Although previously less emphasized than today, servants have been part of Brucemore's interpretation throughout its institutional history. Even before the additional rooms opened in 2000, guides took visitors through the butler's pantry, the kitchen, the servants' hall, and down the servants' staircase. Guides noted the plainness of the servants' wing as well as the fact that the mansion's architecture was designed to separate servants and family. However, they had little background information to discuss servants in their historical contexts, and the only servant with whom guides were consistently familiar was the children's nurse, Ella McDannel, who appears in many of the family's photos and diaries.

The anticipated expansion of the servants' wing interpretation created the need for further research on the household staff. The site's executive director and assistant director strongly supported expanded research and had long been committed to telling a more balanced story of domestic life and work. When the spaces were reclaimed, much of the information gathered during my research became part of the tour. I developed additional training materials that included historical information and techniques for the guides and led training sessions focusing on domestic service in general and at Brucemore. A temporary exhibition, "Help Wanted: Working at Brucemore, 1907–1937," highlighted the lives and work of the site's servants and grounds staff. After the exhibition closed, several of its interpretive panels were installed in some of the mansion's servants' rooms. Over several years, I worked with the program director to develop an outreach lesson for the National Park Service's "Teaching with Historic Places" Web site, which includes maps, photos, excerpts from Ella McDannel's diary, and other primary sources. The lesson "Backstairs at Brucemore: Life as Servants in the Early 20th Century" debuted on the site in March 2003 as part of the agency's spotlight on Women's History Month. This lesson plan offers students all over the world access to the story of Brucemore and its servants.[7]

Archival resources have made the biggest contribution to the understanding of servants at Brucemore; the site's collection includes the diary and two scrapbooks kept by Ella McDannel (known to the family as "Danny the Nanny"). The diary covers five years, 1910–14, and although McDannel's entries are brief, they mention names that have been identified as belonging to servants and provide a picture of daily life, both work and leisure, for McDannel and other household workers. Since personal reflections of domestics are rare, a situation underscored by my survey respondents, Brucemore has the uncommon benefit of a firsthand view from behind the scenes. When this information is combined with Danny's twenty-year residence at Brucemore and her appearance in many photos, her life may be discussed in nearly as much detail as that of the Douglas family.

Her extraordinary connection to the Douglases also provides the opportunity to consider the complexity of servant–employer relationships. Danny and Mrs. Douglas were the same age and spent a lot of time together with and without the presence of the children. Their close relationship was likely a natural extension of Danny's role as the children's nurse. Even after she left the Douglas family and moved to California (where she spent many winters as an employee of the Douglases), she continued to write to Mrs. Douglas and visit her when she came to spend the winter. Although both women appear to have cherished this relationship, their friendship was not likely one of equals. For example, during one of her winters in Santa Barbara, Mrs. Douglas wrote the following to her daughter Margaret: "It has been fun having Danny here the whole week. Socially I hardly know what to do when we are invited out to dinner. Miss Brazelton is near us with Mrs. [illegible] her old employer. Danny goes out with her when I go to a bridge party." However, from Danny's perspective, the Douglases were as close as kin. After Mrs. Douglas's death, she wrote to Margaret, "I do not know what to think or write—But—I do love you and have been thinking of you all, these last few sorrowful days—for you know you are my family—and your mother was a royal friend to me—what wonderful talks and visits we have had over you girls." This is a rare instance where both parties provide insights into the complexity of a mistress–employee relationship that is not elicited when guides simply refer to servants as "like family."[8]

Brucemore also has the advantage of having nearly all its servant spaces open to the public. The only significant servant-related space that remains closed is one bedroom on the third floor. Service rooms are toured on each floor and include both work and living spaces, providing many opportunities to discuss servants in various capacities. Their role as workers may be addressed in the butler's pantry, kitchen, sewing room, and laundry room. Their leisure and amenities may be discussed in the servants' dining room and bedroom, which also presents an example of how the lifestyles of the Douglases' servants differed from servants who worked for middle-class families in Cedar Rapids. A maid-of-all-work was not generally provided with her own dining room, and her bedroom was often a tiny room in the attic, not a relatively large room on the third floor. Such distinctions are important to point out, so visitors do not presume that *all* domestic servants had the amenities offered by upper-class families.

The servants' rooms on the Brucemore tour are essentially unfurnished. As with most house museums, these parts of the house were never photographed, and despite Brucemore's excellent archival documentation, there is little evidence of their early-twentieth-century appearance. In some rooms (Danny's bedroom, the sewing room, and the servants' dining room), interpretive panels from the temporary exhibition help tell the story. Photographs of identified servants, which are displayed on the shelves in the bedroom, help to people these spaces. Architecture and building materials are also used to help visitors understand the ways servants may have experienced these rooms.

During the process of training Brucemore's guides to interpret the domestic servants' perspective, the most frequent concern I encountered was that there was not enough time on a tour of about forty-five minutes to incorporate the new material. Although three rooms were added to the tour, only one was subtracted, so these changes were not without their challenges. I made several suggestions to tighten the tour to free up time for the extra rooms and shared the concerns over its length, but I also felt that if words were chosen carefully, there would be time to include the new material. In many cases, the key is not to add information but to rethink how the room can be interpreted from multiple perspectives.[9]

In addition to the many spaces inside the mansion where domestic service is discussed, the visitor center offers a variety of interpretations of the Douglases' servants. A panel in the permanent exhibition, "Working at the 'Big House,'" illustrates their importance during all three eras of the home's history. Another feature in this exhibition is a short video presentation that illustrates different conceptions of "work" and "play" based on diary entries written during the same period by Mrs. Douglas, Ella McDannel, and a teenaged Margaret Douglas. A temporary exhibition, "Help Wanted," provided an opportunity for visitors to get to know some of the most important but often unseen residents of Brucemore. The fact that the estate has a fair amount of photographs of servants and one of the nanny's diaries gave the exhibition a more intimate feel. A display of early-twentieth-century appliances illustrated the work required to clean a home a hundred years ago. A comparison of a rug beater and an early electric vacuum cleaner served as an illustration of how technology raised expectations of cleanliness that ultimately led to more work. A brightly polished silver tray and tea service sat among the appliances to remind visitors that even items typically associated with owner families required the care of servants.

After this new servant interpretation had been in place at Brucemore for just over a year, I conducted a survey of the tour guides who had attended the training sessions on servants. Nearly half returned the questionnaires. Their responses gave me a good sense of how they use the materials and their perception of the public's reception of them. For the most part I was very pleased with the guides' acceptance of the material, but I also found that like guides at other sites, Brucemore's were also susceptible to the appeal of the ideal.

For the most part, the guides found the material engaging, informative, and of interest to them and visitors. Many commented that they felt the visitors could relate to the servants better than they could the owners, and thus they had enjoyed the servant material. Guides also noted that there had always been questions about the servants, and they now felt better able to answer them. Several remarked that the new information about servants made the interpretation more balanced.

One concern that I did have after reading the survey results was the tour guides' inclination to focus on the positive aspects of domestic service without suggesting the challenges of this position. This is consistent with a tendency at other sites and was mentioned specifically by my respondents. In the Brucemore survey, some responses included: "I feel that most tours have a favorable impression of Douglases and Halls after they hear of working conditions"; "I try to point out that the Douglases and Halls valued the work their servants did and respected them for their contributions and paid them somewhat better than they may have been paid by other employers"; "also mention how servants were treated almost like family." From the research gathered so far, the Douglases do seem to have been good employers. Thus far, the staff has yet to turn up much in the way of servant problems for the Douglases. They had several servants who stayed with the family many years. The two people I have met who remember Mrs. Douglas have wonderful memories of her as a gracious lady. The servants' side of Brucemore, although plain, is large and airy. There were surely employer–servant disagreements during the site's period of emphasis, but there is no documentation of specific conflict. However, that does not mean that guides should not discuss the fact that, despite the perception of closeness between servers and served, these were by definition unequal relationships. As a former member of the Halls' domestic staff once told the executive director, "They were like friends, but you knew your place."

The Brucemore staff's interest in domestic service and the desire to make these important but somewhat ghostly residents more widely known to visitors likely would have resulted in research and integration of this material in the standard tour even without the relocation of visitor services to a separate building, but the ability to reclaim former servants' spaces provided a greater reason to pursue it. Other historic house museum staffs have had similar experiences that allowed for greater balance in the domestic story. At Historic New England, which owns and operates thirty-six historic house museums in five New England states, a similar evolution has taken place. Many of the organization's sites have used and continue to use some of their servants' wings for storage, visitor services, or apartments for resident overseers. However, over time, these areas have been slowly recovered as new opportunities arise. When visitor services or offices can be relocated or a tenant moves out, these spaces are reevaluated and, when possible, opened to visitors.[10]

Since the late 1980s social history has increasingly informed tours at the organization's properties. It has been a gradual evolution, with the initial impetus for creating tours based on themes as opposed to being fully object-centered coming from the newly formed education department. The research staff was redirected to cultivate social history research to support tour themes, and servants increasingly became part of house tours, despite the fact that at many sites these areas of the house were not on view. As these rooms are reclaimed, the servants' stories become more integrated into the everyday visitor experience, and they are regularly the focus of special tours and programs.

The organization has successfully reclaimed servants' rooms at several properties, where the domestic staff is an important part of the daily visitor experience. At Beauport, Sleeper-McCann House, in Gloucester, Massachusetts, the story of the Wonson family provides a layer of reality to the experience of an architectural and interior-design fantasy house. The original portion of the house was built in 1907 for Henry Davis Sleeper, an interior designer of some renown in his own day. Until his death in 1934, Sleeper continually added to and remade Beauport, which came to include forty-five rooms, each with a different decor and theme. He used Beauport as his summer residence and a showplace for his interior-design philosophies, which incorporated creative use of light, color, and arrangement of objects (primarily antiques). Today's visitors tour twenty-six of these rooms, including the Pine Kitchen (a dining room designed in the style of a colonial hall), the Byron Bedroom (featuring objects related to the poet Lord Byron), and the nautically themed Mariner's Room.

The daily tour also includes Beauport's kitchen and the servants' quarters. Here visitors learn about the domestic functions in Sleeper's fantastic home. During his early years at the house, he was regularly frustrated by a series of unreliable servants. In 1919, he hired Mary Wonson to be his cook, and for over the next forty years, the Wonsons came to be associated with Beauport. Mary's husband, George, worked nearby for Sleeper's friend A. Piatt Andrew, and their sons Jack and Tom helped with chores. The family lived in a series of small bedrooms in the main house during the summer and in the off-season relocated to their own home in East Gloucester. The Wonson family had a long history of working as domestics in Eastern Point homes, and Mary and her mother-in-law, known to most as "Madame," were legendary cooks.[11]

Food came to be a well-known part of Sleeper's entertaining; he served meals appropriate to the themes of the five dining rooms, such as New England boiled dinners in the aforementioned Pine Kitchen. These elaborate productions came out of Beauport's kitchen, restored and added to the tour in the early 2000s. In the kitchen, guides share the Wonson family's story and a little about the community of domestics working in the homes of Sleeper's Eastern Point friends and neighbors. Domestics working in summer homes removed from the city often complained of isolation, but those working for Sleeper and his friends often worked together at larger parties and established friendships among themselves. Although the Wonsons were devoted to their employer, the existence of this separate community centered on the kitchens of exclusive summer homes makes it clear that the employers and other house staffs inhabited a separate but intertwined world.

Visitors see the servants' quarters upstairs, a series of five small rooms and one bathroom. Two of the bedrooms have been restored and are open for viewing. These are very simple bedrooms and reflect the standard advice for outfitting and decorating servants' rooms: "A single size enamel bed of the hospital type is most suitable. . . . Beside adequate closet space a worker should have a chiffonier, table or desk and comfortable rocking chair. Generally, it is best to have the walls of light colored tones of paint and to permit each worker to 'decorate' her room as she prefers." All the furnishings are original, and the staff relied on forensic evidence in the rooms and a series of oral histories conducted with the Wonsons to re-create their summer living quarters. The sparseness of these rooms is especially notable, given the decor in the main house, where rooms are filled with objects and color. Sleeper designed this section of the house with traditional single female servants in mind, so when the Wonsons lived there, Mary and George had to have separate rooms. A call bell box located outside of Mary's room serves as a reminder of the relentless nature of domestic work. The servants' quarters are also included on the special "Nooks and Crannies" tour, which visits several additional rooms in the main house that are not included on the regular tour in the interest of time.[12]

By opening the Beauport kitchen and servants' bedrooms to visitors, Historic New England presents a more balanced picture of everyday life at this extraordinary place. House museums where the interpretation of architecture, art, or interior design is the primary focus often ignore these humble areas. Given the overwhelming visual experience of the main house, it is easy to lose oneself in Sleeper's fantasy world. Beauport's back stairs and the Wonsons bring the visitor back to earth.

THE VIEW FROM THE BACK STAIRS—*Servants' Tours*

Even once the basic research for a site's servants is essentially complete and their stories have become part of every visitor's experience, historic house museums can further enhance the interpretation of servants through special programs. These may involve special tours, first-person programs, or dramatic presentations. In recent years, house museums have developed "theme" tours that offer special opportunities to see rarely viewed spaces or unique perspectives. These programs encourage repeat visitation and can also function as membership incentives, either as "member's only programs" or with reduced admission for members. Servants'-perspective tours are excellent ways to expand a site's presentation of domestic service and diversify public programs. I first became acquainted with "servants' tours" at Villa Louis in Prairie du Chien, Wisconsin, and later successfully adapted part of this tour's format at Brucemore.

Located on the banks of the Mississippi River, Villa Louis is an impressive country estate that offers visitors a window into the late Victorian household. Milwaukee architect E. Townsend Mix designed the main residence for H. Louis Dousman, son of a prominent fur trader and entrepreneur, and his mother in 1870. Although the Dousmans were the only family to occupy Villa Louis, their residence was sporadic. When Louis Dousman married Nina Linn Sturgis in 1872, the couple moved to St. Louis to live and start their family. Upon the death of his mother ten years later, the Dousmans moved back to Prairie du Chien. Louis died in 1886, one year after his wife directed an impressive redecoration of the home. Nina and the five Dousman children left the estate for New York, returning in 1893 following the annulment of Nina's second marriage.

The Villa Louis staff has chosen 1893 to 1898 as its interpretive period, a time when the estate reached its zenith in development. This was also a time of great activity for Nina and her children, who entertained frequently, with the hope of securing appropriate marriage partners for the children. The Dousman heirs married and moved to other cities, which marked the beginning of a long transitional period for the estate. Between 1913 and 1951, it was used as a boys' school, a boarding house, and a city-run historic site focusing on Villa Louis's antebellum history (Villa Louis had replaced the earlier "House on the Mound," built by Louis Dousman's father before the Civil War). Finally, in 1952, Villa Louis became Wisconsin's first state historic site and remains under the Wisconsin Historical Society's governance today.[13]

Villa Louis has excellent documentation and collections from its interpretive period, including archival photographs, family and business-related documents, and 90 percent of the home's original furnishings. A multimillion dollar restoration of the home's interiors has recaptured its Victorian glory and 1885 William Morris–inspired British Arts-and-Crafts decor. The site's interpretation of both family and servants also benefits from having good primary sources on hand.[14]

Visitors to Villa Louis experience the mansion through a guided tour led by a costumed interpreter using the third-person technique. Guides begin tours in the Dousman Office Building, known to the family as "The Cottage," which includes the estate manager's office, the billiard room, and second-floor guest rooms (not included on the tour). The tour proceeds to the mansion's front door, where guides describe the custom of social calling and the social activities that took place on this large front porch. The main floor has been completely restored, and visitors may look into the parlor, sitting room, dining room, and guest bedroom over Plexiglas barriers. The family bedrooms on the second floor are also fully restored and viewed from behind similar barriers with small interpretive panels mounted on top. Each panel includes a photograph of the bedroom's occupant and brief room descriptions. The bathroom and the bedroom of Penelope F. McLeod, the head housekeeper, are located on this floor, around the corner from family bedrooms. A reading rail label with a photo of the rather dour Miss McLeod tells the visitor: "She directed the day to day activities of the five to six servants that made up the household staff and in absence of the Dousman family, represented them in making decisions regarding the domestic sphere of the estate." The label indicates the privileged position of Miss McLeod among the staff as indicated by the location of her room in the family wing.[15]

From McLeod's room, the visitors continue down the hall and take two steps down into the servants' wing, which includes three bedrooms, linen closets, a sink in the hall, and a commode in a closet. All servants' bedrooms are open and furnished appropriately for the period. The furnishings are simple, the walls plainly painted, and the floors covered with Japanese matting (a treatment unique to these rooms and based on a surviving fragment). One room is identified as female servants' quarters, another simply as servant quarters, but which likely housed women. Visitors can enter the female servants' quarters and view the room from behind stanchions, which feature short text panels. One panel combines specific and general information about servants at Villa Louis: "Domestic servants cooked, cleaned, served meals, answered the doors and generally attended to the daily needs of the family and guests. At various times the staff included a housekeeper, butler, cook, upstairs maid, waitress, nurse and perhaps a cook's assistant. The work was physically demanding, the hours were long and the rate of pay was low (servants' wages in this household averaged $8.00 a month between 1888 and 1900)." By describing the basic duties of servants and the specialization that one found in a large household, the label suggests the complexity of the household and acknowledges the fact that servants worked very hard for low wages. Visitors often ask how much servants earned, so including the specific wages paid by the Dousmans satisfies a common curiosity. Additional context could make this information even more meaningful by suggesting what servants could have bought with their $8 per month. Another useful comparison would be the wages unskilled women earned in other trades, such as factory work, information that can often be found in reports of state bureaus of labor statistics.

The label on the other stanchion, which includes an excerpt from a Norwegian servant's letter, presumably to family across the ocean, offers a firsthand impression of servant life. Writing from Malta, a town in northern Illinois, she states that "here in this country we don't need to sit up and toil and work all the long winter nights until we are so sleepy we almost faint. No, at most places, the hired girls have almost the whole afternoon free, that is to say, after they have washed up in the afternoon until it is time for supper." While this servant comments on the greater availability of leisure time in the United States compared to Norway, she qualifies having "the whole afternoon free" with a more specific statement suggesting that in reality hired girls had less than their whole afternoon to themselves. However, the letter's upbeat tone provides balance to the long hours and low pay mentioned in the companion label. This positive attitude about working as a hired girl may signify a difference in an immigrant's perspective of domestic service. An American-born girl may have grown up believing that domestic service was undesirable, while in some European countries this stigma did not exist. Joy Lintelman's research on Swedish American domestic servants suggests that Swedish women frequently chose this work without suffering the social stigma perceived by American girls. Wages and working conditions were better in the United States than in Sweden, and the Swedish American community provided strong support for their "serving sisters." Read together, the two labels hint at the complexity of domestic service. It was demanding work that many young women sought to avoid, but for some, such as immigrants starting a new life in a strange country, it could offer improved conditions and an opportunity to acclimate to life in America.[16]

Visitors take the very narrow, tunnel-like servants' stairs down to the kitchen, where they find that a costumed interpreter has fired up the stove. The "cook," interpreting from the third-person perspective, describes the activities in which she is engaged and gives the group an overview of the activities that would have taken place in the kitchen, including the preparation of six meals a day, three meals for the family and three for the servants, following two different menus and using different cuts of meat. She continues, describing the contents of the butler's pantry, adjacent to the kitchen. The kitchen is full of period utensils, plates of imitation food for display, and an open period cookbook, providing visitors with a peek at historical recipes. A small table, with chairs, in the back of the room is set for the servants' meal. Perhaps because of the "living history" techniques used in the kitchen, it is among the warmest and liveliest rooms on the tour. The material presented by the cook and the activity taking place in the room suggest that this was one of the busiest places in the house when the Dousmans were in residence.

The kitchen interpreter also encourages visitors to look into the room of butler Louis LeBrun, a former indentured servant from Canada who worked for the Dousman family for over fifty years. Of particular interest is a large chest of silver with the top open so visitors may see the contents.

One of LeBrun's primary duties was care of the silver, a task he took very seriously. His room also includes wall-to-wall ingrain carpet (compared to the matting in the servants' bedrooms), a double bed, a rocking chair, and pleasant floral wallpaper. The interpreter in the kitchen also points out that LeBrun's room is close to two of his most important workplaces, the dining room and the pantry. Although the quality of his furnishings and important responsibilities indicate LeBrun's higher status among the servants at Villa Louis, he too was never far from his work. Throughout the standard house tour, McLeod and LeBrun serve as reminders that a hierarchy governed the community of domestic servants and influenced relationships with their employers.

Exiting from the kitchen, visitors have the opportunity to look at exhibits in the preserve house, directly behind the main house. From the outside, one can look into the preserve kitchen, where servants canned produce. Inside the building are two exhibits. One room houses equipment from the laundry building (which still exists but is not open to the public). Its label explains that site archives indicate that some servants lived there, but various modifications over the years have made determining the building's original floorplan difficult.

Across the hall is a self-guided exhibition, "Laundress, Nursemaid, Coachman, Cook: Keeping House at the Villa Louis." This one-room exhibition of photographs and charts introduces visitors to the estate's many servants and their world; at the same time, though, it acknowledges the paucity of this information. The title and opening label emphasize the need for a large specialized staff at a country estate like Villa Louis and lists the many kinds of servants needed on a daily, seasonal, or monthly basis. Most of the wall next to this label features a very large reproduction of Charles Van Schaick's photograph of Norwegian domestics from Black River Falls, Wisconsin, which further underscores the variety of specialized servants listed in the title, even though these were not servants from Villa Louis, as the label admits. The Van Schaick photograph is arresting when presented nearly life-size, and it effectively draws visitors in to learn more. The accompanying label calls attention to the fact that this is a posed image and that the subjects are wearing their best clothes. Given the complexity of this image, as I discuss in chapter 3, it offers additional opportunities to consider why and how people photographed servants. Juxtaposed with formal portraits and snapshots of named Dousman servants, this depiction of an anonymous group of domestic servants becomes even more enigmatic.

The wall facing the Van Schaick photograph features an arrangement of five photos with interpretive labels and a series of lists. A visitor beginning at the far left encounters the photographs after another brief introduction, which again highlights the variety within the servants' world: "In a well-run Victorian household, each domestic servant had a specific job description that also carried a status of rank. This status was reflected in the work they did, the clothes they wore, the salary they were paid and the quarters they were assigned to live in." A bulleted list illustrates the differences between different categories of servants (e.g., house servants of various levels and grounds staff) according to where they would have lived on the estate. The label below it describes specific servants on the Villa Louis staff that had positions close to the family, namely, the head housekeeper and the butler: "While many servants worked for a year or more and then moved on, others worked for decades. Penelope McLeod and Louis LeBrun were buried alongside the family in the Dousman cemetery plot. Domestic servants were so integrated into the Dousman's daily living routine that their images were frequently captured by the Dousman's Kodak while their studio portraits were lovingly preserved in family albums."

These images depict a cross section of the specialized workers present at large country estates like Villa Louis and illustrate deeper personal relationships between employers and domestic or estate workers. For example, Peter Nolan was an Irish immigrant who managed the estate and supervised construction during its Artesian Stock Farm phase, in which Louis Dousman started a horse-breeding farm to serve the horse-racing market. After leaving the family's employ, Nolan was elected Crawford County Clerk, and the Dousmans continued to hold him in high regard, so much so that after his death from tuberculosis, they held his wake in the Villa Louis parlor.

To the right of Nolan's image are two photographs, one possibly of Barbara Hagene, a nurse or domestic servant; the other of Fred Standorf, a groundskeeper and stable hand. The identity of Barbara Hagene is described as somewhat speculative, based on its identification in the Dousman family album as "Barbara holding Florence." As the stable hand, Standorf is posed in front of the Dousman's stable with four of the family horses. His employment spanned the end of the Dousman era and the beginning of its varied post-family uses. Standorf is also credited with saving livestock when a fire destroyed the stable not long after the photograph was taken.

The final two photographs are of the aforementioned Louis LeBrun and Penelope F. McLeod. LeBrun casually stands holding a watering can in the garden, while Miss McLeod looks rather severe in her studio portrait. Labels describe their duties, their long tenures that spanned two generations of

Dousmans, and their interment in the Dousman family burial plot. Their personalities are also implied. LeBrun "appears in numerous family photographs, and was obviously well-loved by the Dousmans. He was usually photographed with one or more of the family dogs." McLeod's stern and orderly appearance is accentuated by a Dousman cousin's memory that "[Miss McLeod] was always counting linen and running and doing things and telling the maids what to do."

In these very brief sketches, LeBrun and McLeod are identified as Canadian and Scottish, respectively. A series of charts grouped to the right of the photographs illustrate the ethnic diversity of the Villa Louis servants, who also came from Germany, Norway, France, Ireland, and Bohemia. In many cases, the ethnic backgrounds of the servants are unknown. The chart also includes the job performed by each worker, their wage, and the years they worked at Villa Louis. This material supplements much of the information presented on the tour and in the text panels in the servants' bedrooms. Here, it becomes clear that some positions earned higher wages and commanded greater respect within the staff hierarchy. Census records, household accounts, and family recollections are identified as the sources of this information; however, the panel also indicates that this work is not complete and queries "can you help recover lost names and the stories that go with them?" The open-endedness of this label makes an important point about history research—it is never complete, and any visitor has the potential to add another piece to the puzzle. This is a simple but important point to include, because a great deal of information about domestic servants comes from visitors and through community outreach.[17]

The location of this small exhibition in the preserve house makes it fairly convenient for visitors. The building is located just behind the kitchen door where the tour exits, and curiosity seems to draw visitors in. During one of my visits, a mother read the labels aloud to her child and explained them to her, which led them to spend a fair amount of time with the material. This is a very simple display, and most components were likely produced in-house, but it effectively expands on the information provided in the house and reminds the public that this research is important and ongoing.

The standard tour of Villa Louis offers visitors many opportunities to learn about the servant staff that was the backbone of life at the estate and to see where they lived and worked. Having furnished servant bedrooms and a working period kitchen are definite advantages, even if they are based on general rather than specific information. The photographs on labels for Miss McLeod's and Louis LeBrun's bedrooms also give faces to some of the names in the house. The establishment of the hierarchy on the servants' side suggests the social divisions that existed even among the working classes, adding a layer of complexity to the house's story.

Clearly, the regular tour of Villa Louis offers considerable information about the site's domestic servants, but the staff has also experimented with tours that focus specifically on servant life. In June 2000, I visited Villa Louis to take the special servants' tour, offered the first Saturday in June, July, and August. On these Saturdays, all tours of the house were given from the perspective of the servant. This was the second time the staff had offered these tours, which were later suspended due to state budget cuts. The tour was offered again during three evenings in 2008, and the servant tour approach may be integrated into the daily tour on occasion in coming seasons.[18]

Guides at Villa Louis are typically dressed in period costume; however, for the servants' tours, all wore the afternoon livery of a chambermaid or parlormaid, a long black dress with white apron, cuffs, collars, and cap. Other modifications were made to the standard tour: all rooms—both servant and family sides—were interpreted from the servants' perspective, and the tour flow was reversed to feature the servants' spaces first and family spaces last. Three first-person vignettes further illustrated different aspects of servant life. Overall, the Villa Louis servants' tour effectively described servant life by giving visitors more opportunities to understand some of its nuances.

During house tours at many sites, guides do not address the servants' perspective until they reach the kitchen, laundry, or servants' bedrooms; hence, servants become invisible when the group moves into the family space. This was not the case on the Villa Louis servants' tour. The viewpoint of the servant shaped the interpretation of all rooms in the mansion. On the second floor, an "upstairs maid" would have tended to the personal needs of her employers in addition to making beds, dusting, and other straightening. The front hall is typical of the Victorian era, replete with many patterns, textures, and bric-a-brac, all of which required careful dusting. The etiquette of servers and served also came into play: when serving tea in the parlor, how would a servant be expected to interact with the guests? In all of the family areas, the guide emphasized that while the arranged objects may have been purchased and used by the Dousmans, they did not have complete control over their treasures. This interpretation employs Barbara Carson's method of "perspectivist history," in which artifacts can be interpreted from the point of view of all who came in contact with them. This aspect of the tour also brought visitors in touch with the reality that these items may have been beautiful to look at, but those who had to care for them may have seen them differently, since some required extra care, concern, or labor to maintain. The tour's effectiveness was also significantly enhanced by reversing the tour flow. Most importantly, it allowed plenty of time for thorough interpretation of domestic service, something that is often neglected, since service areas tend to be the last rooms visited. During the servants' tour, it was the family spaces that had to be viewed at a more rapid pace.[19]

The majority of the narrative was presented by the guide in the third person, but in three locations the group encountered first-person vignettes. En route to the servants' entrance of the mansion, the group stopped at the estate manager's office, where they met an interpreter portraying Daniel H. Quilligan. He offered his impression of Villa Louis as a whole, not just as a fancy residence, but as a country estate complete with farms and, at one point, a major horse-breeding operation. The Dousmans also owned other properties and downtown rentals, which Quilligan managed. He also looked after the house and grounds when the Dousmans were away, a rather frequent occurrence. Even when the family left to spend a summer or winter away, some servants or other estate employees usually remained behind to keep things in order. Quilligan spoke of the Dousmans' financial difficulties, noting that "Mrs. Dousman has no head for business." Therefore, he suggested that they may have to sell the farms. "Quilligan's" presentation illustrated intimate knowledge of the family's finances, but he did not elaborate on how he felt about them as employers.

Upon entering the house through the back entrance, the group started the mansion tour in the kitchen, where they met the cook, Miss Hoffman (not a historic character, but a generic persona with the surname of the woman portraying her). The cook's mood was a bit testy, due to her frustration with Katy the Irish scullery maid, who quit in a hurry and absconded with Miss Hoffman's cornucopia mold, which she was in need of at that moment. She explained that she had the benefit of a very modern kitchen with running water, and cold storage in a building nearby, and that because the family could buy their bread in town, she was spared of that labor. Miss Hoffman's interpretation covered the same general topics as the standard third-person interpretation of the kitchen, and she too was engaged in food preparation. Visitors were generally reluctant to interact with either the guide or the first-person personas, but two in this group asked the cook if she had any help (which gave her another opportunity to express her frustration with the quality of scullery girls) and how many she had to cook for (twelve on a regular basis and occasionally fifteen to twenty). She also noted that 900 pieces of china were once used for a meal. Miss Hoffman's presentation illustrated the impact of technology, the beginning of outsourcing food preparation, the "servant problem" regarding her inability to find a quality scullery maid, and the intensity of a job that required her to prepare two different meals (one for servants, one for her employers and their guests), the latter with very elaborate presentations.

The group encountered the final scene in the family side of the house. A maid, portrayed by a girl probably in her mid-teens, stopped the group to ask for help reading a list of chores that Mrs. Dousman had given her. When she interviewed for the job, she did not claim to be able to read (she could sign her name and recognize letters of the alphabet), but she also did not admit to being illiterate. Now that she has this list, she is in a state of panic; she needs this job, so she doesn't want Mrs. Dousman to think she is a liar. She asked the group if someone would help her read the list. None of the visitors offered assistance, instead maintaining a somewhat awkward silence. The maid acting as our guide helped her before resuming the tour of the main floor.

This particular encounter seemed to cause the most unease among group members, especially compared to their responses to the cook and Quilligan. While in those situations they were not overly demonstrative, they seemed more relaxed than with the young parlormaid. Her situation illustrates aspects of domestic service that have greater impact when interpreted using first-person methods. The parlormaid's youth was consistent with the age of many who would have been in her position, and seeing a girl of her age in this somewhat desperate position was compelling. Although this particular servant was not identified as an immigrant, foreign-born servants likely found themselves in similar positions.

The visitors' unwillingness to interact with most of the character interpreters raises an important drawback to using first-person methods. My own experiences visiting Colonial Williamsburg, Conner Prairie, and Plimoth Plantation, and the observations of other museum professionals, suggest that interacting with first-person interpreters can be demanding or confusing for visitors. During a visit to Conner Prairie, an Indiana museum specializing in the state's pioneer history, my husband and I had our first real encounter with "immersion" into historical periods. While I found the experience intriguing, it was also exhausting on many levels. When the character interpreters asked questions of us—although relatively simple and on the order of "What brings you to Prairietown?"—I felt as though we needed historically accurate personas in order to have quality conversations with the "villagers." We also realized how difficult it is to ask the interpreters meaningful questions in a situation in which we were "outsiders" just letting ourselves into these people's homes and businesses. In the "real" world, it is considered impolite to ask strangers about politics, religion, and other personal matters. Strangely, it seemed equally impolite in this fictional setting, whereas we asked such questions freely in third-person interactions.[20]

The most difficult interaction we had was with an African American woman who was watching over her employer's home while he was away. When we came in, she was seated by the back door doing some mending. She asked us if we were there to see her employer and whether he was expecting us. We said no, we were just passing through town and learning about life there. We tried to get her to talk about herself but were unsuccessful for the most part. As much as I wanted to ask her about whether she had been a slave and what she thought of her employer, her standoffishness and our being unprepared to ask such questions in this environment led to some awkward silence. As intriguing as the first-person interactions were, I often found myself wishing I could ask questions of someone from the "present." With adequate "framing" of the first-person interaction by third-person interpreters, the former method seems more effective. During the Villa Louis tour, we always had our tour guide available should we feel uncomfortable asking certain questions of the "personas."

Villa Louis has many resources to interpret the domestic servants who were responsible for the estate's daily upkeep. It has the benefit of having at least a few specific servants whom guides can call by name and use as examples of the hierarchy that existed in the backstairs world. Based on the information in the preserve house exhibit, the site is able to demonstrate the diversity of the staff at the estate and provide faces for some of the names. The presence of this exhibit means that visitors always have the opportunity to learn at least a little more about domestic servants, although they may also choose to ignore it. Like most house museums, site-specific stories about the servants are limited, requiring the staff to rely on some period information, but the general material is employed successfully to create a rich presentation of servant life.

Using the Villa Louis servants' tour as a model, I developed and presented "The View from Back Stairs" tours at Brucemore, which debuted in April 2005. During the month of April, this ninety-minute tour was offered once each Saturday morning. Unlike the Villa Louis tours, the Brucemore version did not include first-person "vignettes" along the way but did feature a costumed guide, which is unlike the standard visitor experience. I wore the costume created for the aforementioned holiday evening tours during this tour. As additional guides took on the tour, similar costumes were made for them. Men guiding the tour chose either the dark suit reminiscent of a butler or the denim and slouch cap of the head gardener. The tour itself was given in third-person interpretation, but the use of the costume was something to which the audience seemed to respond positively, and it provided an opportunity to discuss the function of livery as a way of visually distinguishing servants and their role as an indicator of the family's status.

I also incorporated a variety of primary sources into the tour. In the first year of presenting "The View from Back Stairs," I mounted on foam core quotes and illustrations from etiquette and household manuals, advertisements, photographs of servants at Brucemore, period floor plans from the site, and a few of Ella McDannel's diary entries and placed these pieces throughout the house for reference during the tour. I asked visitors who took the tour to fill out an evaluation, through which I learned that many were interested in the materials but didn't have enough time to view them. They were still present the next year, but I also incorporated most of them into a simple booklet I designed and printed in-house, which visitors could refer to throughout the tour and take with them.

The tour began in the visitor center, where I used several panels in the permanent orientation exhibition as part of a fifteen-minute introduction. I provided an overview of the three families who lived there, basic information on the servant staffs during each period, and a description of Brucemore as a country estate that relied on a large number of specialized workers to care for not just the house and family but also the grounds. In summarizing this content, I introduced the ideas that the Douglases and their servants lived in a period of great social and technological change that made an impact on housekeeping, that most servants were immigrants, and that many women who hired servants experienced the "servant problem," which affected the way mistresses and servants viewed and interacted with each other. In essence, this tour was an opportunity to put into practice several themes that I had developed during my dissertation research: images of ideal and real servants, and the servant problem as an interpretive theme.

While walking the group from the visitor center to the mansion, we made several short stops in front of outbuildings built by the Douglas family in the 1910s. These buildings provided work and living space necessary to maintain the estate, and they have a unified architectural style that creates the look of a small "village" at the same time as it distinguishes them from the more elaborate architecture of the family residence. All of the buildings were built along a service drive, and all but one, a squash court/bookbindery used by the Douglas family (and later used as a residence for the last family's housekeeper), had their doors oriented facing the service drive and served utilitarian functions. The barn (now visitor center) had been the location of horse stalls and later a garage. The servants' duplex was used as a residence for the head gardener and married staff, which offered more privacy than the mansion's third-floor bedrooms but still kept workers on the estate and within summoning range. The greenhouse, next door to the duplex, provided an opportunity to share the story of Archie White, the Douglases' last head gardener, about whom much is known due to contact with his daughter, who had shared her memories of growing up in the duplex, as well as family snapshots.

Before entering the mansion, the group learned more about the way architecture masked the domestic side of a household. When the mansion was built, it was like most Victorian houses: family and guests entered through the front door, and servants and deliveries through the back. However, after the Douglases purchased the house, they made a series of interior and exterior changes that affected domestic traffic; namely, they moved the main entrance to what had been the "back" side of the house. Since family and servants were now entering on the same side, the Douglases enclosed the servants' entrance with a porch and created an adjacent service yard, which allowed the domestic functions of the house to continue without drawing attention to them. A series of photographs and plans illustrated these changes.

Instead of entering using the main entrance, the tour went inside through the service porch and into the basement laundry room. In the basement and in each of the mansion's three floors, the servant rooms were viewed first, followed by the family rooms. This tour flow allowed for more integration of material on servants and their employers. In the servants' spaces, content included the type of work performed there, domestic technology that was still present or may have been found there, names of servants known to have worked there, and specific stories when available. The family spaces were interpreted through the eyes of the domestic staff, such as the interaction between family and servants when meals were served in the dining room, the ceremonial role of servants at the front door and when the Douglases entertained in the public spaces of the mansion, the cleaning and care of public areas, personal service provided by ladies' maids and valets in the bedrooms, and the role of the nurse in a family with children. The final room on the tour was a servants' bedroom, where I discussed living conditions. One of the few documents available for this space is a list of the cost of wallpapers purchased for the home during the 1907 renovation. Eighteen rolls of paper at twenty cents each were purchased for the cook's room ($3.60); 20 rolls of paper at 17 cents each for the maid's room ($3.40); 18 rolls of paper at 65 cents each for the boudoir ($11.70), and 28 rolls of linen damask at $2.50 each for the library walls ($70.00). This information demonstrates the relative significance of decor in the servants' wing, the bedroom floor, and the public area, and the fact that although domestic manuals and articles in women's magazines emphasized that servants' rooms should be pleasant, they should be decorated and furnished inexpensively.

"The View from Back Stairs" allowed for a more detailed interpretation of the estate as a whole than is possible during the average visitor experience. Based on the 2005 visitor surveys, of the seventy-three people who took the tour that month, only ten had never visited the mansion before, which suggests that this type of tour has strong potential for attracting repeat visitation. An added incentive was the fact that members could take the tour for free, while general admission was ten dollars. The tour also offered guides a new way to learn about and present information about domestic service and likely made an impact on their daily house tours. As a way to initiate guide training for the tour, during the first year it was offered, I asked for volunteer "assistants" who worked the back of the group to keep things moving and to observe the tour. Two guides worked each week. When the tour was offered the next year, I created a training packet for assistants who wanted to give the tour, and this group became the next generation of guides for "The View from Back Stairs."

SERVANTS IN LEADING ROLES

Fine furniture and objets d'art are typically the centerpieces of house museum interpretation, but at the James J. Hill House in St. Paul, Minnesota, the lack of these artifacts is actually an asset. While rare and expensive artifact collections frequently attract visitors, without them the guides must mine information from the primary artifact—the house itself. Empty rooms challenge guides to think beyond the inventory and random family anecdotes. Without furniture and art objects to distract the visitor, guides turn to the social history of the house. Although the imposing forty-two-room Richardsonian Romanesque mansion on St. Paul's fashionable Summit Avenue is nearly empty of furniture, its impressive servants' quarters and mechanical systems provide the basis for a fascinating tale of family and servant life, one that gets a dramatic treatment each holiday season.

James J. Hill, who would become known as the "Empire Builder," earned his wealth through shipping and transportation ventures. When he arrived in Saint Paul in 1856, Hill was seventeen years old and had only recently left his native Canada. He started as a riverboat shipping clerk, but the railroad business made him rich. He and several partners purchased a bankrupt railroad in 1878, extended the tracks north to Canada, and reorganized it as the St. Paul, Minneapolis, and Manitoba, later known as the Great Northern Railroad. During Hill's lifetime, the railroad reached the Pacific and made St. Paul a major transportation and wholesale center. In 1888, Hill hired Peabody, Stearns, and Furber of Boston and St. Louis to design a new monumental residence for his family. Hill, his wife Mary Theresa Mehegan Hill, and their ten children lived at the Summit Avenue house between 1891 and 1921. In 1925, four years after Mary Hill's death, four of her daughters gave the estate to the Archdiocese of St. Paul and Minneapolis. Church officials used the house as an office building until the archdiocese consolidated its offices in 1978, at which point the house was offered to the Minnesota Historical Society, which owns and operates the site today.[21]

Before the house even opened to the public, plans for interpreting the site and its working inhabitants were described in print. An article in the AASLH publication *History News* highlighted the Hill House and the Raynham Hall Museum in Oyster Bay, New York, as "good examples of the way interpretation has changed to incorporate the social history movement and to shed light on the other side." Elisabeth Doermann, an early administrator at the Hill House, noted that some staff favored the "great man" approach, others the social history approach. After this initial disagreement, concern for interpreting the lives of *all* the Hill House's residents became a priority.[22]

The interpretive tour of the Hill House gradually expanded over time. Originally, visitors toured only the ground floor and basement; today, they see all three main floors and the basement, which provides them with a thorough view of the role of servants in the Hill household. Guides describe the roles of servants in both the family and servants' areas of the house: a servant stood behind the Christmas tree with a pail of water after the candles were lit; a signal on the pipe organ alerted a servant in the basement to pump the bellows; and a cook or maid earned $5 to $7 a week versus the $1 an hour earned by the woodcarver who crafted the elaborate carvings found in the main hall. Noting the presence of servants throughout the house instead of just in their work and living areas reminds visitors that servants, especially in a large house like the Hills', were literally everywhere.[23]

At many sites, unfurnished servants' rooms have a barren feeling compared to spaces filled with furniture on the family side. At the Hill House, the emptiness of *all* the rooms allows for consistent interpretation throughout the residence. The third-floor servants' rooms have pine finishes and simple trim. The bedrooms have many windows, one with a view of Saint Paul Cathedral, which prompts the story of a head cook who married one of the cathedral's construction workers. Despite the many windows, the rooms have the odd shapes and slanted ceilings typical of top-floor servant bedrooms. Two servants shared each room, and Mrs. Hill hung a plaque stating their duties on the wall, which provided a constant reminder of their work even during their personal time. These plaques are not present today, but if it were possible to replicate them, they would further emphasize the family's control of the servants' lives.

The basement working spaces are particularly revealing locations to describe the labor necessary to run such a large household. A large kitchen provides an opportunity to discuss two well-documented cooks who worked for the Hills, Celia Tauer and Lena Peterson. The working areas are integrated with several staff common areas, reminding visitors that servants were part of a separate community within the household. The servants' hall provided a place for leisure, as evident in a humorous anecdote about cook Lena's three suitors who all called on the same evening. A well-equipped laundry room is a testament to the backbreaking nature of the labor, which may have contributed to the surly personality of Irish laundress Helen Murphy. Throughout the tour, one is continually reminded of the intertwined lives of these very different groups of people, not only the differences between upstairs and downstairs, but the variety of personalities living and working together as a staff. House museum personnel frequently cite the lack of artifacts related to servants as a reason for not interpreting domestic servants or doing it in a limited capacity. The Hill House serves as an example of how such obstacles can be not only overcome, but turned into assets.

Historic houses often utilize their interiors for bringing stories of their residents to life. Dramatic presentations appear to be quite popular with visitors; at Colonial Williamsburg, a slate of dramatic "evening programs" regularly sells out. While many sites use first-person interpretation during the guided tour to allow different members of the household to present their impressions of the house, some have created scripted performances based on site documentation that feature servants in prominent roles.

The Hill House may be unfurnished, but the site is still able to populate the rooms and halls with servants that are as three-dimensional as their employers. After the house became a public historic site, a handful of former Hill House servants participated in oral history interviews and offered their photographs and personal documents for study. The most creative way of sharing their stories is the program "Hill House Holidays," a very popular play performed in the mansion each holiday season for over twenty years. Visitors are asked to assume the role of an applicant for a waitress position at the Hill House. The audience follows the actors, who portray various documented Hill House servants, through the rooms on the first floor and basement as they prepare the house for a holiday party. Each room offers the actors an opportunity to discuss how the family and servants related to the space, and a setting for introducing other servant "characters" who would have worked there.

"Hill House Holidays" is a lighthearted production full of humorous stories told by the servants about their misadventures and interactions with their employers. When new servant characters are introduced to the audience, an actor reads from a "biography book," which includes such information as the servants' ethnic backgrounds, duties, and personality traits. Stories about servant life at the Hill House gathered from oral histories and other research are also integrated into the narrative. When Jack Hasslen is introduced, as he hangs paintings in the picture gallery, he relates the following story:

> Nothing so unnerving as having Jim Hill fix his glare on you while you do your job. . . . Finally I got 'em [the new paintings from Paris] all straight and perfect. Hill was feeling good, and it looked like he was going to give me a tip. He was wearing a white vest with four white pockets, and he reached into one and came out with a $20 bill. That must have been too much for me. He put it back. He pulled out some $10 bills, and shoved them back in his pockets, too. He found a $50 and more $20s, and finally gave up trying to find a $1 bill, so he patted me on the shoulder and said, 'Very satisfactory indeed' . . . and left.

Following Jack's speech, the action freezes and another servant reads from the biography book about the story's source, an interview with Jack published in the *Minneapolis Tribune* in 1980. The biographical note also mentions that Jack got work for his sister Clara as a pantry maid, and throughout the production her character fantasizes about what it must be like to be peers of the Hills, to the extent that she neglects her duties. The Hills are never seen during the production; but occasionally Mrs. Hill's voice is heard gently scolding Clara for forgetting her work. "Hill House Holidays" effectively reverses the traditional turn-of-the-century household by bringing the activities of the workers into the spotlight and relegating the owner families to offstage voices.[24]

The more difficult aspects of servant life are relayed through the "job interview." Since the actors interact with the audience as if they were seeking a job in the Hill household, throughout the program they make reference to some of the less appealing aspects of servant life and the expectations that Mrs. Hill has for her staff. At the beginning of the program, the "guide" (who acts as a narrator of sorts) tells the audience,

"So, if you are looking for long hours, low pay, and no benefits . . . you've come to the right place." Once the group has reached the servants' realm downstairs, the characters reveal more about the expectations Mrs. Hill has, by sharing her interview questions, putting visitors to work peeling apples and potatoes, and looking at their hands for signs that they are used to demanding labor. Although the program as a whole provides an upbeat picture of servant life at the Hill House, the hardships are shown to lurk just beneath the surface. A twelve-person servant staff shared both the good and bad parts of their lives and work with one another, and "Hill House Holidays" capably incorporates personal anecdotes to remind visitors that although work was hard, within their "community" some prospects for enjoyment existed.[25]

As my survey respondents indicated, some sites use first-person interpretation for tours and special programs. While not technically "theater," this technique incorporates theatrical elements (in fact, many such interpreters have previous theater experience), although unlike the Hill House program, it is improvised rather than scripted. The Alexander Ramsey House, a second St. Paul house museum owned and operated by the Minnesota Historical Society, uses first-person interpretation to introduce the stories of domestic servants, which were researched quite thoroughly in a master's thesis by a student in the Cooperstown Graduate Program. Servants' work and living spaces are part of the tour, and a kitchen interpretation program brings one aspect of domestic service to life.[26]

In the kitchen, we were greeted by Annie, the cook, who was in the process of making cookies from one of Mrs. Ramsey's recipes. Annie talked about scientific management in the kitchen as endorsed by Catherine Beecher and explained how the call bell panel that summoned servants worked. She also described the labor-saving advantages of the icebox and the privilege of access to the latest technology. Annie gave a very informative overview of a cook's experiences of the period during our tour; however, she also could have addressed the complexities of some of the objects she pointed out. For example, the call-bell panel could prompt a description of how she or other servants felt about the disruption of being called in the middle of a task, and about always being at the beck and call of their employers. The icebox could provide a chance to question to what extent such labor-saving devices actually eased servants' work or, conversely, increased it by raising expectations of their productiveness. It is possible that other first-person interpreters in the kitchen (not always Annie; sometimes there is a family member looking for one of the servants) do address these issues; ours was just one example of the experience offered in the Ramsey kitchen.[27]

The first-person interpretation is successful at the Ramsey House and certainly has the potential to be adapted by others. One of its great advantages is its ability to bring life into what are usually static spaces. Historic house museums tend to be very "hands-off" places, so the activity and aromas produced in the kitchen program engage senses normally dormant during a guided tour. On a basic level, the visitor is reminded that this house was lived in as a home, something easily forgotten when viewing rooms from behind ropes or Plexiglas barriers. The kitchen program focuses on tasks that are easy for the visitor to relate to, but the danger is that it can easily become influenced by nostalgia. First-person interpretations tend to be task-based demonstrations of baking, making candles, sewing, or other activities that often lead visitors to think that the past was a "simpler" time, despite the intentions of the interpreters. These presentations can address much more than how servants did their work, including how they felt about it, how it segregated them from the family, and how their status as servants affected their relationships overall.

The performance-based interpretations can be powerful visitor experiences when well executed. Scripted programs like "Hill House Holidays" have the benefit of being more predictable: the actors are more likely to be trained, which usually means higher-quality performances, and the use of a script ensures consistent content. The kitchen program at the Ramsey House is a slice of what a visitor experiences on a grand scale at living history sites like Conner Prairie and Colonial Williamsburg but is less overwhelming from the visitor's perspective. One benefit of confining the living history interpretation to one room is that the regular tour guide (speaking from the perspective of the present) has the opportunity to fill in the historical context and use the character interpreter's presentation to describe changes over time.

"Fourth wall" presentations, in which visitors watch the interaction of two or more character interpreters, with an audience discussion after the performance, may be the best approach to using "living history." The now-closed Baltimore City Life Museum's program "Steps in Time" offered audiences the opportunity to contemplate the issues of race, class, and religion without having to be directly involved with the performance. Like "Hill House Holidays," the program combined a guided tour with a scripted theatrical performance. As groups moved through the eight-room house, they were able to "eavesdrop" on various conversations taking place within: "John Hutchinson argued with his servant [a free African American] and boarder about colonialism and abolition. The brother and fiancé of the African American servant disagreed heatedly about the prospects for a free black man who had lost his job in the shipyards due to competition from Irish immigrants. The Catholic Hutchinsons and their Protestant boarder disputed over an 1839 riot at a Carmelite convent." An audience discussion followed the tour, which allowed them to ask questions and talk about what they had seen. The Villa Louis servants' tour took an approach similar to "Steps in Time," but the fact that tours had to run on a regular schedule meant that the guide needed to worry as much about finishing the tour within a particular frame of time as she did about engaging the visitors in discussion; the former concern typically won out, and it usually does at most house museums when time is an issue.[28]

BEHIND THE SCENES

Tours like the Villa Louis servant tours and "The View from Back Stairs" are two examples of expanded tour options that allow visitors to see a historic house museum from a different perspective. Another popular "special interest" tour that can either fully focus on or provide a more balanced interpretation of domestic servants is the "behind the scenes" tour, which takes visitors into areas of the house that are normally closed to the public. These "nooks and crannies" tours are common at very large house museums in which it is impossible for a visitor to see the whole house during a standard visit of forty-five to sixty minutes. They are also opportunities to bring small numbers of visitors into areas that are being used for storage or are more "raw" or unrestored than the rooms typically presented on the standard tour. Visitors always want to see what is behind closed doors, and often they will pay slightly higher ticket prices for the privilege.

Stan Hywet Hall & Gardens in Akron, Ohio, started offering "Nooks and Crannies" as a special tour but made it a daily offering in 2006. Built for F. A. Seiberling, a co-founder of the Goodyear Tire and Rubber Company, and his family, between 1912 and 1915, this impressive Tudor Revival manor house features more than sixty-five rooms and is sited on seventy acres of landscaped grounds (a fraction of its original acreage, but enough to isolate it from the surrounding residential area). Like Brucemore, Stan Hywet preserves the significant elements of an early-twentieth-century country estate such as gardens, facilities for family leisure, and support buildings such as a gate lodge, greenhouse/conservatory, gardener's cottage, carriage house, and stables. After Seiberling's death in 1955, his heirs donated the property to a nonprofit organization to ensure its preservation and enjoyment as a cultural and educational center for the community.

Stan Hywet's staff has an extensive base of research for the material they present on domestic servants. The Seiberling family left all of the house's furnishings intact (including those once present in the servants' wing) and an extensive family archive. Because the house was built and lived in during the first half of the twentieth century, the staff has been able to conduct oral histories with several former domestic employees, so a certain level of specificity is possible. The archives also include numerous pieces of personal correspondence to and from Stan Hywet's domestics as well as letters about them. Perhaps most importantly, the archives also include photos of domestics, including several taken when the Seiberlings hosted a Shakespearean ball and all the servants were dressed in appropriate costume.

Each day, visitors have several options for touring the Manor House. They may choose the guided tour or opt for a self-guided experience accompanied by a brochure and supplemented by information provided by staff in the house. Stan Hywet has an expansive and elaborate servants' wing. The principal work areas—the butler's pantry, kitchen, cook's pantry, and breakfast room pantry—are part of both guided and self-guided visitor experiences. A large and impressive kitchen, featuring a cooking range that could be fueled by gas, coal, and wood, offers one location for guides to discuss the domestic side of life at Stan Hywet Hall. Although Mrs. Seiberling likely spent little if any time in the kitchen, her education at the Lasell Seminary for Young Women, located outside of Boston, one the first schools to offer domestic science courses, and at Fannie Farmer's cooking school, perhaps prepared her better than most of her peers to manage a staff of servants. At the end of the tour, the group may browse a series of interpretive panels in the basement, several of which address aspects of life and work for the Seiberlings' domestic employees. These panels incorporate photographs of the site's domestic staff and period advertisements.[29]

Those who have visited before or prefer a "behind the scenes" perspective can take the "Nooks and Crannies" tour, offered three times each day. This tour explores areas not included on the standard manor house tour, such as the service areas, some of which are now restored, and others that are still used for offices and collections storage. "Nooks and Crannies" expands the visitor's understanding of domestic workers by providing greater access to rooms primarily lived in by the employees and more time to discuss the details of their work and everyday life. A series of female staff bedrooms have been part of this special tour for several years, but in 2008 the staff began presenting them as period rooms. All the furnishings are original, although the museum staff relied on educated conjecture in determining furniture placement and which pieces to use in each room. One former female-staff bedroom has been made into a "hands-on" room featuring early-twentieth-century domestic technology, while another offers a glimpse at sports and leisure of the country house era. A series of interpretive panels hang in the hallways to provide contextual information and quotes from archival materials. Like the panels in the basement, they are illustrated with photographs and period advertisements from Stan Hywet's collections.

Tour content combines site-specific information, including the number of staff employed by the Seiberlings, the specialized positions present there in a typical backstairs hierarchy, and names and stories related to specific personalities, with general background material culled from domestic and etiquette manuals. Themes present in the tour include the ethnic backgrounds of the servants, the difference between living in and living out, the varying lengths of staff tenures, and the fact that while the domestic staff interacted with the family and their spaces, they also inhabited a world of their own. The goal of Stan Hywet Hall's "Nooks and Crannies" tour is to offer unique insights and personalized stories for visitors so that they can have a more authentic experience of the life of the domestic staff during the height of the Gilded Age. The opening of the additional servants' rooms for this tour has helped the site achieve this goal.

Several of Historic New England's house museums also offer behind-the-scenes tours that focus on domestic service. Phillips House in Salem, Massachusetts, has an extraordinary early-twentieth-century collection of domestic equipment and technology, large and small. The kitchen features a built-in range, a call bell and intercom system, and a large cabinet filled with all manner of tools and gadgets. The basement laundry room has a large sink, washboards, wringers, a set kettle, and a laundry stove with irons. Phillips House staff members have documented many of the men and women who worked at the house, several of whom had extraordinarily long tenures. As a result of the strong presence of original domestic objects and stories of real people, interpretation of the domestic staff is an important part of all tours at Phillips House, but additional opportunities are occasionally offered to give visitors a glimpse of the laundry room and the servants' bedrooms, which are not currently part of the everyday tour. Visitor interest in these areas has led to adding an empty servants' bedroom to the daily tour.

"The Way They Were," a special tour at Hamilton House in South Berwick, Maine, focuses on a general history of domestic service at the house in the early twentieth century, in addition to taking visitors into the attic servants' area. Information about servants during this period is quite fragmentary, but period domestic manuals are used to describe a typical household at a summer estate and the way servants and employers may have interacted. The tour focuses on the attic, which includes several bedrooms, a bathroom, and a hatch that provides a stunning view of the surrounding grounds. Only one of the bedrooms is open, and although it is now being used for storage, it gives visitors a sense of what these spaces are like, and the physical experience of being in the servants' living quarters. In most cases, people are delighted simply to have access to areas that are not normally seen, so these are great opportunities both to provide a special visitor experience and to deepen education about the lives of domestic workers.[30]

RESTORING BALANCE TO THE DOMESTIC STORY

Maymont, a Gilded Age estate in Richmond, Virginia, has thus far been the most ambitious in its development of a fully nuanced interpretation of domestic service. Although a significant number of southern historic houses have started to interpret slavery on the antebellum plantation, Maymont is an excellent example of a site where visitors learn about the lives of African American servants during the post–Civil War era. In May 2005, Maymont staff completed the long process of implementing an impressive and extensive restoration and interpretation of the basement service areas. The resulting period rooms and accompanying permanent exhibition allow Maymont to feature one of the most complete interpretations of domestic service in the country. This project was in the making for over twenty years, but the site's curatorial staff overcame the common hurdles in bringing this history to the public.

Maymont House sits on a 100-acre site on the banks of the James River in Richmond, Virginia. James Henry Dooley, lawyer, financier, and civic leader, purchased the property in 1886. Several years later, ground was broken for the massive stone house, which combined Romanesque Revival and Queen Anne styles. James and his wife, Sallie May Dooley, both in their forties, moved into the new residence in 1893 and called it home for the remainder of their lives. The couple had no children, and after Mrs. Dooley's death in 1925, the estate passed to the city of Richmond and opened to the public as a museum.[31]

The city operated Maymont from 1926 to 1975 as a free museum and park. The mansion interiors and gardens remained much as they had been during the residential period. However, the city developed part of the large acreage into a small zoo and emphasized the estate's function as a public park. The city transferred management and operation to the nonprofit Maymont Foundation in 1975, with a stipulation that the site must remain a free attraction as it had during the city's management. Since that time, Maymont has developed in two directions simultaneously. A children's farm, animal exhibits, and a new nature/visitor center are located on the north section of the grounds, and Maymont House and its gardens occupy the south section. Each area has separate staff. Some visitors come to the site without even seeing the historic mansion, and many Richmonders know Maymont only as a park and zoo.[32]

Maymont's location has the potential to draw a more diverse audience than the typical house museum. It is located adjacent to a lower-middle-class, predominantly African American neighborhood in a city that has a nonwhite population of 57 percent. Of the students that participated in school programs at Maymont House, 80 percent were from the Richmond public school system, which is 91 percent African American. Nearly half of Maymont's visitors come from the Greater Richmond area, which has nonwhite representation of 30 percent. A 1995 phone survey found that a considerable number of African American visitors came from the Greater Richmond area. This audience is far different from that represented in a 1996 survey on visitation to historic sites in the Hudson Valley, New York, in which visitor demographics recorded 50 percent of visitors as over fifty years old, with only 4 percent younger than twenty-five, 62 percent earning above $50,000 a year and holding college degrees, and presumably predominantly white.[33]

When Maymont first opened to the public, the interpretive focus was on the Dooleys and their lifestyle. When Dale Wheary joined the staff as curator in 1979, she began investigating the history of Maymont's domestic staff and conducting oral history interviews, in addition to planning and fundraising for ongoing renovation of the family spaces and collections conservation. Unfortunately, documents such as diaries, letters, and ledgers that are usually key sources for research on any aspect of a family's residence at a historic place are virtually nonexistent. A 1926 entry in an early museum log indicates that "all papers and plans at the Maymont home (now 'Dooley Museum') were burned by the Dooleys' former maid, Fannie Waddy, at the order of Mrs. Dooley's nieces." In 1982, a small NEH grant, however, provided funds for a school outreach lesson on Victorian servant life. The site also began offering a monthly focus tour—The Victorian Servant Life Backstairs Tour—which was extremely popular. These tours led to additional connections for the project, including oral history referrals and donations of period household manuals and artifacts. From the beginning, the public showed a great deal of interest in and support for the interpretation of servant life at Maymont.[34]

Members of Richmond's community have played important roles in the planning stages as site staff reached toward higher goals for their servant interpretation. The site sponsored five community roundtables between

1995 and 2000, which brought together diverse groups of civic and church leaders, historians, representatives from other museums, universities and archives, Maymont neighbors, and former domestic servants to discuss their concerns and ideas related to the proposed domestic service project. In its January 2002 NEH Implementation Grant Proposal, the Maymont Foundation reported, "At the first roundtable in 1995, twenty participants were introduced to newly gathered research and documentation and then asked to discuss how an exhibition containing potentially controversial content would be received in the community. The supportive and positive reaction of the group encouraged staff to move forward." African American scholars and community leaders were valuable members of these groups and offered support and assistance as the staff worked to interpret the lives of African American servants during a period when Jim Crow laws limited the freedoms they had won through emancipation. Throughout the long planning process, the Maymont staff took advantage of the time by cultivating positive relationships with stakeholders and expanding their network of friends, supporters, and informants.[35]

Maymont's goal of restoring the basement service areas inched closer to realization during the 1990s as staff consulted the community, conducted oral history research, and worked with architects to mine the basement for information relevant to its previous use. Maymont staff engaged several scholars during this time, including Barbara Carson and Elizabeth O'Leary, who served as the project's guest curator. A thorough architectural investigation conducted by Charles Phillips documented the basement spaces, which had suffered from serious deterioration, in order to preserve as much original fabric as possible and to accurately reproduce that which could not be salvaged. During this time the staff also engaged in extensive fundraising in addition to receiving NEH planning and implementation grants to support the installation of the 3,000-square-foot permanent exhibition "In Service and Beyond: Domestic Work and Life in a Gilded Age Mansion."

The new exhibition and period rooms have greatly improved the basic visitor experience. Prior to completion of the belowstairs project, visitors waited at the mansion's entrance at the posted tour times. Visitors now enter via a modified and handicap-accessible version of the original subterranean servants' entrance, are sheltered from inclement weather, and as they wait for their tour, they may browse the permanent exhibition. Here, they have access to an orientation space with exhibit panels and short introductory videos and seven fully restored period rooms: the kitchen, pantry, laundry room, cold room, butler's bedroom, wine cellar, and maid's room. The newly restored butler's pantry is viewed during the upstairs tour. Each room is an exhibition in its own right, featuring furnishings, appliances, product packaging, household items, and other artifacts and ephemera that would have been found in such areas circa 1910. Visitors encounter an informative series of "reading rail" panels mounted on three-foot-high barriers that protect the collection and allow visitors to view the period rooms and interpretive material in a complementary manner. Throughout the exhibition, visitors have opportunities to supplement the information from the reading rails and exhibit panels with various interactive and auditory experiences.

The former furnace room has been transformed into a central orientation room. A series of wall panels provides visitors with the historical context necessary to fully appreciate the nuances of domestic servant life in the Jim Crow era South and introduces some of the most difficult content. Issues such as race, ethnicity, the "servant problem," and segregation are addressed sensitively but honestly. For example, under the heading "Southern Service in Black and White," exhibition text describes the racial divisions of the Dooleys' world: "James and Sallie Dooley, raised in slave-owning households before the Civil War, were accustomed to service from black attendants. As adults they witnessed the transformation of the master–slave relationship to one of employer–employee. By the time they built Maymont in 1893, slavery had been abolished for nearly thirty years. Nevertheless, an entrenched racial system remained fully in place." The introductory panels also acknowledge, "The Maymont era coincided with the beginning of the Age of Jim Crow, one of the most violent and repressive periods in American race relations." Such issues are challenging to present in public, although necessary for a full understanding of the world the Dooleys and their domestic staff inhabited. Other panels in this central area address more general content relative to the domestic realm, including the impact of new domestic technology like electricity, central heating, plumbing, and lighting. The orientation space also features a selection of videos that introduce visitors to the Gilded Age, the Dooleys, the house, the estate, and domestic service. Tucked in a private corner of this central space, a book of tributes to those who worked in domestic service is available for those who wish to contribute their own reflections on domestic service based on their personal histories.

Additional general subject matter is covered in the back hall. Here, visitors learn about the differences between living in and living out, an important aspect of Maymont's domestic story. Most of Maymont's domestic employees lived out, which is different from the situation at many historic house museums, which more often interpret live-in servants. As the label text points out, this practice became more common throughout the United States after 1920, but it started much earlier in the South. Because the Maymont employees had homes and families outside of their workplace, it is easier to see their work as just one part (albeit a very significant part) of their lives. However, some members of the domestic staff traveled with the Dooleys to their summer home, where they spent the whole season away from their families. The back hall panels also inform visitors that the days of domestic workers were long, that the work was labor-intensive and relentless. A series of panels invites visitors to guess how many staff members and hours were required when Sallie Dooley invited four friends for tea (seven staff, fourteen hours and forty-five minutes), when James Dooley got up, had breakfast with his wife, and left for the office (six staff, twelve hours), or when the Dooleys hosted an evening dinner party for six guests (seven staff, forty-six hours).

The restoration of the adjacent period rooms is meticulous and fully immersive. The sound of a ticking clock and the historically accurate dim lighting in the kitchen are subtle but effective ways of bringing the visitor into this world. Each room features richly illustrated interpretive reading-rail panels that are engaging and informative. The panels describe the work that took place in the room, the domestic technology in place there in 1910, the names of staff who worked in the room, when known, and in several cases more extensive biographical information. A wide selection of visual material, including photographs, advertisements, illustrations from period domestic manuals, and cookbooks, provide depth and nuance to the story related by the text. While the upstairs rooms are furnished almost entirely with original objects and artworks, the majority of the approximately 933 furnishings and artifacts displayed in the period rooms are not original to Maymont but were in use during the interpretive period. A local family trust provided financial support for acquisition of the objects, which were found in antique stores or purchased through eBay. The period rooms are treated with such detail in the comprehensive collection of objects—all manner of period-appropriate appliances, and food and other packaging—that the spaces become "real" in a way that use of only what was "original" could never achieve. While Maymont staff have gained a great deal of site-specific knowledge about their domestic realm, as with most historic house museums, this information is still fragmentary. Yet they have re-created the world belowstairs in a rich and compelling way.[36]

Naturally, however, some of the most powerful content and artifacts are those with direct connections to Maymont. In the kitchen, visitors are introduced to the Walker family. Frances Twiggs Walker worked as the head cook between 1919 and 1925, and six of her children worked at

Maymont as teens and young adults. Visitors are also asked, "Can you find Gloria?" Upon closer inspection of the kitchen, they will find a doll, who belonged to Frances Twiggs Walker's granddaughter, nestled in a box cradle. They also learn that it is through the memories of such grandchildren and other family that descriptions of the kitchen survived. Another very powerful object is found in the butler's room, where visitors meet William Dilworth, the butler between 1919 and 1925. A reproduction of the print "Jesus Died for Both," which shows Christ blessing a black child and a white child, was given by his descendants, and although the original hung in his family home and not at Maymont, it is a testament to the role of the church in his life and others in the African American community. The words of several descendants of Maymont employees are found throughout the exhibition, either in quotes on text panels or in audio components. In an excerpt of an oral history interview that may be listened to in the maid's room, Frances Twiggs Walker's niece, Virgie Payne, described her memory of meeting the lady of the house: "Mrs. Dooley told me, 'I want you to grow up a fine cook, like your Aunt.' And my aunt said, 'Well, I don't want her to be a cook.'"[37]

The visitor finds plenty to read (perhaps a little too much for the average "streaker" or "stroller"), but even those with less time or interest in the reading material are sufficiently introduced to the people and activities that made the gilded life upstairs possible, and those with a greater inclination can learn even more. A well-written and illustrated gallery guide is available to visitors to take away, a piece that reflects the balance that now exists in the site's interpretation. Upon opening the four-panel guide, the reader learns "Maymont House Tells Two Stories . . ." and both the "Upstairs" and "Downstairs" stories are presented in brief. When the guide is fully unfolded, one finds condensed information from the exhibition about the separate but dependent domains within the house, domestic technology, an overview of domestic service, and the specific characteristics of domestic service in the Jim Crow South. Photographs and illustrations add visual interest, and a map provides short descriptions of the period rooms.

The project's guest curator, Elizabeth O'Leary, published a scholarly treatment of the exhibition's content, *From Morning to Night: Domestic Service in Maymont House and the Gilded Age South* (2003), for those with a particularly strong interest in the material. This well-researched book also allows the Maymont story to become more well known beyond the Greater Richmond area and allows the extensive research behind the exhibition to be presented with additional depth. Like the exhibition, O'Leary's book provides a balanced approach to Maymont's domestic story and covers much the same material, but with the benefit of more detail and scholarly apparatus. A panel exhibition on domestic service that travels to other historic houses and museums further expands the knowledge gained through the project.[38]

The extensive treatment of domestic work at Maymont has also made an impact on the interpretation upstairs. New docent training materials recommended how to incorporate the servant perspective into their interpretation of the family rooms, and ways to cross-reference upstairs and downstairs. Training sessions also helped guides make the transition. Maymont's guides, who are both paid and volunteer, have eagerly embraced the more balanced approach, despite initial skepticism by some. Visitors have also responded with great enthusiasm; visitation increased substantially once the exhibition opened, and these higher visitation numbers have been sustained over the subsequent three years.[39]

"In Service and Beyond" and the new period rooms have raised Maymont to a well-deserved position as a model site for domestic service interpretation. The exhibit itself addresses the subject matter with the richness and detail it deserves without placing the burden of additional information and time constraints on guides who interpret the "upstairs" realm. Visitors will be able to view as much or as little of the exhibition as they choose, but they *must* enter these areas in order to go on the mansion tour (guides take groups upstairs on the half hour), and they have less opportunity to completely avoid the exhibit (as they might at Villa Louis, or at Brucemore). This is an intentional aspect of its design—regardless how much or how little the guides discuss domestic service in the family spaces, the logistics of the exhibit guarantee that visitors will have some level of exposure to the subject. As part of the overall tour experience, the exhibition promotes a more balanced representation of life at Maymont House, which now bills itself as a "Gilded Age Showplace and Domestic Workplace."

All of these case study sites have developed their interpretation of domestic servants for tours and special programs over a period of time, sometimes many years. In most cases, these interpretive projects developed incrementally: first by completing research, then by reclaiming spaces (often one room at a time) and incorporating the material into daily tours, and finally, by expanding interpretation to include exhibitions, special tours, and programs. Because most sites, and most of those described in the case studies, have small or medium staffs and budgets, well-developed servant interpretation is usually the product of many years of perseverance and dedication to the topic.

While some of the tours and programs described in the case studies address more of the social history topics I included in my mail survey than do others, they all have found ways to make their average visitor experience more balanced and authentic by making the most of "original" stories, people, architecture, and material culture. These house museums have also learned that supplementing original material with more general period detail adds richness and texture to their interpretations of servant life. They have demonstrated that behind-the-scenes spaces and the stories associated with them have the potential to create opportunities for repeat visitation and also resonate with new visitors. What sites like Maymont, Villa Louis, and Brucemore are discovering is that potential house museum audiences are seeking different ways to see and understand history. Given the current conversations about the need for change in history museum practice and the financial strains that result from increased competition for visitors' leisure time, new ideas are needed. Amplifying the "voices from the back stairs" may be one way to draw visitors in for a unique, meaningful, fully "real" experience of the past.

Photo Essay II

Contemporary Interpretations

of Domestic Service

■ At Brucemore, servants' rooms are interpreted unfurnished. The servants' bedrooms are large but would have been shared by at least two people. The building materials and decorative treatments used for these rooms were less expensive than those used in the family side of the house.

Courtesy of Brucemore, Cedar Rapids, Iowa; National Trust for Historic Preservation

■ An exhibit panel and "standup" from the temporary exhibition, "Help Wanted: Working at Brucemore, 1907–1937," became a display in Ella McDannel's bedroom after the exhibition closed.

Courtesy of Brucemore, Cedar Rapids, Iowa; National Trust for Historic Preservation

Courtesy of Brucemore, Cedar Rapids, Iowa; National Trust for Historic Preservation

■ Domestic servants from all three eras of Brucemore's residential history are discussed in the orientation exhibition in the visitor center.

Kitchen, Beauport, Sleeper-McCann House, Gloucester, Massachusetts. Courtesy of Historic New England, Boston, Massachusetts; photograph by David Carmack, 2004

■ Entertaining was an important part of life at Beauport in the early twentieth century. The newly restored kitchen provides the backdrop for discussing the work behind the impressive dinners created and served by the Wonson family at Henry Davis Sleeper's parties.

■ Servant Room, Beauport,
Sleeper-McCann House, Gloucester, Massachusetts.

Courtesy of Historic New England, Boston, Massachusetts; photograph by David Carmack, 2004

Photograph by the author

■ Guides dressed in traditional
servants' uniforms presented the
Villa Louis "Servants' Tours" in
June 2000.

■ "Servants" preparing for "Hill
House Holidays" at the James J.
Hill House, St. Paul, Minnesota.

Courtesy of Steve Woit/www.stevewoit.com

Courtesy of Maymont Foundation; photograph by Dennis McWaters

■ The orientation room in Maymont's exhibition "In Service and Beyond" introduces visitors to the world of the domestic workers whose work spaces are now authentically and carefully restored.

■ The kitchen was a hub of activity for domestic workers at Maymont Mansion. Their visiting family members also remembered this room, including head cook Frances Twiggs Walker's grand-daughter, whose doll Gloria "sleeps" in a box cradle under the window.

Courtesy of Maymont Foundation; photograph by Dennis McWaters

■ An informative series of reading rail panels, which are richly illustrated with photographs and ephemera, provide context for Maymont's restored servant rooms.

Maymont Mansion, Maid's Room. Courtesy of Maymont Foundation; photograph by 1717 Design Group

Text of Mail Questionnaire Sent to Historic House Museums

Survey of Historic Houses and Interpretation of Domestic Servants

For the purpose of this survey, the following terms are defined as follows

The **standard tour** is the daily tour given to the average walk-in visitor.

Domestic servants or **servants** are any persons whose primary occupations are activities related to the care and comfort of their employers and their family, and cleaning and maintenance of their employers' home and its contents. This includes such persons as those engaged in personal service (butlers, lady's maids), housekeeping and cleaning, food preparation and serving, and childcare.

YOUR SITE

Name of Institution

Location

Governance   Year this site opened for public tours

Staff size Number   full-time   part-time

Seasonal staff Number   full-time   part-time

Number of full-time volunteers

Number of part-time volunteers

Number of tour guides   paid staff   volunteers

What is your site's interpretive period?

What are your site's interpretive themes?

If your site interprets <u>only</u> periods <u>before</u> 1865, please stop now and return this survey. Thank you for your help!

SERVANTS AT YOUR SITE

1. Were servants present at your site during the interpretive period?

    Yes

    No

If no, please stop now and return this survey.
Thank you for your help!

2. How many servants worked at your site during its interpretive period?

3. Which categories of servants were present at your site?

Butler	Head housekeeper	Parlormaid
Chambermaid	Chef	Cook
Kitchen maid	Scullery maid	Children's nurse
Governess	Footman	Chauffeur
Head gardener	Maid-of-all-work	Lady's maid
Other; please indicate		
Unknown		

4. Where did the domestic servant(s) live? (check all that apply)

    In the house   Elsewhere on site   Off site

5. The following is a list of the most common ethnic groups working in domestic service according to the 1900 census. Which ethnic groups are represented at your site?

Native-born white	African American	Austrian
Bohemian/Czech	Canadian (English)	Canadian (French)
Danish	English	French
German	Hungarian	Irish
Italian	Norwegian	Polish
Russian	Scottish	Swedish
Native-born of foreign parentage		Swiss
Other ethnicities; please indicate		

We do not know the ethnic backgrounds of any of the servants who worked at our site.

6. Is information about the domestic servant(s) part of your site's standard tour?

    Yes

    No   **If no, please continue with question 34.**

INTERPRETATION OF SERVANTS AT YOUR SITE

7. Which interpretive method(s) are used for your site's standard tour?
(mark all that apply)

   Third-person interpretation
   First-person interpretation
   Self-guided – labels or exhibit-style panels in the rooms
   Self-guided – written brochure
   Acoustiguide or similar recorded tour with headphones
   Stationary guides posted throughout the house
   Other (please describe)

7a) Which of the above methods are used to interpret domestic servants?

8. Are service areas (kitchen, servants' hall, servants' bedrooms)
part of the standard tour?

   Yes   Please identify
   No

8a) Are any of the above rooms restored as "period rooms"?

   Yes   Please identify
   No

9. May visitors tour support buildings used by servants
(i.e., stables, greenhouses, etc.)?

   Yes
   No
   Not applicable

10. Does your site have artifact collections relevant to servants who worked there?

   Yes   Please describe
   No

11. Does your site have archival collections relevant to servants
who worked there?

   Yes   Please describe
   No

12. Has your staff conducted off-site research about the site's servants?

   Yes   Please describe
   No

13. Does your site include information about domestic service in its tours that is **not** site-specific?

        Yes   a) If yes, which of the following have been the most significant sources?

                    Histories of domestic service

                    Regional history collections

                    Period etiquette/household manuals

                    Period newspapers

                    Period magazines

              b) Which statement best describes your site's use of general sources?

                    They are our primary resources for interpreting servants.

                    We use them to supplement what we know about actual servants at the site.

                    We use them sparingly.

        No   (Comments)

PLEASE INDICATE THE SIGNIFICANCE OF THE FOLLOWING TOPICS IN THE STANDARD TOUR

5 = Very significant   *1 = Not significant*

14. Difficulty of servants' work   5 4 3 2 1
15. Use of domestic appliances and technology   5 4 3 2 1
16. Ethnic backgrounds of servants   5 4 3 2 1
17. Working conditions of servants   5 4 3 2 1
18. Living conditions of servants   5 4 3 2 1
19. Social stigma of domestic service   5 4 3 2 1
20. Friendship between servants and employers   5 4 3 2 1
21. Conflict between servants and employers   5 4 3 2 1
22. Ethnic or racial prejudices of the era   5 4 3 2 1
23. Gender of domestic servants   5 4 3 2 1
24. The "servant problem"   5 4 3 2 1
25. Benefits of domestic service   5 4 3 2 1
26. Servants' uniforms   5 4 3 2 1

(Comments)

27. How would you describe the site's tour guides' reactions to interpreting domestic service?

      Enthusiastic   Favorable   Indifferent

      Resistant   Other; Please describe

(Comments)

28. How would you describe the visitors' reactions to hearing about domestic service?

      Enthusiastic   Favorable   Indifferent

      Resistant   Other; Please describe

(Comments)

SPECIAL PROGRAMS

29. Does your site currently offer special programs for the general public that focus on domestic service?

      Yes

      No   **If no, please continue with question 33.**

30. These programs are offered   seasonally   year-round

(Comments)

31. How frequent are these programs during the season or year?

      Daily   Weekly   Monthly

      Once each season/year   Occasionally, not on any specific schedule

32. Please provide a brief description of domestic service related programs

33. Does your site offer school programs that focus on the domestic servants?

      Yes   If yes, please provide a brief description

      No

      Please note any final comments in the section below.

SITES NOT INTERPRETING DOMESTIC SERVICE

34. Which of the following circumstances prevent interpretation of domestic service at your site? (check all that apply)

      The subject does not fit within our mission or interpretive objectives.

Financial resources are limited or unavailable.

Personnel resources are limited or unavailable.

This site lacks the necessary artifacts and archives to address the issue as we would like.

Board, staff, and/or volunteers are resistant to the idea.

This issue would be too sensitive to address in this community or region.

Other; Please describe

34a) Which of the above is the primary reason for not interpreting servants?

35. Are there plans to develop interpretation of domestic service in the future?
Yes
No

ADDITIONAL COMMENTS

36. Please add any additional comments you have about the interpretation of domestic servants at your historic house museum

APPENDIX 2

Additional Resources

The following is a select list of resources that provides a solid starting point for historic house museum staff members who wish to learn more about the history of domestic service. This is not an exhaustive list but includes most of the primary and secondary sources that have been most useful in my research on late-nineteenth- and early-twentieth-century domestic service. David Katzman and Daniel Sutherland also include extensive annotated bibliographies in their books, which I recommend for additional research material.

Perhaps the most exciting development in domestic service research in recent years has been the digitization of many primary sources related to the topic. Books once accessible only through a major university library or through interlibrary loan are now available free for download. I have found four sites particularly useful: Harvard Libraries Open Collections Program's "Women Working, 1800–1930," http://ocp.hul.harvard.edu/ww; Cornell University Mann Library's "Home Economics Archive: Research, Tradition, and History (HEARTH)," http://hearth.library.cornell.edu; Michigan State University Library and Michigan State University Museum's "Feeding America: The Historic American Cookbook Project," http://digital.lib.msu.edu/projects/cookbooks; and the Google Books Library Project, http://www.google.com/books. Many of the books listed below are available on one of these sites, but there are many more wonderful resources there, which I encourage those interested in domestic service to explore. Rather than including individual links in the citations, I have indicated at which site they are available as follows: Women Working (WW), HEARTH (HEARTH), Feeding America (FA), and Google Books (GB).

Primary Sources

Government Reports

Dempsey, Mary Veronica. *Occupational Progress of Women*. Washington, DC: GPO, 1922. (WW)

Hill, Joseph A. *Women in Gainful Occupations, 1870–1920*. Washington, DC: GPO, 1929. (WW)

Johnson, Borghild Eleanor. *Household Employment in Chicago*. Washington, DC: GPO, 1933. (WW)

Manning, Caroline. *The Immigrant Woman and Her Job*. Washington, DC: GPO, 1930. (WW)

Massachusetts Bureau of Statistics of Labor. *Social Statistics of Working Women*. Boston, 1901. (WW)

Pidgen, Charles F. *Trained and Supplemental Employees for Domestic Service*. Boston: Wright & Potter, 1906. (WW)

Reading List of References on Household Employment. Washington, DC: GPO, 1936. (WW)

Robinson, Mary V. *Domestic Workers and Their Employment Relations*. Washington, DC: GPO, 1924.

Smith, Mary Gove. *Immigration as a Source of Supply for Domestic Workers*. Boston: Women's Education and Industrial Union, 1906. (WW)

United States Bureau of the Census. *Statistics of Women at Work*. Washington, DC, 1907. (WW)

Watson, Amey E. *Household Employment in Philadelphia*. Washington, DC: GPO, 1932. (WW)

Domestic Service—General

Anderson, Mary. "Domestic Service in the United States." *Journal of Home Economics* 20 (January 1928): 7–12.

Barker, C. Hélène. *Wanted, a Young Woman to Do Housework: Business Principles Applied to Housework*. New York: Moffat, Yard, 1915. (WW)

Bentley, Mildred Maddocks. "The Psychology of Servants." *Ladies' Home Journal*, December 1925, 159–62, 165.

Campbell, Helen. *Prisoners of Poverty*. Boston: Roberts Bros., 1889. (WW)

"Employer–Employee Relationships in the Home." *Good Housekeeping*, February 1929, 104.

Frederick, Christine. "Suppose Our Servants Didn't Live with Us." *Ladies' Home Journal*, October 1914, 102.

Gale, Zona. "The Eight-Hour Home Assistant." *Ladies' Home Journal*, April 1919, 35.

Greene, Dorothea Pearson. "My Experiences with My Servants." *Ladies' Home Journal*, March 1914, 38.

Hervey, Antoinette. "The Saints in My Kitchen." *Outlook*, February 17, 1912, 367–71.

Higginson, Mary T. "My Summer with Japanese Servants." *Good Housekeeping*, August 1911, 188–92.

Hotchkiss, T. W. "Advice to Employers." *Good Housekeeping*, September 1909, 244.

Kellor, Frances A. "The Housewife and Her Helper." *Ladies' Home Journal*, November 1905, 24.

———. "The Housewife and Her Helper." *Ladies' Home Journal*, October 1905, 21.

———. "The Intelligence Office." *Atlantic Monthly*, October 1904, 458–64.

———. "The New Department: The Housewife and Her Helper." *Ladies' Home Journal*, September 1905, 17.

———. *Out of Work*. New York: G. P. Putnam's Sons, 1904.

Klink, Jane Seymour. "Put Yourself in Her Place." *Atlantic Monthly*, February 1905, 169–77.

Parloa, Maria. "The Young Couple with a Maid." *Ladies' Home Journal*, September 1905, 36.

Preston, Erie L. "Service Rooms of Modern Homes." *House and Garden,* November 1907, 185–90.

Robb, Juliet Everts. "Our House in Order." *Outlook,* June 18, 1910, 353–60.

Rorer, Mrs. S. T. "How to Treat and Keep a Servant." *Ladies' Home Journal,* May 1900, 26.

Salmon, Lucy Maynard. *Domestic Service.* New York: Macmillan, 1901. (GB)

———. *Progress in the Household.* Boston: Houghton Mifflin, 1906. (GB)

Trueblood, Mary E. "Housework versus Shop and Factories." *Independent,* November 13, 1902, 2691–93.

Household Manuals and Domestic Advice—General

Beecher, Catherine Esther. *Letters to Persons Who Are Engaged in Domestic Service.* New York: Leavitt & Trow, 1842. (WW)

Beecher, Catherine, and Harriet Beecher Stowe. *The American Woman's Home; or, Principles of Domestic Science.* New York: J. B. Ford, 1869. (FA)

Beecher, Mrs. Henry Ward [Eunice]. *Motherly Talks with Young Housekeepers.* New York: J. B. Ford, 1873. (WW)

"The Correct Apron for Maids." *Ladies' Home Journal,* March 1910, 47.

Frederick, Christine. *The New Housekeeping: Efficiency Studies in Home Management.* Garden City: Doubleday, Page, 1926. (WW)

Harland, Marion, ed. *Home Making.* Boston: Hall and Locke, 1911. (WW)

Herrick, Christine Terhune. *Housekeeping Made Easy.* New York: Harper & Brothers, 1888. (WW)

Holt, Emily. *The Complete Housekeeper.* Garden City, NY: Doubleday, Page, 1917. (HEARTH)

Pattison, Mary. *The Business of Home Management.* New York: Robert M. McBride, 1918.

Prince, Jane. *Letters to a Young Housekeeper.* Boston: Houghton Mifflin, 1917.

"Servants and Housekeepers." *Good Housekeeping,* May 1921, 125–26, 128.

"Servants and Labor-Saving Devices." *Good Housekeeping,* November 1912, 859–60.

"Service without Servants." *Good Housekeeping,* September 1925, 89, 220–21.

Sheldon, Rev. Charles M. "Servant and Mistress." Independent, December 1900, 3018–21.

Tachau, Hanna. "Furnishing the Servants' Rooms." *House Beautiful,* October 1920, 288–89, 316.

Tarbell, Ida. "What Shall We Do for Maids?" *Good Housekeeping,* November 1917, 22–23, 102, 105, 106, 109.

White, Charles E., Jr. "The Servant in the Little House." *Ladies' Home Journal,* November 1915, 54.

———. "Where Does Your Servant Live?" *House Beautiful,* April 1913, 136–38.

White, Sallie Joy. *Housekeepers and Home-Makers.* Boston: Jordan, Marsh, 1888. (WW)

Van de Water, Virginia Terhune. *From Kitchen to Garret.* New York: Sturgis & Walton, 1910. (GB)

Household Manuals—Focusing on Servants

Beecher, Mrs. Henry Ward [Eunice]. *The Law of the Household*. Boston: Small, Maynard, 1912. (WW)

Carter, Mary Elizabeth. *Millionaire Households and Their Domestic Economy*. New York: D. Appleton, 1903. (WW)

Herrick, Christine Terhune. *The Expert-Maid Servant*. New York: Harper & Brothers, 1904. (GB)

Hill, Janet McKenzie. *The Up-to-Date Waitress*. Boston: Little, Brown, 1908. (HEARTH)

Seely, Mrs. [Lida]. *Mrs. Seely's Cook Book: A Manual of French and American Cookery with Chapters on Domestic Servants, Their Rights and Duties and Many Other Details of Household Management*. New York: Macmillan, 1914. (GB)

Springsteed, Anne Francis. *The Expert Waitress: A Manual for the Pantry and Dining Room*. New York: Harper & Brothers, 1911. (GB)

Wadhams, Caroline Reed. *Simple Directions for the Chambermaid*. New York: Longmans, Green, 1917. (WW)

———. *Simple Directions for the Cook*. New York: Longmans, Green, 1917. (WW)

———. *Simple Directions for the Laundress*. New York: Longmans, Green, 1917. (WW)

Etiquette Manuals

Holt, Emily. *Encyclopedia of Etiquette: What to Write, What to Do, What to Wear, What to Say: A Book for Everyday Use*. New York: Doubleday, Page, 1921. (WW)

Post, Emily. *Etiquette*. New York: Funk & Wagnalls, 1928.

Roberts, Helen Lefferts. *Putnam's Handbook of Etiquette*. New York: G. P. Putnam, 1913. (WW)

Sherwood, Mary Elizabeth Wilson. *Manners and Social Usages*. New York: Harper's, 1918.

Servant Problem

Allen, Annie Winsor. "Both Sides of the Servant Question." *Atlantic Monthly*, April 1913, 496–506.

Civic Federation of New Haven, Section on Household Economics. *Are You Interested in the Servant Question?* New Haven: Printed at the United Workers Boys' Club, 1917. (WW)

Forrester, Izola. "The 'Girl' Problem." *Good Housekeeping*, September 1912, 374–82.

Frederick, Christine. "It Works like a Charm: Scientific Management and the Servant Problem." *Ladies' Home Journal*, December 1912, 16, 79.

Howe, Frederic C. "The Vanishing Servant Girl: The Problem That Confronts the Woman with Help in Her Home." *Ladies' Home Journal*, May 1918, 48.

McCracken, Elizabeth. "The Problem of Domestic Service: I. From the Standpoint of the Employer." *Outlook*, February 15, 1908, 368–73.

———. "The Problem of Domestic Service: II. From the Standpoint of the Employee."

Outlook, February 29, 1908, 493–99.

Rubinow, I. M. "Household Service as a Labor Problem." *Journal of Home Economics* 3 (April 1911): 130–40.

——. "The Problem of Domestic Service." *Journal of Political Economy* 14 (October 1906): 502–19.

Rubinow, I. M., and Daniel Durant. "The Depth and Breadth of the Servant Problem." *McClure's Magazine,* March 1910, 576–85.

Sherwood, Mary Elizabeth Wilson. "The Lack of Good Servants." *North American Review* 153 (November 1891): 546–58.

Spofford, Harriet Prescott. *The Servant Girl Question.* Boston: Houghton Mifflin, 1881. (WW)

Stone, Mrs. C. H. *The Problem of Domestic Service.* St. Louis: Nelson Printing, 1892.

Vrooman, Anne L. "The Servant Question in Social Evolution." *Arena* 25 (June 1901): 643–52.

First-Person Accounts by Servants

"A Butler's Life Story." *Independent,* July 14, 1910, 77–82.

"The Confession of a Japanese Servant." *Independent,* September 21, 1905, 661–68.

"The Experiences of a Hired Girl." *Outlook,* April 6, 1912, 778–80.

Godman, Inez. "Ten Weeks in a Kitchen." *Independent,* October 17, 1901, 2549–64.

Goritzina, Kyra. *Service Entrance: Memoirs of a Park Avenue Cook.* New York: Carrick & Evans, 1939.

M., Agnes. "The True Life Story of a Nurse Girl." *Independent,* 24 September 1903, 2261–66.

Pettengill, Lillian. *Toilers of the Home: The Record of a College Woman's Experience as a Domestic Servant.* New York: Doubleday, Page, 1905. (GB)

"The Story of an Irish Cook." *Independent,* March 30, 1905, 715–17.

"A Washerwoman." *Independent,* November 10, 1904, 1073–76.

SECONDARY SOURCES

Working Women and Domestic Service—General

Clark-Lewis, Elizabeth. *Living In, Living Out: African American Domestics in Washington, D.C., 1910–1940.* Washington, DC: Smithsonian Institution Press, 1994.

——. "'This Work Had an End': African-American Domestic Workers in Washington, D.C., 1910–1940." In Carol Groneman and Mary Beth Norton, eds., *To Toil the Livelong Day: America's Women at Work, 1780–1980,* 196–212. Ithaca: Cornell University Press, 1987.

Dudden, Faye E. *Serving Women: Household Service in Nineteenth-Century America.* Hanover, NH: Wesleyan University Press, 1981.

Groneman, Carol, and Mary Beth Norton, eds. *To Toil the Livelong Day: America's Women at Work, 1780–1980.* Ithaca: Cornell University Press, 1987.

Hotten-Somers, Diane M. "Relinquishing and Reclaiming Independence: Irish Domestic Servants, American Middle-Class Mistresses, and Assimilation, 1850–1920." *Eire-Ireland* 36 (2001): 185–201.

Jones, Jacqueline. *Labor of Love, Labor of Sorrow: Black Women, Work, and the Family from Slavery to the Present*. New York: Basic Books, 1985.

Katzman, David M. *Seven Days a Week: Women and Domestic Service in Industrializing America*. New York: Oxford University Press, 1978.

Kessler-Harris, Alice. *Out to Work: A History of Wage-Earning Women in the United States*. New York: Oxford University Press, 1982.

Lintelman, Joy K. "'America is the woman's promised land': Swedish Immigrant Women and American Domestic Service." *Journal of American Ethnic History* 8 (Spring 1989): 9–23.

———. "'Our Serving Sisters': Swedish-American Domestic Servants and Their Ethnic Community." *Social Science History* 15, no. 3 (1991): 381–95.

Lynch-Brennan, Margaret. "The Servant Slant: Irish Women Domestic Servants and Historic House Museums." In *Her Past around Us: Interpreting Sites for Women's History,* edited by Polly Welts Kaufman and Katherine T. Corbett, 121–43. Malabar, FL: Krieger, 2003.

O'Leary, Elizabeth L. *At Beck and Call: The Representation of Domestic Servants in Nineteenth-Century American Painting*. Washington, DC: Smithsonian Institution Press, 1996.

Palmer, Phyllis. *Domesticity and Dirt: Housewives and Domestic Servants in the United States, 1920–1945*. Philadelphia: Temple University Press, 1989.

Rollins, Judith. *Between Women: Domestics and Their Employers*. Philadelphia: Temple University Press, 1985.

Romero, Mary. *Maid in the USA*. New York: Routledge, 1992.

Stigler, George J. *Domestic Servants in the United States: 1900–1940*. New York: National Bureau of Economic Research, 1946.

Strasser, Susan. *Never Done: A History of American Housework*. New York: Henry Holt, 2000.

Sutherland, Daniel. *Americans and Their Servants: Domestic Service in the United States from 1800 to 1920*. Baton Rouge: Louisiana State University Press, 1981.

Tucker, Susan. *Telling Memories among Southern Women*. Baton Rouge: Louisiana State University Press, 1988.

Domestic Servants in Houses Now Open to the Public

Callahan, Helen C. "Upstairs–Downstairs in Chicago 1870–1907: The Glessner Household." *Chicago History* 6, no. 4 (1977/78): 195–209.

Linsley, Judith W. "Main House, Carriage House: African-American Domestic Employees at the McFaddin-Ward House in Beaumont, Texas, 1900–1950." *Southwestern Historical Quarterly* 53 (July 1999): 16–51.

Molloy, Mary Alice. *Prairie Avenue Servants: Behind the Scenes in Chicago's Mansions,*

1870–1920. St. Clair Shores, MI: Palindrome Press, 1995.

O'Leary, Elizabeth L. *From Morning to Night: Domestic Service in Maymont House and the Gilded Age South*. Charlottesville: University of Virginia Press, 2003.

Seale, William. "Upstairs and Downstairs: The 19th-Century White House." *American Visions*, February/March 1995, 16–20.

Shoemaker, Linda. "Backstage at Beauport." *Historic New England* 5 (Summer 2004): 2–7.

West, Patricia. "Irish Immigrant Workers in Antebellum New York: The Experience of Domestic Servants at Van Buren's Lindenwald." *Hudson Valley Regional Review* 9 (September 1992): 112–26.

Cultural History and Technology

Brewer, Priscilla J. *From Fireplace to Cookstove: Technology and the Domestic Ideal in America*. Syracuse, NY: Syracuse University Press, 2000.

Carlisle, Nancy, and Melinda Talbot Nasardinov. *America's Kitchens*. Boston: Historic New England, 2008.

Cowan, Ruth Schwartz. *More Work for Mother: The Ironies of Household Technology from the Open Hearth to the Microwave*. New York: Basic Books, 1983.

Foy, Jessica, and Thomas J. Schlereth. *American Home Life, 1880–1930: A Social History of Spaces and Services*. Knoxville: University of Tennessee Press, 1994.

Green, Harvey. *The Light of the Home: An Intimate View of the Lives of Women in Victorian America*. New York: Pantheon Books, 1983.

Ierley, Merritt. *The Comforts of Home: The American House and the Evolution of Modern Convenience*. New York: Clarkson Potter, 1999.

Leavitt, Sarah A. *From Catherine Beecher to Martha Stewart: A Cultural History of Domestic Advice*. Chapel Hill: University of North Carolina Press, 2002.

Nylander, Jane C. *Our Own Snug Fireside: Images of the New England Home, 1760–1860*. New York: Alfred A. Knopf, 1993.

Pond, Catherine Seiberling. *The Pantry: Its History and Modern Uses*. Salt Lake City: Gibbs Smith, 2007.

Shapiro, Laura. *Perfection Salad: Women and Cooking at the Turn of the Century*. Berkeley: University of California Press, 2009.

Shenone, Laura. *A Thousand Years over a Hot Stove: A History of American Women Told through Food, Recipes, and Remembrances*. New York: W. W. Norton, 2003.

Notes

INTRODUCTION

1. In his book *Lies across America: What Our Historic Sites Get Wrong,* James Loewen outlines the history of the logs that became known as those of Lincoln's birthplace cabin (James W. Loewen, *Lies across America: What Our Historic Sites Get Wrong* [New York: New Press, 1999], 166–69). In 2004, dendrochronology established that the oldest log dated to 1848. The Park Service, which operates and maintains the site, now refers to it as the "symbolic cabin" (Sandy Brue, "Preparing for a National Celebration of Abraham Lincoln's Bicentennial," *CRM: The Journal of Heritage Stewardship* 5 [Winter 2008]: 22).

2. After the building was damaged by fire in 2001, the interior paint colors were reassessed and reinterpreted in a richer neoclassical palette before reopening in May 2006.

3. Eric Foner, "The Historian in the Museum," *Museum News* 85 (March–April 2006): 47.

4. "Over half the respondents assigned museums a score of 9 or 10 on the 10-point trustworthiness scale." The average rating was 8.4, with 79.9 percent rating museums between 8 and 10. (Roy Rosenzweig and David Thelen, *The Presence of the Past: Popular Uses of History in American Life* [New York: Columbia University Press, 1998], 21–22, 32, 105–8.) "As with modern intrusions, visitors to outdoor history museums seem to have mixed feelings about sanitized history. When we asked, 'Sometimes history is not pleasant. How do you want difficult issues of the past such as slavery, racism, or religious intolerance, presented at an Outdoor History Museum,' sixty-two percent selected 'openly,' but almost one-third selected 'delicately'" (Susie Wilkening and Erica Donnis, "Authenticity? It Means Everything," *History News* 63 [Autumn 2008]: 20).

5. Hal K. Rothman, "Museums and Academics: Thoughts toward an Ethic of Cooperation," *Journal of American Culture* 12 (Summer 1989): 37–38; Michael Ettema, "History Museums and the Culture of Materialism," in *Past Meets Present: Essays about Historic Interpretation and Public Audiences,* ed. Jo Blatti (Washington, DC: Smithsonian Institution Press, 1987), 62–85; Carol Kammen, "Tripping over History," *History News* 63 (Autumn 2008): 3.

6. Spencer R. Crew and James E. Sims, "Locating Authenticity: Fragments of a Dialogue," in *Exhibiting Cultures: The Poetics and Politics of Museum Display,* ed. Ivan Karp and Steven D. Lavine (Washington, DC: Smithsonian Institution Press, 1991), 164–66. The literature discussing the impact of the "new social history" on history museums includes, but is not limited to: Susan Porter Benson, Stephen Brier, and Roy Rosenzweig, eds., *Presenting the Past: Essays on History and the Public* (Philadelphia: Temple University Press, 1986); Steven C. Dubin, *Displays of Power: Memory and Amnesia in the American Museum* (New York: New York University Press, 1999); Warren Leon and Roy Rosenzweig, eds., *History Museums in the United States: A Critical Assessment*

(Urbana: University of Illinois Press, 1989); Catherine M. Lewis, *The Changing Face of Public History: The Chicago Historical Society and the Transformation of an American Museum* (DeKalb: Northern Illinois University Press, 2005); Edward T. Linenthal and Tom Englehardt, eds., *History Wars: The Enola Gay and Other Battles for the American Past* (New York: Metropolitan Books, 1996); Michael Wallace, *Mickey Mouse History and Other Essays on American Memory* (Philadelphia: Temple University Press, 1996).

7. Crew and Sims, "Locating Authenticity," 169, 172.

8. Ibid., 173.

9. Richard Handler and Eric Gable, *The New History in an Old Museum: Creating the Past at Colonial Williamsburg* (Durham, NC: Duke University Press, 1997), 221–22.

10. Eric Gable, Richard Handler, and Anna Lawson, "On the Uses of Relativism: Fact, Conjecture, and Black and White Histories at Colonial Williamsburg," *American Ethnologist* 19, no. 4 (1992): 798–800.

11. Handler and Gable, *New History in an Old Museum*, 84, 114–15.

12. Ibid., 222–23; Antoinette J. Lee, "An Interview with William Seale," *CRM: The Journal of Heritage Stewardship* 1 (Summer 2004): 24.

13. Rex M. Ellis, "Interpreting the Whole House," in *Interpreting Historic House Museums*, ed. Jessica Foy Donnelly (Walnut Creek, CA: AltaMira Press, 2002), 63.

CHAPTER 1

1. Donna Ann Harris, *New Solutions for House Museums: Ensuring the Long-Term Preservation of America's Historic Houses* (Lanham, MD: AltaMira Press, 2007). The symposium "New Audiences for Old Houses: Building a Future with the Past" was held in Boston on September 28, 2007; the session "Future Options for Historic House Museums" was part of the Mass History conference "Sustaining the Future of Massachusetts History," held in Worcester, Massachusetts, on June 9, 2008; the Associated Press story "Twain, Wharton homes join others in financial peril," was posted on the AASLH Historic House Museum Listserv on June 19, 2008; Susie Wilkening, "Family Visitation at Museums: Historic Sites and History Museums," *Dispatch,* January 2008, 2, 4; the Forum on Historic Site Stewardship in the 21st Century resulted in a special issue of the National Trust publication *Forum Journal* entitled "America's Historic Sites at a Crossroads" (vol. 22 [Spring 2008]).

2. Gerald George, "Historic House Museum Malaise: A Conference Considers What's Wrong," *History News* 57 (Autumn 2002): 22–23.

3. Thomas J. Schlereth, *Artifacts and the American Past* (Walnut Creek, CA: AltaMira Press, 1996), 115; Charles B. Hosmer, Jr., *Presence of the Past: A History of the Preservation Movement in the United States before Williamsburg* (New York: G. P. Putnam's Sons, 1965), 112.

4. Cunningham used the moniker "A Southern Matron" in her "Appeal to Ladies of the South," in which she advocated saving the home and tomb of George Washington. This letter was published in newspapers throughout the South (Patricia West, *Domesticating History: The Political Origins of America's House Museums* [Washington, DC: Smithsonian Institution Press, 1999], 7); "We neither desire nor intend sectionality,"

quoted in West, *Domesticating History*, 10. West's book provides one of the best and most detailed histories of the founding of Mount Vernon, Orchard House, Monticello, and the Booker T. Washington Birthplace.

5. West, *Domesticating History*, 2, 43; Mary C. Dorris, *Preservation of the Hermitage, 1889–1913* (Nashville: Ladies' Hermitage Association, 1915), quoted in Hosmer, *Presence of the Past*, 71.

6. Hosmer, *Presence of the Past*, 138, 264–66; West, *Domesticating History*, 72–73.

7. Hosmer, *Presence of the Past*, 243, 254; Edward P. Alexander, "Sixty Years of Historic Preservation: The Society for the Preservation of New England Antiquities," *Old-Time New England* 61 (1970–71): 15–16.

8. William H. Truettner and Thomas Andrew Denenberg, "The Discreet Charm of the Colonial," in *Picturing Old New England: Image and Memory*, ed. William H. Truettner and Roger B. Stein (New Haven: Yale University Press, 1999), 89–90.

9. Carl R. Nold, "The Future of the Historic House Museum," *Historic New England*, Summer 2008, 7; Historic New England Web site, http://www.historicnewengland.org/about/WhatsNew.asp (accessed April 20, 2007). For more on Historic New England's rebranding, see Diane Viera, *"Strike up the Brand": Creating or Enhancing Your Museum's Brand Identity*, American Association for State and Local History Technical Leaflet #232, 2005.

10. Harris, *New Solutions for House Museums*, 7–8. Charles Hosmer, *Preservation Comes of Age: From Williamsburg to the National Trust, 1926–1949* (Charlottesville: University of Virginia Press, 1980), 471; Patrick H. Butler III, "Past, Present, and Future: The Place of the House Museum in the Museum Community," in *Interpreting Historic House Museums*, ed. Jessica Foy Donnelly (Walnut Creek, CA: AltaMira Press, 2002), 26; Michael Kammen, *Mystic Chords of Memory: The Transformation of Tradition in American Culture* (New York: Vintage Books, 1993), 460–61, 468–69.

11. Hosmer, *Preservation Comes of Age*, 573, 565; Ron Thomson and Marilyn Harper, "Telling the Stories: Planning Effective Interpretive Programs for Properties Listed in the National Register of Historic Places," *National Register Bulletin* (Washington, DC: National Park Service, 2000), http:www.cr.nps.gov/nr/publications/bulletins/interp/int2.htm.

12. Public Law 81-408, quoted in Elizabeth D. Mulloy, *The History of the National Trust for Historic Preservation* (Washington, DC: Preservation Press, 1976), 12. Today, the National Trust does not have any federal government affiliation and receives no federal moneys. It operates as a private nonprofit organization.

13. Diane Barthel, *Historic Preservation: Collective Memory and Historic Identity* (New Brunswick, NJ: Rutgers University Press, 1996), 6.

14. Patricia Chambers Walker and Thomas Graham, *Directory of Historic House Museums in the United States* (Walnut Creek, CA: AltaMira Press, 2000), 15. Regarding relevance, consider the theme of the 2007 AASLH annual meeting: "Relevance = The Bottom Line." The conference included sessions entitled "Relevance, Public History, and Community History" and "Relevance: Reinterpreting the House Museum."

15. James Oliver Horton, "Slavery in American History: An Uncomfortable National Dialogue," in *Slavery and Public History: The Tough Stuff of American Memory*,

ed. James Oliver Horton and Lois E. Horton (New York: New Press, 2006), 36–37.

16. Jennifer L. Eichstedt and Stephen Small, *Representations of Slavery: Race and Ideology in Southern Plantation Museums* (Washington, DC: Smithsonian Institution Press, 2002). Other book-length "travelogues" that have raised awareness of the omissions and mistruths at historic sites are Philip Burnham, *How the Other Half Lived: A People's Guide to American Historic Sites* (Boston: Faber and Faber, 1995), and James Loewen, *Lies across America: What Our Historic Sites Get Wrong* (New York: New Press, 1999). These books address the blunders of a wide variety of historic sites as well as monuments and markers. Both are very accessible to general audiences and have the potential to educate visitors of historic sites.

17. Eichstedt and Small, *Representations of Slavery,* 4, 10.

18. Ibid., 107–9; Michael S. Durham, "The Word Is 'Slaves,'" *American Heritage,* April 1992, 89–99.

19. Eichstedt and Small, *Representations of Slavery,* 113–20, 127–29.

20. Joanne Melish, "Recovering (from) Slavery: Four Struggles to Tell the Truth," in *Slavery and Public History: The Tough Stuff of American Memory,* ed. James Oliver Horton and Lois E. Horton (New York: New Press, 2006), 106–9.

21. Eichstedt and Small, *Representations of Slavery,* 147–49.

22. Ibid., 151, 153–54; Loewen, *Lies across America,* 341.

23. Eichstedt and Small, *Representations of Slavery,* 161–63, 166–67.

24. Ibid., 170, 174–75, 201.

25. James Oliver Horton, "Presenting Slavery: The Perils of Telling America's Racial Story," *Public Historian* 21, no. 4 (Fall 1999): 28.

26. Lois E. Horton, "Avoiding History: Thomas Jefferson, Sally Hemings, and the Uncomfortable Public Discussion on Slavery," in *Slavery and Public History: The Tough Stuff of American Memory,* ed. James Oliver Horton and Lois E. Horton (New York: New Press, 2006), 140.

27. Eichstedt and Small, *Representations of Slavery,* 204.

28. Quoted in ibid., 215. As of this writing, the removal of the later DuPont wings of the mansion and restoration of the building to its Madison-era appearance were largely complete. It is likely that when regular tours resume (during the restoration tours focused heavily on the how and why of the restoration), interpretation will reintroduce the interpretation of slavery discussed here, if not enhance it, based on the restored physical surroundings. For more on the restoration of Montpelier, see Christopher Shea, "Uncovering Montpelier's Hidden Past," *Preservation,* September/October 2008, 28–35.

29. The narration includes the following: "It's hard today to put ourselves in the mind of a man like Madison. He condemned what he called 'the original sin of slavery.' A few of his friends and family members, acting on similar beliefs, freed their slaves. Madison, whose comfortable existence at Montpelier depended on slave labor, did not. By all accounts, he was a humane master. But the philosopher-statesman who fought to create a government of free men remained a slave owner his whole life" (Eichstedt and Small, *Representations of Slavery,* 218). A less expensive, but perhaps equally effective,

way to incorporate audio tours is through the use of cell-phone audio tours, which are currently offered by several companies at fairly reasonable rates.

30. Eichstedt and Small, *Representations of Slavery,* 203, 205. Lucia Stanton, *Free Some Day: The African American Families of Monticello* (Charlottesville, VA: Thomas Jefferson Foundation, 2000).

31. Horton, "Avoiding History," 138.

32. The majority of the information on the Monticello house tour is based on field notes taken during my visit on March 16, 2003.

33. I took Monticello's plantation tour on September 17, 2005. One interpreter interviewed by James and Lois Horton estimated that only 6 percent of Monticello visitors took the plantation tour (Horton, "Avoiding History," 140).

34. Daniel P. Jordan, "Statement on the TJF Research Committee Report on Thomas Jefferson and Sally Hemings, January 26, 2000," http://www.monticello.org/plantation/hemingscontro/reportstatement.html; Horton, "Avoiding History," 143–45.

35. Lower East Side Tenement Museum, "About Us," http://www.tenement.org/about.html. Information about tours is available at http://www.tenement.org/tours.html. Attendance for the Lower East Side Tenement Museum has increased from 16,000 in 2004 to 128,513 in 2007 (Amy Webb and Carolyn Brackett, "Cultural Heritage Tourism Trends Affecting Historic Sites," *Forum Journal* 22 [Spring 2008], 32).

36. Margaret Garb, "Lower East Side Tenement Museum," *Journal of Urban History* 26 (November 1999): 109–11; R. J. Lambrose, "East Side Story" in "The Abusable Past," *Radical History Review* 43 (January 1989): 143.

37. Somini Sengupta, "Immigrants Tell Their New York Stories," *New York Times,* late ed., final, May 6, 1996, B2.

38. Ruth J. Abram, "Kitchen Conversations: Democracy in Action at the Lower East Side Tenement Museum," *Public Historian* 29 (Winter 2007): 59–76.

39. Ruth J. Abram, "Harnessing the Power of History," in *Museums, Society, Inequality,* ed. Richard Sandell (London: Routledge, 2002), 136.

40. Charles Hardy III, "Exhibition Reviews: The Lower East Side Tenement Museum," *Journal of American History* 84, no. 3 (December 1997): 1013.

CHAPTER 2

1. Patricia West, "'The New Social History' and Historic House Museums: The Lindenwald Example," *Museum Studies Journal* 2 (Fall 1986): 22.

2. Patricia West, "Irish Immigrant Workers in Antebellum New York: The Experience of Domestic Servants at Van Buren's Lindenwald," *Hudson Valley Regional Review* 9 (September 1992): 112–26.

3. Jim McKay and Gregg Berninger, "Interpreting Servants at the Martin Van Buren NHS," *Cultural Resource Management* 20, no. 3 (1997): 48.

4. Sherry Butcher-Younghans, *Historic House Museums: A Practical Handbook for Their Care, Preservation, and Management* (New York: Oxford University Press, 1993), 188, 184; Barbara Abramoff Levy, Sandra Mackenzie Lloyd, and Susan Porter Schreiber,

Great Tours! Thematic Tours and Guide Training for Historic Sites; Jessica Foy Donnelly, ed., *Interpreting Historic House Museums* (Walnut Creek, CA: AltaMira Press, 2002); Ron Thomson and Marilyn Harper, "Telling the Stories: Planning Effective Interpretive Programs for Properties Listed in the National Register of Historic Places," *National Register Bulletin* (Washington, DC: National Park Service, 2000), 15.

Polly Welts Kaufman and Katherine T. Corbett, ed., *Her Past around Us: Interpreting Sites for Women's History* (Malabar, FL: Krieger, 2003); Gail Lee Dubrow and Jennifer B. Goodman, eds., *Restoring Women's History through Historic Preservation* (Baltimore: Johns Hopkins University Press, 2003).

5. These scholars included Jane C. Nylander, author of *Our Own Snug Fireside: Images of the New England Home, 1760–1860* (New York: Alfred A. Knopf, 1993); Faye E. Dudden, author of *Serving Women: Household Service in Nineteenth-Century America* (Hanover, NH: Wesleyan University Press, 1983); Jacqueline Jones, author of *Labor of Love, Labor of Sorrow: Black Women, Work, and the Family from Slavery to the Present* (New York: Basic Books, 1985); Phyllis Palmer, author of *Domesticity and Dirt: Housewives and Domestic Servants in the United States, 1920–1945* (Philadelphia: Temple University Press, 1989); and Judith Rollins, author of *Between Women: Domestics and Their Employers* (Philadelphia: Temple University Press, 1985); Barbara A. Levy and Susan Schreiber, "The View from the Kitchen," *History News* 50 (March/April 1995): 19; Jane Brown Gillette, "Breaking the Silence," *Historic Preservation*, March/April 1995, 42; Barbara A. Levy and Susan Schreiber, "The View from the Kitchen," 16–20.

6. Her survey focused on house museums interpreted as single-family homes not part of museum villages; 57.9 percent interpreted free servants, 15.8 enslaved servants, and 26.3 both free and enslaved (which Walker refers to as "combination" sites) (Patricia Chambers Walker, "A More Complete History: Interpreting Domestic Servants at Historic House Museums" [master's thesis, John F. Kennedy University, 1996], 63–64, 66, 79, 109, 189).

7. In June 2003, I mailed 691 questionnaires to historic house museums in all but two states and the District of Columbia. I drew my survey population from Patricia Chambers Walker and Thomas Graham's *Directory of Historic House Museums in the United States* (2000), which lists each house's interpretive period (if provided by the respondent). I did not mail the survey to sites that clearly would not have had domestic servants, such as pioneer homesteads and log cabins. I received 358 completed surveys, a preliminary response rate of 51.8 percent. Twenty-two surveys were returned as undeliverable, making the final response rate 53.5 percent. To encourage candid responses, I guaranteed that any comments included in the dissertation would be identified only by state or region. I divided the returned surveys into regional categories, based on those used in the 1900 census aggregate statistics. These regions were manageable to work with as well as being relatively consistent in terms of geography, settlement, and immigration patterns. Only two regions had responses lower than 50 percent, the Eastern South Central (33.3 percent) and the Noncontiguous States (44.4 percent). Many individual states had response rates between 60 and 100 percent.

8. In 1989, the American Association of Museums (AAM) conducted a survey of all museums, from zoos to historic sites to art museums. The result was an impres-

sive collection of data about annual budgets and finances, governance, age of the institutions, and general descriptions of collections, visitation, facilities, and human resources. The survey report, *Museums Count,* influenced some questions I asked in my survey, particularly about the age of institutions, percentages of paid and volunteer staff, and the content of collections. As this larger survey was under way, Peggy Coats of the Campbell House in California attempted to define the basic characteristics of house museums as a subsection of the museum community. She gathered information about personnel and financial resources, annual visitation, and the services that house museums provided their constituents. Her sample size was very small, but she concluded that house museums offer many services to the public despite being understaffed and underfunded (although one would be hard-pressed to find many museums not in this situation). Coats did not address interpretive issues, which were my main concern, but her survey did suggest that insufficient resources, in part, explained the slow progress of social history at historic house museums. Coats's survey offered an example to follow and a reference point for my study nearly fifteen years later (American Association of Museums, *Museums Count* [Washington, DC: American Association of Museums, 1994]); Peggy Coats, "Survey of Historic House Museums," *History News* 45 (January 1990): 26–28.

9. I broke the states down into the following regions: New England (Maine, New Hampshire, Massachusetts, Connecticut, Rhode Island, Vermont); Southern North Atlantic (New Jersey, New York, Pennsylvania); Northern South Atlantic (Delaware, District of Columbia, Maryland, Virginia); Southern South Atlantic (North Carolina, South Carolina, Georgia, Florida); Eastern North Central (Ohio, Indiana, Michigan, Illinois, Wisconsin); Western North Central (Iowa, Minnesota, Missouri, North Dakota, South Dakota, Nebraska, Kansas); Eastern South Central (Kentucky, Tennessee, Alabama, Mississippi); Western South Central (Oklahoma, Arkansas, Louisiana, Texas); Rocky Mountain (Colorado, Montana, Wyoming, Idaho); Basin and Plateau (Arizona, Utah); Pacific (California, Oregon, Washington); and Noncontiguous (Hawaii, Alaska).

10. Jennifer L. Eichstedt and Stephen Small, *Representations of Slavery: Race and Ideology in Southern Plantation Museums* (Washington, DC: Smithsonian Institution Press, 2002), 133; Walker, "More Complete History," 139.

11. American Association of Museums, *Museums Count,* 33, 46.

12. Peggy Coats, "Survey of Historic House Museums," 28. Coats mailed her survey to 200 house museums selected from the American Association of Museums *Official Museum Directory* using the category HISTORY/Houses—Buildings. She achieved a 50 percent response rate. Three hundred two sites responding to my survey indicated the number of full-time staff.

13. Two hundred ninety-four respondents indicated the number of part-time volunteers at their sites; 197 respondents reported the number of full-time volunteers at their site.

14. Barbara Abramoff Levy, Sandra Mackenzie Lloyd, Susan Porter Schreiber, *Great Tours!* 131. In their essay about living-history museums, Warren Leon and Margaret Piatt discuss this problem as it relates to a prominent Wisconsin historic site. "Old World Wisconsin, which is open only seasonally, does not offer its interpreters year-round employment; many stay for just a single season. In that time, they can learn only

a modest amount of the information the researchers have gathered and cannot develop a complete range of teaching techniques for presenting what they know to the public. . . . The unfortunate result is that even serious visitors to Old World Wisconsin are not likely to detect the subtle differences between cultures presented at various farms." (Warren Leon and Margaret Piatt, "Living-History Museums," in *History Museums in the United States: A Critical Assessment,* edited by Warren Leon and Roy Rosenzweig [Urbana and Chicago: University of Illinois Press, 1989], 80).

15. Two hundred forty-eight sites indicated the number of paid guides; percentages are based on a total 308 respondents reporting the makeup of their guide staff.

16. Although I considered the data for all respondents in tallying the information for the first section, "Your Site," beginning with the second section, "Servants at Your Site," 8.7 percent of the total returns did not fit my criteria and were not counted. The discarded sites included those with interpretive periods prior to 1865, those that functioned as something other than traditional house museums (e.g., art gallery or rental facility), and a small number that had closed to the public. Three hundred twenty-seven sites fit the survey criteria. Some 65.2 percent of respondents in the Western South Central region (Arkansas, Louisiana, Oklahoma, Texas) had servants during their interpretive period; 57.2 percent of those in the Basin and Plateau region (Arizona, Utah) did; as did 25.0 percent in the Noncontiguous States.

17. I considered only respondents who answered "yes" to question 6 for questions 7 through 33. A small number of sites that answered "no" to question 6 answered questions intended for sites that interpret domestic service. My assumption is that servants are mentioned at these sites, but the staff does not consider them as significant parts of their interpretation. I felt it was more accurate to discard these responses when considering answers to questions 7 through 33.

18. Furniture, clothing, and other personal items were occasionally given to servants, usually when the employer no longer had use for them.

19. Some excellent volumes devoted solely to domestic service include: Mary Elizabeth Carter, *Millionaire Households and Their Domestic Economy* (New York: D. Appleton, 1903); Christine Terhune Herrick, *The Expert Maid-Servant* (New York: Harper & Brothers, 1904). A later reference includes a significant chapter on domestic servants: Emily Post, *Etiquette* (New York: Funk & Wagnalls, 1928), 132–63. Many period household and etiquette manuals are now easily accessible online.

20. One example is Mildred Maddocks Bentley's "The Psychology of Servants," *Ladies' Home Journal,* December 1925, 159–62+. Bentley offers two sample schedules, one for the house with one maid, the other for the house with two maids. Women in charge of larger servant staff often found schedule recommendations in manuals such as Carter's and Herrick's, which are noted above.

21. For more on the history of American kitchens, see Nancy Carlisle and Melinda Talbot Nasardinov, *America's Kitchens* (Boston: Historic New England, 2008).

22. Spencer R. Crew and James E. Sims, "Locating Authenticity: Fragments of a Dialogue," in *Exhibiting Cultures: The Poetics and Politics of Museum Display,* ed. Ivan Karp and Steven D. Levine (Washington, DC: Smithsonian Institution Press, 1991), 172.

23. Ruth Schwartz Cowan, *More Work for Mother: The Ironies of Household Technology from the Open Hearth to the Microwave* (New York: Basic Books, 1983).

24. For more on the transition from "help" to "domestics," see Faye E. Dudden, *Serving Women: Household Service in Nineteenth-Century America* (Hanover, NH: Wesleyan University Press, 1981).

25. For example, Cedar Rapids has a large and very proud community of Czech people. The Douglas family employed several Czechs at Brucemore, although not in some of the most visible and prestigious positions. One guide told me that she felt awkward talking about hierarchy according to ethnicity, because she might offend a member of the Czech community.

26. Thank you to Margherita Desy, who was the site manager at Phillips House when I started at Historic New England, for sharing this observation.

27. "If it is possible, they should have a place in which to meet their friends. Where there is space it is becoming more and more the custom to provide a sitting-room for the servants in which their visitors can be received. To many housekeepers such an arrangement as this would be impossible. In such cases there should at least be an effort to render the kitchen as pleasant as the circumstances will permit. It may be clean and neat, there may be a couple of chairs that are tolerably comfortable, and any little attempt the maid may wish to make to add to the attractiveness of the apartment should be encouraged" (Herrick, *Expert Maid-Servant,* 103). On the challenges of sharing bathroom facilities with employers, see "A Washerwoman," *Independent,* November 10, 1904, 1073–76. On homes in the country: "I would like to add my testimony to that given in the 'Domestic Symposium' as to the reason why women and girls accustomed to city life are unwilling to take good places in the country. My experience as a trained nurse, often called to patients in the country, within an hour's ride of New York perhaps, gives me sympathy with these other workingwomen who are asked to leave the friends and privileges of New York life to go to equally good homes in the country, but where they would be separated from these associations, and where it might be a long time before they would form new ones" (E.A.C.P., "A Day's Mail," *Christian Union,* June 12, 1890, 838).

28. Lillian Pettengill, *Toilers of the Home: The Record of a College Woman's Experience as a Domestic Servant* (New York: Doubleday, 1905), 375–76; I. M. Rubinow and Daniel Durant, "The Depth and Breadth of the Servant Problem," *McClure's Magazine,* March 1910, 579.

29. One respondent reported "We stress longevity of service of several servants (40–50 years) to indicate loyalty and good relationships." Another mentioned, "Service staff were considered extended family to the founders. In the family's later years, the staff were the primary inhabitants of the house and grounds."

30. Annie Winsor Allen, "Both Sides of the Servant Question," *Atlantic Monthly,* April 1913, 505; Elizabeth O'Leary, *From Morning to Night: Domestic Service in Maymont House and the Gilded Age South* (Charlottesville: University of Virginia Press, 2003), 123.

31. Thomas J. Schlereth, "Causing Conflict, Doing Violence," *Museum News* 63 (October 1984), 47–48.

32. Barbara Abramoff Levy, Sandra Mackenzie Lloyd, and Susan Porter Schreiber, *Great Tours!* 116.

33. Freeman Tilden, *Interpreting Our Heritage*, 3rd ed. (Chapel Hill: University of North Carolina Press, 1977), 32–33.

34. Two recent anthologies about interpreting and preserving women's history include essays about domestic servants: Margaret Lynch-Brennan, "The Servant Slant: Irish Women Domestic Servants and Historic House Museums," in *Her Past around Us: Interpreting Sites for Women's History*, ed. Polly Welts Kaufman and Katharine T. Corbett (Malabar, FL: Kreiger, 2003), 121–43; Patricia West, "Uncovering and Interpreting Women's History at Historic House Museums," in *Restoring Women's History through Historic Preservation*, ed. Gail Lee Dubrow and Jennifer B. Goodman (Baltimore: Johns Hopkins University Press, 2003), 83–95.

35. Pettengill, *Toilers of the Home*, 362. In a study of 100 working women in Massachusetts, researchers found that "on the whole, saving and assistance of relatives seem to be least common among those working in shops and most general among the waitresses and houseworkers" (Massachusetts Bureau of Statistics of Labor, *Social Statistics of Working Women* [Boston, 1901], 15).

36. I assigned each response a weighted point value. A rating of 5 equaled 5 points, 4 equaled 4 points, and on down. I divided the total by the number of responses (discounting all "non-responses") to get an average rating for each question.

37. One respondent noted, "We lack the necessary research to base a good interpretation on. Even in a university with a good history department, we lack research, and as a staff of one, I cannot devote enough time to do all the research myself. Information in this little town is scarce"; John Durel and Anita Nowery Durel, "A Golden Age for Historic Properties," *History News* 62 (Summer 2007): 9.

CHAPTER 3

1. Harriet Prescott Spofford, *The Servant Girl Question* (Boston: Houghton Mifflin, 1881), 15.

2. For some servants, help-wanted ads that offered a good home and treatment as part of the family were red flags, because they often meant poor wages (I. M. Rubinow, "The Problem of Domestic Service," *Journal of Political Economy* 14 [October 1906], 512).

3. United States Bureau of the Census, *Statistics of Women at Work* (Washington, DC: 1907), 9, 32, 39, 50. Rubinow, "Problem of Domestic Service," 505.

4. *Statistics of Women at Work*, 9–11, 34; Daniel Sutherland, *Americans and Their Servants: Domestic Service in the United States from 1800 to 1920* (Baton Rouge: Louisiana State University Press, 1981), 47. The aggregate census statistics use the following categories: native white of native-born parentage, native white of foreign or mixed parentage, and foreign-born white; the data for marital status included the unknown in the "single" category (*Statistics of Women at Work*, 36, 38, 40). Thorstein Veblen, *The Theory of the Leisure Class* (1899; reprinted New Brunswick, NJ: Transaction, 1992), 54; Mary Elizabeth Carter, *Millionaire Households and Their Domestic Economy* (New York: D. Appleton, 1903), 119.

5. States included in "New England" were Maine, New Hampshire, Vermont, Massachusetts, Rhode Island, and Connecticut. The Southern North Atlantic states included New York, New Jersey, and Pennsylvania (*Statistics of Women at Work,* 42–43).

6. Elizabeth Clark-Lewis, *Living In, Living Out: African American Domestics in Washington, D.C., 1910–1940* (Washington, DC: Smithsonian Institution Press, 1994); David M. Katzman, *Seven Days a Week: Women and Domestic Service in Industrializing America* (New York: Oxford University Press, 1978), 198–99.

7. The Thor Electric Washing Machine advertisement appeared in the *Ladies' Home Journal,* April 1909, 100; the advertisement for the Coffield Motor Washer Company in *House Beautiful,* August 1920, 123. This point is central to Ruth Schwartz Cowan's *More Work for Mother: The Ironies of Household Technology from the Open Hearth to the Microwave* (New York: Basic Books, 1983).

8. Elizabeth O'Leary, *At Beck and Call: The Representation of Domestic Servants in Nineteenth-Century American Painting* (Washington, DC: Smithsonian Institution Press, 1996), 125; Veblen, *Theory of the Leisure Class,* 57, 59.

9. Many women included "No laundry" in the advertisements they placed in the "help wanted" column, as an incentive.

10. Of the 205 articles indexed by the *Reader's Guide* during this period, 59 ran between 1905 and 1909; 86 between 1910 and 1914; 31 between 1915 and 1918; and 29 between 1919 and 1921. The decline in articles about servants matches housewives' decreasing dependence on this labor. One should also keep in mind that some articles were not indexed in the *Reader's Guide,* nor were images of servants that appeared in advertisements.

11. Frances A. Kellor, *Out of Work* (New York: G. P. Putnam's Sons, 1904), 123–24, 126; Elizabeth McCracken, "The Problem of Domestic Service: I: From the Standpoint of the Employer," *Outlook,* February 15, 1908, 372.

12. Sutherland, *Americans and Their Servants,* 26; Faye E. Dudden, *Serving Women: Household Service in Nineteenth-Century America* (Hanover, NH: Wesleyan University Press, 1981), 12–43.

13. Faye E. Dudden, *Serving Women,* 44–71; Lucy Maynard Salmon, *Domestic Service* (New York: Macmillan, 1901), 151; Allen, "Both Sides of the Servant Question," *Atlantic Monthly,* April 1913, 498; Richard Ohmann, *Selling Culture: Magazines, Markets, and Class at the Turn of the Century* (London: Verso Books, 1996), 165.

14. Jane Seymour Klink, "Put Yourself in Her Place," *Atlantic Monthly,* February 1905, 170; Sutherland, *Americans and Their Servants,* 3.

15. Sutherland, *Americans and Their Servants,* 6–7; Lucy Maynard Salmon, "Recent Progress in the Study of Domestic Service," *Atlantic Monthly,* November 1905, 628–29; Klink, "Put Yourself in Her Place," 170.

16. Dudden, *Serving Women,* 16. At the same time that urban women wistfully remembered "help" in the pre-industrial period, rural women of the early twentieth century also experienced the servant problem. A 1913 report by the U. S. Department of Agriculture documented the difficulties of farm women. Their comments closely paralleled those made by their urban counterparts. According to an Illinois woman, "The woman in town can always hire some one to help by the day at least, but in the country

that is not so—if she hires help she must make a companion of the girl and often take her along when she goes to town. There is no family privacy in the farm home where help is kept." Farm women also reported a change in the type of "hired man" employed on the farm, which is remarkably similar to the shift from "help" to "domestics" observed by many commentators on the servant problem: "One great trouble perhaps the greatest is the fact that here in New England whatever help is employed on the farm must to some extent be taken into the house. Formerly the 'hired man' was the son of a neighbor or perhaps the cousin or relative of the proprietor, so was not so bad; but now the help that it is possible to obtain is usually a very undesirable member of the household besides being another for the housewife to provide food for" ("Dissatisfied with the Lives They Live: Farm Women Describe Their Work in a 1913 U.S. Department of Agriculture Report," History Matters: The U.S. Survey Course on the Web, http://historymatters.gmu.edu/d/101).

17. Mary E. Trueblood, "Housework versus Shop and Factories," *Independent,* November 13, 1902, 2693.

18. Regarding the dislike for the term *servant,* Harriet Prescott Spofford countered: "But why should the term 'servant' be offensive to those who undertake the duties that term describes? To hand your dishes, to prepare your food, to cleanse your rooms and scrub your floors, to wash and iron your clothes, to dress your hair and your feet—all that is service, and they who render it serve, and are exactly and precisely servants; and we are at a loss to see why the English language should be changed to suit a false pride on their part should they dislike to hear their work called by its own name" (Spofford, *Servant Girl Question,* 11; Ruth Dunbar, "Not Wanted: Girl for General Housework," *Saturday Evening Post,* May 31, 1919, 52).

19. Carolyn Kitch, *The Girl on the Magazine Cover: The Origins of Visual Stereotypes in American Mass Media* (Chapel Hill: University of North Carolina Press, 2001), 3, 40; Lois Banner, *American Beauty* (New York: Knopf, 1983).

20. Banner, *American Beauty,* 20; Katzman, *Seven Days a Week,* 237; Mrs. [Lida] Seely, *Mrs. Seely's Cook Book: A Manual of French and American Cookery with Chapters on Domestic Servants, Their Rights and Duties and Many Other Details of Household Management* (New York: Macmillan, 1914).

21. Salmon, *Domestic Service,* 157; Ophilia Simpson, who had been a servant in Washington, D.C., made this comment in an oral history interview with Elizabeth Clark-Lewis (Elizabeth Clark-Lewis, "'This Work Had an End': African-American Domestic Workers in Washington, D.C., 1910–1940," in *To Toil the Livelong Day: America's Women at Work, 1780–1980,* ed. Carol Groneman and Mary Beth Norton [Ithaca: Cornell University Press, 1987], 202–3).

22. O'Leary, *At Beck and Call.*

23. Jennifer Scanlon, *Inarticulate Longings:* The Ladies' Home Journal, *Gender, and the Promises of Consumer Culture* (New York: Routledge, 1995), 34; "The Correct Apron for Maids," *Ladies' Home Journal,* March 1910, 47.

24. Ellen Gruber Garvey, *The Adman in the Parlor: Magazines and the Gendering of Consumer Culture, 1880s to 1910s* (New York: Oxford University Press, 1996), 68–69, 72.

25. Roland Marchand, *Advertising the American Dream: Making Way for Modernity, 1920–1940* (Berkeley: University of California Press, 1985), 166, 202.

26. Spofford, *Servant Girl Question,* 159–60. McCracken, "Problem of Domestic Service," 373.

27. Rubinow, "Problem of Domestic Service," 506; "MAID—WHITE RELIABLE, FOR GENERAL housework in small apt.; Protestant preferred;" "MAID—EXPERIENCED LADIES' MAID, handy with needle; French preferred; only first class applicant need apply; references required" (*Chicago Sunday Tribune,* May 18, 1919, p.10, part 9); Carter, *Millionaire Households,* 217; Spofford, *Servant Girl Question,* 17.

28. Mary Elizabeth Wilson Sherwood, *Manners and Social Usages* (New York: Harper's, 1918), 310.

29. Hasia Diner, *Erin's Daughters in America: Irish Immigrant Women in the Nineteenth Century* (Baltimore: Johns Hopkins University Press, 1983), xiv, 85; Spofford, *Servant Girl Question,* 25–26.

30. Sutherland, *Americans and Their Servants,* 59; [Mrs.] Christine Frederick, *The New Housekeeping: Efficiency Studies in Home Management* (Garden City: Doubleday, Page, 1925), 115. I. M. Rubinow also mentions that the advantages of immigrant servants are one exception in the case of immigration restrictions: "even such an authoritative body as the Industrial Commission sees one great objection to the educational test for immigrants. It would keep out the virtuous and industrious Irish girls who come to this country, seeking positions as domestic servants" (Rubinow, "Problem of Domestic Service," 507).

31. Izola Forrester, "The 'Girl' Problem," *Good Housekeeping,* September 1912, 374–82.

32. The illustration was also published in *International Studio* 35 (July 1908): xxix; O'Leary, *At Beck and Call,* 254–55.

33. William R. Linneman, "Immigrant Stereotypes: 1880–1900," *Studies in American Humor* 1, no. 1 (April 1974): 28; Fairfax Davis Downey, *Portrait of an Era as Drawn by C. D. Gibson* (New York: Charles Scribner's Sons, 1936), 146.

34. Katzman, *Seven Days a Week,* 184, 189.

35. Ibid., 189, 192.

36. Clark-Lewis, *Living In, Living Out,* 105–6.

37. O'Leary, *At Beck and Call,* 146, 149.

38. Advertisement for Aunt Jemima pancake flour, *Ladies' Home Journal,* May 1929, 80.

39. The backdrop for the photograph of the Norwegian servants is present in at least one Van Schaick image reproduced in Michael Lesy, *Wisconsin Death Trip* (New York: Pantheon Books, 1973). The image has been used in Hasia Diner's *Erin's Daughters in America,* and the catalogue for an art museum exhibition entitled *Dirt & Domesticity: Constructions of the Feminine* (New York: Whitney Museum, 1992).

40. Brucemore and the James J. Hill House in St. Paul, Minnesota, also have group photographs of their servant staffs.

41. Inez Godman, "Ten Weeks in a Kitchen," *Independent,* October 17, 1901, 2459.

42. Ibid.

43. Ibid.

44. Lillian Pettengill, *Toilers of the Home: The Record of a College Woman's Experience as a Domestic Servant* (New York: Doubleday, Page, 1905), v.

45. Ibid., 5, 48.

46. Ibid., 20–21, 30, 55.

47. Ibid., 206, 229, 258, 337–38.

48. Ibid., 248–52, 263–64, 286–88.

49. Ibid., 359–63, 373–76, 392.

50. David M. Katzman and William M. Tuttle Jr., eds., *Plain Folk: The Life Stories of Undistinguished Americans* (Urbana: University of Illinois Press, 1982), xi, 195–98.

51. "The Story of an Irish Cook," *Independent,* March 30, 1905, 716.

52. Agnes M., "The True Life Story of a Nurse Girl," *Independent,* September 24, 1903, 2262.

53. Ibid.," 2263, 2264, 2265.

54. "A Butler's Life Story," *Independent,* July 14, 1910, 78–79.

55. Ibid., 80–81.

56. "The Confession of a Japanese Servant," *Independent,* September 21, 1905, 664, 666–67.

57. "A Washerwoman," *Independent,* November 10, 1904, 1073–74.

58. Ibid., 1074, 1075.

59. "More Slavery at the South: A Negro Nurse," in *Plain Folk: The Life Stories of Undistinguished Americans,* 177–78. This life story was originally in the *Independent,* January 25, 1912, 196–200, 178.

60. Ibid., 179.

61. Ibid., 178, 180–81; Katzman, *Seven Days a Week,* 216–18.

CHAPTER 4

1. Gerald George, "Historic House Museum Malaise: A Conference Considers What's Wrong," *History News* 57 (Autumn 2002): 21–25; see also Candace Tangorra Matelic, "Understanding Change and Transformation in History Organizations," *History News* 63 (Spring 2008): 7–13.

2. Jessica Foy Donnelly, "Introduction," in *Interpreting Historic House Museums,* ed. Jessica Foy Donnelly (Walnut Creek, CA: AltaMira Press, 2002), 9; AASLH Performance Management Program, http://www.aaslh.org/perfmanagement.htm.

3. Barbara Franco, "What's New in Exhibits?" *Cultural Resource Management* 23, no. 5 (2000): 48. Within the past ten years, the National Park Service has done some exceptional work with community members in terms of soliciting recommendations from those who live with and use the site. Many of the resulting reports are published on NPS Web pages, which provide excellent models for other public historians. For one example, see William Blair Curtis, "General Management Plan: Summary of Public

Scoping Workshops, September 15 and October 27, 1998," Hampton National Historic Site, 23 January 2003, http://www.nps.gov/hamp/GMP/gmp3.htm.

4. Historic House Museums Listserv, http://groups.yahoo.com/group/historic housemuseums. As of April 20, 2007, the list had 591 members. Other lists, such as MUSEUM-L and H-MUSEUM provide broader topical and international coverage. The National Trust for Historic Preservation hosts the "PreservationNation Blog," http://blogs.nationaltrust.org/preservationnation; Max van Balgooy, the National Trust's director of Interpretation and Education, keeps a blog to facilitate communication with the organization's network of historic sites, which is also a valuable resource for other house museum and historic site professionals, http://historicsites.wordpress.com.

5. Kim Moon, "'Raising Our Sites': Integrating Women's History into Museums," *Cultural Resource Management* 20, no. 3 (1997): 22–24. The fourteen sites included the Chester County Historical Society, West Chester; Drake Well Historic Site, Titusville; Folklife Demonstration Center for Gender Studies, Seton Hill College; Library Company of Philadelphia; Historical Society of Western Pennsylvania; Lycoming County Historical Society, Williamsport; Lehigh County Historical Society, Allentown; Lackwanna County Historical Society, Scranton; Landis Valley Museum, Lancaster; Hopewell Furnace National Historic Site, Elverson; Hershey Museum; Old Economy Village, Ambridge; Joseph Priestly House, Northumberland; Pennsbury Manor, Morrisville.

6. Belle Grove, Montpelier, Oatlands, and Woodlawn (all in Virginia), Cliveden (Philadelphia), and the Decatur House (Washington, D.C.). Two other plantation sites, Shadows-on-the-Teche (Louisiana) and Drayton Hall (Charleston, South Carolina) participated on a long-distance basis; Susan P. Schreiber, "Interpreting Slavery at National Trust Sites: A Case Study," *Cultural Resource Management* 23, no. 5 (2000): 52.

7. Excellent online resources for research on domestic service include: Open Collections [Harvard University]: Women Working, http://ocp.hul.harvard.edu/ww; HEARTH Home Economics Archive: Research, Tradition, and History, http://hearth.library.cornell.edu; and Feeding America, http://digital.lib.msu.edu/projects/cookbooks/. All feature a wealth of period materials that can be downloaded for no charge. Domestic manuals have many contemporary parallels that can be used to make this point clearer to visitors. For example, *Martha Stewart Living,* Home and Garden Television, and other sources provide domestic ideals for today's audience. However, most readers and viewers probably don't have the lifestyle these sources encourage. Instead, they create standards that some can only aspire to.

8. In *Selling Culture: Magazines, Markets, and Class at the Turn of the Century* (London: Verso, 1996), Richard Ohmann gives a good example of the regional bias of mass publications. "The *Journal* ran a series (in 1897–98) of photographs taking readers 'Inside of a Hundred Homes,' in 'all parts of the country.' The May 1898 installment depicted twenty rooms, porches, and terraces. Seventeen were in the metropolitan East and its suburban penumbra, or in California. One of the others was a vacation cottage. That left just two homes from the rest of the country, one in Michigan and one in Hamilton, Ohio, the latter standing as the lone representative of the small-town

heartland. . . . For the most part, the contemporary U.S. appeared in these magazines as the eastern seaboard from Washington to Boston, with less frequent glimpses of California, Chicago, the aristocratic South, the scenic or untamed West" (231). In addition to servants who lived and worked in private households, others lived and worked in hotels and boardinghouses. When setting up a tally like the one I described for Cedar Rapids, one should consider whether and how to count servants that did not work in private households.

9. The James J. Hill House displays framed photographs on a fireplace mantel in the servants' hall. Brucemore exhibits photographs (mounted on foam core) in the servants' bedroom.

10. Rex M. Ellis, "Interpreting the Whole House," in *Interpreting Historic House Museums,* ed. Jessica Foy Donnelly (Walnut Creek, CA: AltaMira Press, 2002), 67.

11. Barbara Abramoff Levy, Sandra Mackenzie Lloyd, and Susan Porter Schreiber, *Great Tours! Thematic Tours and Guide Training for Historic Sites* (Walnut Creek, CA: AltaMira Press, 2001).

12. This approach has also been used successfully at another National Trust site, Cliveden, in the Germantown section of Philadelphia. A detailed description of their development of interpretive storylines and themes is presented in Sandra Mackenzie Lloyd, "Creating Memorable Visits: How to Develop and Implement Theme-Based Tours," in *Interpreting History House Museums,* ed. Jessica Foy Donnelly (Walnut Creek, CA: AltaMira Press, 2002), 210–30.

13. Anne L. Vrooman, "The Servant Question in Social Evolution," *Arena* 25 (June 1901): 645.

14. Barbara A. Levy and Susan Schreiber, "The View from the Kitchen," *History News* 50 (March/April 1995): 20.

15. Barbara Carson and Cary Carson, "Things Unspoken: Learning Social History from Artifacts," in *Ordinary People and Everyday Life,* ed. James B. Gardner and George Rollie Adams (Walnut Creek, CA: AltaMira Press, 1996), 194.

16. Mildred Maddocks Bentley, "The Psychology of Servants," *Ladies' Home Journal,* December 1925, 159; "Servants and Labor-Saving Devices," *Good Housekeeping,* December 1912, 860.

17. Erie L. Preston, "Service Rooms of Modern Homes," *House and Garden,* November 1907, 185.

18. Patricia West, "Uncovering and Interpreting History at Historic House Museums," in *Restoring Women's History through Historic Preservation,* ed. Gail Lee Dubrow and Jennifer B. Goodman (Baltimore: Johns Hopkins University Press, 2003), 93–94.

19. "A Washerwoman," *Independent,* November 10, 1904, 1073–76. Clark-Lewis notes that live-in servants hoping to make the transition to day work needed to earn the laundresses' respect before they could hope to win them as allies. But once they did, laundresses provided support and encouragement, as in the experience of Mayme Gibson: "After a while I could talk to the laundress. See, they worked house-to-house, always, and they didn't care. They'd do it and didn't feel like it was just picking up work neither. They really made good and didn't have that woman on they backs day *and*

night. Now they'd know where jobs was. Not doing piecework, too. This one called Dee helped me find my very first work out. She was nice, but it was over a year before she helped me and another girl get set and in some day work" (Elizabeth Clark-Lewis, *Living In, Living Out: African American Domestics in Washington, D.C., 1910–1940* [Washington, DC: Smithsonian Institution Press, 1994], 141).

20. Some experts on housekeeping espoused the ideas of Frederick Taylor by encouraging efficiency and scientific management in the home. Christine Frederick applied these methods in solving the servant problem (*The New Housekeeping: Efficiency Studies in Home Management* [Garden City: Doubleday, Page & Company, 1925]).

21. Charles E. White, Jr., "The Servant in the Little House," *Ladies' Home Journal,* November 1915, 54.

22. Hanna Tachau, "Furnishing the Servants' Rooms," *House Beautiful,* October 1920, 288–89, 316. Other authors offered similar advice on servants' accommodations and warned housekeepers that using the excuse that servants were used to poverty to avoid giving them nice rooms was not acceptable. T. W. Hotchkiss gave the following "Advice to Employers" in the September 1909 issue of *Good Housekeeping*: "It is not sufficient answer for any employer to allege that, in the servant's home in the 'old country,' the pigs lived in the kitchen. Good, plain food, clean living rooms which are well lighted, warmed and aired, good beds and clean bedding, bathing facilities and extra time free, are among the ordinary rights for which every servant in this country should stipulate when making an engagement; they should not be classed as special privileges" (244). Finally, when the "Visiting Housekeeper" is asked for help solving the servant problem, she noted the following after seeing the servant's room: "I knew the room was one of those cold, dreary boxes which are arranged for servants on the top floor of many big apartments. . . . The comparison between the sunny house downstairs and this homeless place under the eaves was sharp enough for a child to see. The first girl had made a pitiful effort at arranging the furniture. There was a colored print from the butcher's and a cheap calendar pinned to the dingy white wall. . . . Mrs. McHenry shrugged angry shoulders. 'It's very good for a servant; they are used to this sort of thing. At home they live in slums'" ("The Visiting Housekeeper: I. She Answers a 'Hurry Call' from a Servantless Home," *Good Housekeeping,* March 1911, 341).

23. Massachusetts Bureau of Statistics of Labor, *Social Statistics of Working Women* (Boston, 1901), 17–18; Lillian Pettengill, *Toilers of the Home: The Record of a College Woman's Experience as a Domestic Servant* (New York: Doubleday, Page, 1905), 314–15.

24. Ellis, "Interpreting the Whole House," 67.

25. Carol E. Kohan, *Historic Furnishings Report for "Lindenwald"* (Washington, DC: GPO, 1986), 35–36, 272–77; David Wallace, *Sagamore Hill Historic Furnishings Report,* vol. 2 (Washington, DC: GPO, 1991).

26. Elizabeth O'Leary, *From Morning to Night: Domestic Service in Maymont House and the Gilded Age South* (Charlottesville: University of Virginia Press, 2003), 127–48. Developing such biographies for slaves and servants is also recommended by the authors of *Great Tours!*

27. James Loewen, *Lies across America: What Our Historic Sites Get Wrong* (New

York: New Press, 1999), 339; Jennifer L. Eichstedt and Stephen Small, *Representations of Slavery: Race and Ideology in Southern Plantation Museums* (Washington, DC: Smithsonian Institution Press, 2002), 107, 134–37. Mentioning the names of servants can also lead to a discussion of the fact that servants were typically addressed by their Christian names, while they addressed their employers formally. Many servants objected to this convention. One respondent to Lucy Maynard Salmon's survey wrote the following: "A woman who had been for years a domestic employee left her place on account of sickness, and ultimately opened a small bakeshop. Her former employer called on her one day, and said, 'Well, Sarah, how do you like your work?' She replied, 'I never thought of it before, but now that you speak, I think the reason I like it so well is because everybody calls me "Miss Clark"'" (*Domestic Service* [London: Macmillan, 1901], 157, fn. 1).

28. Pettengill, *Toilers of the Home*, 365–66.

29. Stacy F. Roth, *Past into Present: Effective Techniques for First-Person Historical Interpretation* (Chapel Hill: University of North Carolina Press, 1998), 9.

30. Margaret Lynch-Brennan, "The Servant Slant: Irish Women Domestic Servants and Historic House Museums," in *Her Past around Us: Interpreting Sites for Women's History,* ed. Polly Welts Kaufman and Katherine T. Corbett (Malabar, FL: Krieger, 2003), 124–30.

31. The only promotions for the living history aspect of the tour were via staff when people called to inquire about holiday tours and a photograph of me dressed in costume holding up a tray of cookies that ran in the local newspaper the day before our first Wednesday evening. The attendance on those three Wednesdays far exceeded the evening tour attendance of any previous year.

32. In December 2008, as this manuscript was nearing completion, Brucemore staff presented a new program, "Douglas Family Christmas," which featured interpreters portraying the Douglas family and several servants describing their preparations for the holidays.

33. "NCPH Award Winners," *Public History News* 23 (Summer 2003): 6; "The Campbell House Story, Revised Narrator's Script," 2002. Thanks to the staff at the Campbell House for providing me with a copy of their work. For a detailed description of how the Campbell House staff, consultants, and a graduate student seminar collaborated on the development of this tour, see Janice Williams Rutherford and Steven E. Shay, "Peopling the Age of Elegance: Reinterpreting Spokane's Campbell House: A Collaboration," *Public Historian* 26 (Summer 2004): 27–48.

34. Barbara and Cary Carson, "Things Unspoken," 192.

35. Karen Lee Davis and James G. Gibb, "Unpuzzling the Past: Critical Thinking in History Museums," *Museum Studies Journal* 3, no. 2 (Spring/Summer 1988), 41. When I describe the duties of a maid-of-all-work, some visitors comment, "Today this person is called 'Mom'!"

36. George, "Historic House Museum Malaise," 18.

37. Barbara Ehrenreich, "Maid to Order: The Politics of Other Women's Work," *Harper's Magazine,* April 2000, 60–62.

38. Ibid., 64.

39. Barbara Ehrenreich, *Nickel and Dimed: On (Not) Getting By in America* (New York: Henry Holt, 2001), 93.

40. Ibid., 100.

41. Conny Graft, "Listen, Evaluate, Respond! The Colonial Williamsburg Visitor Research Story," *History News* 62 (Spring 2007): 14.

CHAPTER 5

1. Patricia Chambers Walker and Thomas Graham, *Directory of Historic House Museums in the United States* (Walnut Creek, CA: AltaMira Press, 2000).

2. Jennifer L. Eichstedt and Stephen Small, *Representations of Slavery: Race and Ideology in Southern Plantation Museums* (Washington, DC: Smithsonian Institution Press, 2002), 19.

3. Some of these sites include: Glensheen, Duluth, MN; the Pabst Mansion, Milwaukee; the Glessner House, Chicago; the Clarke House, Chicago; the Dana-Thomas House, Springfield, IL; Ellwood House, DeKalb, IL; Salisbury House, Des Moines; Montauk, Clermont, IA; Mathais Ham House, Dubuque, IA; Arbor Lodge, Nebraska City, NE; the Maggie Lena Walker National Historic Site, Richmond, VA; Lindenwald, Kinderhook, NY; Naumkeag, Stockbridge, MA; Chesterwood, Stockbridge, MA; The Mount, Lenox, MA; Gibson House Museum, Boston; John Fitzgerald Kennedy National Historic Site, Brookline, MA; Old Manse, Concord, MA.

4. My description of Brucemore's National Trust era history is based on informal conversations with Brucemore staff members between 1998 and 2006, especially those related to a 2001 temporary exhibition I coordinated that interpreted the site's twenty-year anniversary as a public historic site. Peggy Whitworth, the site's first executive director, contributed a great deal to my understanding of Brucemore's recent past.

5. Wiss, Janney, Elstner Associates, Inc., *Historic Structure Report for Brucemore, Cedar Rapids, Iowa,* 1991.

6. The approach to creating thematic tours used at Brucemore is the same published by Barbara Abramoff Levy et al. in *Great Tours!* One of the authors, Susan Schreiber, was the director of Interpretation and Education at the National Trust when I started working at Brucemore.

7. http:www.cr.nps.gov/nr/twhp/wwwlps/lessons/105Brucemore/105brucemore. htm.

8. Irene Hazeltine Douglas to Margaret Douglas Hall, January 20, Hall Collection correspondence, days of the week only, folder 4, Brucemore archives; Ella McDannel to Margaret Douglas Hall, January 10, 193[7], Borden Stevens Collection, Box 4, Folder 7, Brucemore archives.

9. Closing the door of the "preschool room" also caused some objections. Although the room is not restored and is basically used to store extra books from the library restoration, two juvenile portraits of George Bruce Douglas and his brother Walter hang in the room. Some guides objected to closing this room because they used the portrait of Walter to tell the story of his death in the *Titanic* disaster. The staff offered

other suggestions for incorporating this material, and eventually the issue died out.

10. Much of the background information on changes in interpretation at SPNEA/ Historic New England and the reclamation and subsequent interpretation of servant spaces at the organization's properties was provided by Peter Gittleman, team leader, visitor experience, Historic New England, during an interview conducted in November 2008.

11. Linda Shoemaker, "Backstage at Beauport," *Historic New England* 5 (Summer 2004): 4.

12. Christine Frederick, *Household Engineering: Scientific Management in the Home* (Chicago: American School of Home Economics, 1920), 436; Shoemaker, "Backstage at Beauport," 7.

13. *Villa Louis* (Prairie du Chien, WI: Friends of Villa Louis, 2002), 28, 31–32.

14. "Visitor Guide, Villa Louis, Prairie du Chien, Wisconsin" (Wisconsin Historical Society, n.d.), n.p.; Governor's Commission on Historic Sites, *History Where It Happened: Wisconsin's Historic Sites* (Madison: Wisconsin Historical Society, 2002), 14.

15. Information about the guided tour of Villa Louis is based on field notes taken during visits on June 3, 2000, and June 8, 2003. Additional information was provided by Michael Douglass, site administrator, and Sarah Hoffman, lead interpreter, on June 2, 2000 and June 3, 2000, respectively. Thank you to Mr. Douglass for answering follow-up questions regarding recent restorations to the servants' wing as I was preparing the final draft of this manuscript.

16. Joy K. Lintelman, "'Our Serving Sisters': Swedish-American Domestic Servants and Their Ethnic Community," *Social Science History* 15, no. 3 (Fall 1991): 381–95; "'America Is the Woman's Promised Land': Swedish Immigrant Women and American Domestic Service," *Journal of American Ethnic History* 8 (Spring 1989): 9–23.

17. While it may seem like a long shot that a random visitor might be able to fill in the gaps of a site's domestic history, one of my own experiences reveals that it can indeed occur. I happened to be at Brucemore one Saturday morning, training guides about interpreting domestic service, when one of the staff found me and told me that a woman on the current house tour had said that her father had been the Douglases' chauffeur. Such stories are rather common for the later period of Brucemore's residential history; it seems like everyone in Cedar Rapids has either worked for or is related to someone who worked for Mr. and Mrs. Hall. However, stories from the Douglas era are less common. I caught the woman and her husband at the end of the tour and asked her some questions. She had with her photographs of her father, the Douglases' Santa Barbara home, and the Douglas daughters, as well as a book that had been signed and given to her father by Mr. Douglas. As it turned out, her father had worked for the Douglases briefly. When she told me his last name was Horn, I immediately remembered reading about a "Horn" in some of the family diaries. She told me that her father had been hired to drive for the Douglases during their 1913 vacation in England. Mr. Douglas liked his work so much that he asked him to come to America, hiring him away from the lord mayor of London. The visitor's story was consistent with our archival information, and not only were we able to add a fascinating anecdote to our stories about servants, but she provided us with some wonderful photographs of her

father from the period in which he had been employed by the Douglases.

18. Michael Douglass, personal communication with the author, December 14, 2008.

19. At the National Trust for Historic Preservation workshop "View from the Kitchen," Carson described this method: "The object of perspectivist history is to consider something—a place, event, person, or group of people—from several points of view" (Jane Brown Gillette, "Breaking the Silence," *Historic Preservation,* March/April 1995, 42).

20. In his review of programs at Colonial Williamsburg based on the site's "Choosing Revolution" storyline, Edward Ayers describes the confusion or discomfort of visitors as they interact with character interpreters. For example, he describes a first-person program at a military encampment where Governor Dunmore's regiment of freed slaves is being trained: "A character interpreter portraying a newly arrived runaway slave approached the visitors and began asking their advice concerning his dilemma. If he joined the governor's regiment to gain his freedom, what would happen to his wife and children left behind to face the wrath of his master? The character interpreter tended to overact at times, but in general gave a convincing performance. The visitors, however, seemed unsure how to react to his confronting them while in character" (Edward Ayers, "Colonial Williamsburg's Choosing Revolution Storyline" *Public Historian* 20, no. 3 [Summer 1998]: 88).

21. Elisabeth Doermann and Ellen M. Rosenthal, "Introducing the Hill House," *Minnesota History* 46, no. 8 (Winter 1979): 328–30; Barbara Ann Carson, "The James J. Hill House: Symbol of Status and Security," *Minnesota History* 55, no. 6 (Summer 1997): 236.

22. "Shedding Light on the Other Side," *History News* 36 (September 1981): 9, 12; Candace Floyd, "Upstairs Downstairs: Minnesota Society Tells Story of James J. Hill House," *History News* 36 (September 1981).

23. These were some of the things pointed out by the guide during my tour of the site on May 31, 2000.

24. Craig Johnson, "Hill House Holidays" script, 1998, 6; in the play's list of characters, Mary and James Hill are described as "an off-stage noise." Thank you to Craig Johnson for providing me with a copy of the script.

25. "Hill House Holidays" script, 2.

26. Lisa Craig, "Servants Who Worked for the Alexander Ramsey Family: 1872–1903" (master's thesis, Cooperstown Graduate Program in Museum Studies, 1994).

27. Ruth Schwartz Cowan's *More Work for Mother: The Ironies of Household Technology from the Open Hearth to the Microwave* (New York: Basic Books, 1983) is the primary source for such an interpretation.

28. Stacy F. Roth, *Past into Present: Effective Techniques for First-Person Historical Interpretation* (Chapel Hill: University of North Carolina Press, 1998), 166; Ron Thomson and Marilyn Harper, "Telling the Stories: Planning Effective Interpretive Programs for Properties Listed in the National Register of Historic Places," *National Register Bulletin* (Washington, DC: National Park Service, 2000).

29. Maria Parloa, Fannie Farmer, and Mary Lincoln were among the instructors at Lasell (Catherine Seiberling Pond, *The Pantry: Its History and Modern Uses* [Salt Lake City: Gibbs Smith, 2007], 54).

30. The Elms, one of the Newport mansions, offers the "Rooftop and Behind-the-Scenes Tour" hourly during the house's regular operating schedule. According to the Preservation Society of Newport County's Web site, the tour allows visitors to "See and hear how the other half lived as you tour the 'back stairs' and roof top of this Gilded Age mansion. Walk through the kitchens, coal cellar and boiler room, laundry room and wine cellar, then up stairs to the third-floor staff quarters." When weather permits, tours also visit the roof; http://www.newportmansions.org/page3559.cfm. In 2008, The Old Manse, in Concord, Massachusetts, offered special behind-the-scenes tours of the attic, formerly home to servants, students, and family members.

31. Dale Wheary, "Maymont: Gilded Age Estate," *Maymont Notes* 1 (Fall 2001): 11. The name Maymont (also written May Mont) comes from Mrs. Dooley's maiden name and *mont* for "hill."

32. Conversation with Elizabeth O'Leary, guest curator, Maymont, March 17, 2003.

33. Maymont Foundation, Implementation Grant Proposal to the National Endowment of the Humanities, January 2002, 13; quoted in Frank E. Sanchis III, "Looking Back or Looking Forward? House Museums in the 21st Century," *An Athenaeum of Philadelphia Symposium on Historic House Museums*, December 4–5, 1998, http://phila athenaeum.org/hmuseum/sanchis/htm.

34. Quoted in Wheary, "Maymont," endnote 8; Maymont Foundation, Implementation Grant Proposal, 5.

35. Maymont Foundation, Implementation Grant Proposal, 7–8.

36. Elizabeth O'Leary, guest curator, Maymont, personal communication with the author, July 16, 2002.

37. Maymont Foundation, Exhibition Walkthrough, 12, 7, Elizabeth O'Leary, "Making the Invisible Visible: Domestic Employees at Maymont House" *Maymont Notes* 1 (Fall 2001): 17.

38. Elizabeth O'Leary, *From Morning to Night: Domestic Service in Maymont House and the Gilded Age South* (Charlottesville: University of Virginia Press, 2003). Past, current, and future hosts of the traveling panel exhibition "From Morning to Night: Domestic Service in the Gilded Age South" include the Valentine Richmond History Center, Sweet Briar College (VA), the Alexandria [VA] Black History Museum, the Catawba County Museum (NC), Hay House Museum (GA), and the Scott Joplin House (MO). As of this writing, the exhibition is booked through early 2009.

39. Maymont Foundation, *Final Performance Report, NEH Implementation Grant, Maymont House Museum Domestic Service Exhibition and Interpretation Project* (December 2005).

Works Cited

PRIMARY SOURCES

Allen, Annie Winsor. "Both Sides of the Servant Question." *Atlantic Monthly,* April 1913, 496–506.

Bentley, Mildred Maddocks. "The Psychology of Servants." *Ladies' Home Journal,* December 1925, 159–62, 165.

"A Butler's Life Story." *Independent,* July 14, 1910, 77–82.

Carter, Mary Elizabeth. *Millionaire Households and Their Domestic Economy.* New York: D. Appleton, 1903.

"The Confession of a Japanese Servant." *Independent,* September 21, 1905, 661–68.

"The Correct Apron for Maids." *Ladies' Home Journal,* March 1910, 47.

Dunbar, Ruth. "Not Wanted: Girl for General Housework." *Saturday Evening Post,* May 31, 1919.

E.A.C.P. "A Day's Mail." *Christian Union,* June 12, 1890, 838.

Forrester, Izola. "The 'Girl' Problem." *Good Housekeeping,* September 1912, 374–82.

Frederick, Christine. *Household Engineering: Scientific Management in the Home.* Chicago: American School of Home Economics, 1920.

———. *The New Housekeeping: Efficiency Studies in Home Management.* Garden City: Doubleday, Page, 1926.

Godman, Inez. "Ten Weeks in a Kitchen." *Independent,* October 17, 1901, 2549–64.

Herrick, Christine Terhune. *The Expert Maid-Servant.* New York: Harper & Brothers, 1904.

Hotchkiss, T. W. "Advice to Employers." *Good Housekeeping,* September 1909, 244.

Kellor, Frances A. *Out of Work.* New York: G. P. Putnam's Sons, 1904.

Klink, Jane Seymour. "Put Yourself in Her Place." *Atlantic Monthly,* February 1905, 169–77.

M., Agnes. "The True Life Story of a Nurse Girl." *Independent,* 24 September 1903, 2261–66.

Massachusetts Bureau of Statistics of Labor. *Social Statistics of Working Women.* Boston, 1901.

McCracken, Elizabeth. "The Problem of Domestic Service: I. From the Standpoint of the Employer." *Outlook,* February 15, 1908, 368–73.

Pettengill, Lillian. *Toilers of the Home: The Record of a College Woman's Experience as a Domestic Servant.* New York: Doubleday, Page, 1905.

Post, Emily. *Etiquette.* New York: Funk and Wagnalls, 1928.

Preston, Erie L. "Service Rooms of Modern Homes." *House and Garden,* November 1907, 185–90.

Rubinow, I. M. "The Problem of Domestic Service." *Journal of Political Economy* 14 (October 1906): 502–19.

Rubinow, I. M., and Daniel Durant. "The Depth and Breadth of the Servant Problem." *McClure's Magazine,* March 1910, 576–85.

Salmon, Lucy Maynard. *Domestic Service*. New York: Macmillan, 1901.

———. "Recent Progress in the Study of Domestic Service." *Atlantic Monthly*, November 1905, 628–35.

Seely, Mrs. [Lida]. *Mrs. Seely's Cook Book: A Manual of French and American Cookery with Chapters on Domestic Servants, Their Rights and Duties and Many Other Details of Household Management*. New York: Macmillan, 1914.

"Servants and Labor-Saving Devices." *Good Housekeeping*, December 1912, 860.

Sherwood, Mary Elizabeth Wilson. *Manners and Social Usages*. New York: Harper's, 1918.

Spofford, Harriet Prescott. *The Servant Girl Question*. Boston: Houghton Mifflin, 1881.

"The Story of an Irish Cook." *Independent*, March 30, 1905, 715–17.

Tachau, Hanna. "Furnishing the Servants' Rooms." *House Beautiful*, October 1920, 288–89, 316.

Trueblood, Mary E. "Housework versus Shop and Factories." *Independent*, November 13, 1902, 2691–93.

United States Bureau of the Census. *Statistics of Women at Work*. Washington, DC, 1907.

Veblen, Thorstein. *The Theory of the Leisure Class*. 1899. Reprint, New Brunswick, NJ: Transaction, 1992.

"The Visiting Housekeeper: I. She Answers a 'Hurry Call' from a Servantless Home." *Good Housekeeping*, March 1911, 340–42.

Vrooman, Anne L. "The Servant Question in Social Evolution." *Arena* 25 (June 1901): 643–52.

"A Washerwoman." *Independent*, November 10, 1904, 1073–76.

White, Charles E., Jr. "The Servant in the Little House." *Ladies' Home Journal*, November 1915, 54.

SECONDARY SOURCES

Abram, Ruth J. "Harnessing the Power of History." In *Museums, Society, Inequality*, edited by Richard Sandell, 125–41. London: Routledge, 2002.

———. "Kitchen Conversations: Democracy in Action at the Lower East Side Tenement Museum." *Public Historian* 29 (Winter 2007): 59–76.

Alexander, Edward P. "Sixty Years of Historic Preservation: The Society for the Preservation of New England Antiquities." *Old-Time New England* 61 (1970–71): 14–19.

American Association of Museums. *Museums Count*. Washington, DC: American Association of Museums, 1994.

Ayers, Edward. "Colonial Williamsburg's Choosing Revolution Storyline." *Public Historian* 20, no. 3 (Summer 1998): 77–92.

Banner, Lois. *American Beauty*. New York: Knopf, 1983.

Barthel, Diane. *Historic Preservation: Collective Memory and Historic Identity*. New Brunswick, NJ: Rutgers University Press, 1996.

Benson, Susan Porter, Stephen Brier, and Roy Rosenzweig, eds. *Presenting the Past: Essays on History and the Public*. Philadelphia: Temple University Press, 1986.

Brue, Sandy. "Preparing for a National Celebration of Abraham Lincoln's Bicentennial."

CRM: Journal of Heritage Stewardship 5 (Winter 2008): 18–30.

Burnham, Philip. *How the Other Half Lived: A People's Guide to American Historic Sites*. Boston: Faber and Faber, 1995.

Butcher-Younghans, Sherry. *Historic House Museums: A Practical Handbook for Their Care, Preservation, and Management*. New York: Oxford University Press, 1993.

Butler, Patrick H. III. "Past, Present, and Future: The Place of the House Museum in the Museum Community." In *Interpreting Historic House Museums*, edited by Jessica Foy Donnelly, 18–42. Walnut Creek, CA: AltaMira Press, 2002.

Carlisle, Nancy, and Melinda Talbot Nasardinov. *America's Kitchens*. Boston: Historic New England, 2008.

Carson, Barbara Ann. "The James J. Hill House: Symbol of Status and Security." *Minnesota History* 55, no. 6 (Winter 1979): 234–49.

Carson, Barbara, and Cary Carson. "Things Unspoken: Learning Social History from Artifacts." In *Ordinary People and Everyday Life*, edited by James B. Gardner and George Rollie Adams, 191–203. Walnut Creek, CA: AltaMira Press, 1996.
Clark-Lewis, Elizabeth. *Living In, Living Out: African American Domestics in Washington, D.C., 1910–1940*. Washington, DC: Smithsonian Institution Press, 1994.

———. "'This Work Had an End': African-American Domestic Workers in Washington, D.C., 1910–1940." In Carol Groneman and Mary Beth Norton, eds., *To Toil the Livelong Day: America's Women at Work, 1780–1980*, 196–212. Ithaca: Cornell University Press, 1987.

Coats, Peggy. "Survey of Historic House Museums." *History News* 45 (January 1990): 26–28.

Cowan, Ruth Schwartz. *More Work for Mother: The Ironies of Household Technology from the Open Hearth to the Microwave*. New York: Basic Books, 1983.

Craig, Lisa. "Servants Who Worked for the Alexander Ramsey Family: 1872–1903." Master's thesis, Cooperstown Graduate Program in Museum Studies, 1994.

Crew, Spencer R., and James E. Sims. "Locating Authenticity: Fragments of a Dialogue." In *Exhibiting Cultures: The Poetics and Politics of Museum Display*, edited by Ivan Karp and Stephen D. Lavine, 159–73. Washington, DC: Smithsonian Institution Press, 1991.

Davis, Karen Lee, and James G. Gibb. "Unpuzzling the Past: Critical Thinking in History Museums." *Museum Studies Journal* 3 (Spring/Summer 1988): 41–45.

Diner, Hasia. *Erin's Daughters in America: Irish Immigrant Women in the Nineteenth Century*. Baltimore: Johns Hopkins University Press, 1983.

Doermann, Elisabeth, and Ellen M. Rosenthal. "Introducing the Hill House." *Minnesota History* 46, no. 8 (Winter 1979): 328–35.

Donnelly, Jessica Foy, ed. *Interpreting Historic House Museums*. Walnut Creek, CA: AltaMira Press, 2002.

Downey, Fairfax Davis. *Portrait of an Era as Drawn by C. D. Gibson*. New York: Charles Scribner's Sons, 1936.

Dubin, Steven C. *Displays of Power: Memory and Amnesia in the American Museum*. New York: New York University Press, 1999.

Dubrow, Gail Lee, and Jennifer B. Goodman. *Restoring Women's History through Historic Preservation*. Baltimore: Johns Hopkins University Press, 2003.

Dudden, Faye E. *Serving Women: Household Service in Nineteenth-Century America*. Hanover, NH: Wesleyan University Press, 1981.

Durel, John, and Anita Nowery Durel. "A Golden Age for Historic Properties." *History News* 62 (Summer 2007): 7–16.

Durham, Michael S. "The Word Is 'Slaves.'" *American Heritage,* April 1992, 89–99.

Ehrenreich, Barbara. "Maid to Order: The Politics of Other Women's Work." *Harper's Magazine,* April 2000, 59–70.

———. *Nickel and Dimed: On (Not) Getting By in America*. New York: Henry Holt, 2001.

Eichstedt, Jennifer L., and Stephen Small. *Representations of Slavery: Race and Ideology in Southern Plantation Museums*. Washington, DC: Smithsonian Institution Press, 2002.

Ellis, Rex M. "Interpreting the Whole House." In *Interpreting Historic House Museums,* edited by Jessica Foy Donnelly, 61–80. Walnut Creek, CA: AltaMira Press, 2002.

Ettema, Michael. "History Museums and the Culture of Materialism." In *Past Meets Present: Essays about Historic Interpretation and Public Audiences,* edited by Jo Blatti, 62–85. Washington, DC: Smithsonian Institution Press, 1987.

Floyd, Candace. "Upstairs Downstairs: Minnesota Society Tells Story of James J. Hill House." *History News* 36 (September 1981): 10–13.

Foner, Eric. "The Historian in the Museum." *Museum News* 85 (March–April 2006): 45–49.

Franco, Barbara. "What's New in Exhibits?" *Cultural Resource Management* 23, no. 5 (2000): 46–48.

Gable, Eric, Richard Handler, and Anna Lawson. "On the Uses of Relativism: Fact, Conjecture, and Black and White Histories at Colonial Williamsburg." *American Ethnologist* 19, no. 4 (1992): 791–805.

Garb, Margaret. "Lower East Side Tenement Museum." *Journal of Urban History* 26, no. 1 (November 1999): 108–11.

Garvey, Ellen Gruber. *The Adman in the Parlor: Magazines and the Gendering of Consumer Culture, 1880s to 1910s*. New York: Oxford University Press, 1996.

George, Gerald. "Historic House Museum Malaise: A Conference Considers What's Wrong." *History News* 57 (Autumn 2002): 21–25.

Gibb, James G., and Karen Lee Davis. "History Exhibits and Theories of Material Culture." *Journal of American Culture* 12, no. 2 (Summer 1989): 27–33.

Gillette, Jane Brown. "Breaking the Silence." *Historic Preservation,* March/April 1995, 38–43.

Governor's Commission on Historic Sites. *History Where It Happened: Wisconsin's Historic Sites*. Madison: Wisconsin Historical Society, 2002.

Graft, Conny. "Listen, Evaluate, Respond! The Colonial Williamsburg Visitor Research Story." *History News* 62 (Spring 2007): 14.

Handler, Richard, and Eric Gable. *The New History in an Old Museum: Creating the Past at Colonial Williamsburg*. Durham, NC: Duke University Press, 1997.

Hardy, Charles, III. "Exhibition Reviews: Lower East Side Tenement Museum." *Journal of American History* 84, no. 3 (December 1997): 1009–13.

Harris, Donna Ann. *New Solutions for House Museums: Ensuring the Long-Term Preservation of America's Historic Houses.* Lanham, MD: AltaMira Press, 2007.

Horton, James Oliver. "Presenting Slavery: The Perils of Telling America's Racial Story." *Public Historian* 21, no. 4 (Fall 1999): 19–38.

———. "Slavery in American History: An Uncomfortable National Dialogue." In *Slavery and Public History: The Tough Stuff of American Memory,* edited by James Oliver Horton and Lois E. Horton, 35–55. New York: New Press, 2006.

Horton, James Oliver, and Lois E. Horton, eds. *Slavery and Public History: The Tough Stuff of American Memory.* New York: New Press, 2006.

Horton, Lois E. "Avoiding History: Thomas Jefferson, Sally Hemings, and the Uncomfortable Public Discussion on Slavery." In *Slavery and Public History: The Tough Stuff of American Memory,* edited by James Oliver Horton and Lois E. Horton, 135–49. New York: New Press, 2006.

Hosmer, Charles B. *Presence of the Past: A History of the Preservation Movement in the United States before Williamsburg.* New York: G. P. Putnam's Sons, 1965.

———. *Preservation Comes of Age: From Williamsburg to the National Trust, 1926–1949.* Charlottesville: University of Virginia Press, 1980.

Jones, Jacqueline. *Labor of Love, Labor of Sorrow: Black Women, Work, and the Family from Slavery to the Present.* New York: Basic Books, 1985.

Kammen, Carol. "Tripping over History." *History News* 63 (Autumn 2008): 3–4.

Kammen, Michael. *Mystic Chords of Memory: The Transformation of Tradition in American Culture.* New York: Vintage, 1993.

Katzman, David M. *Seven Days a Week: Women and Domestic Service in Industrializing America.* New York: Oxford University Press, 1978.

Katzman, David M., and William M. Tuttle, eds. *Plain Folk: The Life Stories of Undistinguished Americans.* Urbana: University of Illinois Press, 1982.

Kaufman, Polly Welts, and Katharine T. Corbett, eds. *Her Past around Us: Interpreting Sites for Women's History.* Malabar, FL: Krieger, 2003.

Kitch, Carolyn. *The Girl on the Magazine Cover: The Origins of Visual Stereotypes in American Mass Media.* Chapel Hill: University of North Carolina Press, 2001.

Kohan, Carol E. *Historic Furnishings Report for "Lindenwald."* Washington, DC: GPO, 1986.

Lambrose, R. J. "East Side Story" in "The Abusable Past." *Radical History Review* 43 (January 1989): 143.

Lee, Antoinette J. "An Interview with William Seale." *CRM: The Journal of Heritage Stewardship* 1 (Summer 2004): 20–33.

Leon, Warren, and Margaret Piatt. "Living-History Museums." In *History Museums in the United States: A Critical Assessment,* edited by Warren Leon and Roy Rosenzweig, 64–97. Urbana: University of Illinois Press, 1989.

Leon, Warren, and Roy Rosenzweig, eds. *History Museums in the United States: A Critical Assessment.* Urbana: University of Illinois Press, 1989.

Levy, Barbara Abramoff, Sandra Mackenzie Lloyd, and Susan Porter Schreiber. *Great Tours! Thematic Tours and Guide Training for Historic Sites*. Walnut Creek, CA: AltaMira Press, 2001.

Levy, Barbara A., and Susan Schreiber. "The View from the Kitchen." *History News* 50 (March/April 1995): 16–20.

Lewis, Catherine M. *The Changing Face of Public History: The Chicago Historical Society and the Transformation of an American Museum*. DeKalb: Northern Illinois University Press, 2005.

Linenthal, Edward T., and Tom Englehardt, eds. *History Wars: The Enola Gay and Other Battles for the American Past*. New York: Metropolitan Books, 1996.

Linneman, William R. "Immigrant Stereotypes: 1880–1900." *Studies in American Humor* 1, no. 1 (April 1974): 28–39.

Lintelman, Joy K. "'America Is the Woman's Promised Land': Swedish Immigrant Women and American Domestic Service." *Journal of American Ethnic History* 8 (Spring 1989): 9–23.

———. "'Our Serving Sisters': Swedish-American Domestic Servants and Their Ethnic Community." *Social Science History* 15, no. 3 (Fall 1991): 381–95.

Lloyd, Sandra Mackenzie. "Creating Memorable Visits: How to Develop and Implement Theme-Based Tours." In *Interpreting Historic House Museums*, edited by Jessica Foy Donnelly, 210–30. Walnut Creek, CA: AltaMira Press, 2002.

Loewen, James W. *Lies across America: What Our Historic Sites Get Wrong*. New York: New Press, 1999.

Lynch-Brennan, Margaret. "The Servant Slant: Irish Women Domestic Servants and Historic House Museums." In *Her Past around Us: Interpreting Sites for Women's History*, edited by Polly Welts Kaufman and Katherine T. Corbett, 121–43. Malabar, FL: Krieger, 2003.

Marchand, Roland. *Advertising the American Dream: Making Way for Modernity, 1920–1940*. Berkeley: University of California Press, 1985.

Matelic, Candace Tangorra. "Understanding Change and Transformation in History Organizations." *History News* 63 (Spring 2008): 7–13.

Maymont Foundation. Final Performance Report, NEH Implementation Grant, Maymont House Museum Domestic Service Exhibition and Interpretation Project. December 2005.

———. Implementation Grant Proposal to the National Endowment for the Humanities. January 2002.

McKay, Jim, and Gregg Berninger. "Interpreting Servants at the Martin Van Buren NHS." *Cultural Resource Management* 20, no. 3 (1997): 48.

Melish, Joanne. "Recovering (from) Slavery": Four Struggles to Tell the Truth." In *Slavery and Public History: The Tough Stuff of American Memory*, edited by James Oliver Horton and Lois E. Horton, 103–33. New York and London: New Press, 2006.

Moon, Kim. "'Raising Our Sites': Integrating Women's History into Museums." *Cultural Resource Management* 20, no. 3 (1997): 22–24.

Mulloy, Elizabeth D. *The History of the National Trust for Historic Preservation*. Washington, DC: Preservation Press, 1976.

Nold, Carl R. "The Future of the Historic House Museum." *Historic New England* 9 (Summer 2008): 5–9.

Nylander, Jane C. *Our Own Snug Fireside: Images of the New England Home, 1760–1860.* New York: Alfred A. Knopf, 1993.

Ohmann, Richard. *Selling Culture: Magazines, Markets, and Class at the Turn of the Century.* London: Verso Books, 1996.

O'Leary, Elizabeth L. *At Beck and Call: The Representation of Domestic Servants in Nineteenth-Century American Painting.* Washington, DC: Smithsonian Institution Press, 1996.

———. *From Morning to Night: Domestic Service in Maymont House and the Gilded Age South.* Charlottesville: University of Virginia Press, 2003.

———. "Making the Invisible Visible: Domestic Employees at Maymont House." *Maymont Notes* 1 (Fall 2001): 15–19.

Palmer, Phyllis. *Domesticity and Dirt: Housewives and Domestic Servants in the United States, 1920–1945.* Philadelphia: Temple University Press, 1989.

Pond, Catherine Seiberling. *The Pantry: Its History and Modern Uses.* Salt Lake City: Gibbs Smith, 2007.

Rollins, Judith. *Between Women: Domestics and Their Employers.* Philadelphia: Temple University Press, 1985.

Rosenzweig, Roy, and David Thelen. *The Presence of the Past: Popular Uses of History in American Life.* New York: Columbia University Press, 1998.

Roth, Stacy F. *Past into Present: Effective Techniques for First-Person Historical Interpretation.* Chapel Hill: University of North Carolina Press, 1998.

Rothman, Hal K. "Museums and Academics: Thoughts toward an Ethic of Cooperation." *Journal of American Culture* 12 (Summer 1989): 35–41.

Rutherford, Janice Williams, and Steven E. Shay. "Peopling the Age of Elegance: Reinterpreting Spokane's Campbell House: A Collaboration." *Public Historian* 26 (Summer 2004): 27–48.

Sanchis, Frank E. III. "Looking Back or Looking Forward? House Museums in the 21st Century." American House Museums: An Athenaeum of Philadelphia Symposium, 4–5 December 1998, http://www.philaathenaeum.org/hmuseum/sanchis.htm.

Scanlon, Jennifer. *Inarticulate Longings:* The Ladies' Home Journal, *Gender, and the Promises of Consumer Culture.* New York: Routledge, 1995.

Schlereth, Thomas J. *Artifacts and the American Past.* Walnut Creek, CA: AltaMira Press, 1996.

———. "Causing Conflict, Doing Violence." *Museum News* 63 (October 1984): 45–52.

Schreiber, Susan P. "Interpreting Slavery at National Trust Sites: A Case Study." *Cultural Resources Management* 23, no. 5 (2000): 49–52.

Sengupta, Somini. "Immigrants Tell Their New York Stories." *New York Times,* late ed., final, May 6, 1996: B2.

Shea, Christopher. "Uncovering Montpelier's Hidden Past." *Preservation,* September/October 2008, 28–35.

"Shedding Light on the Other Side." *History News* 36 (September 1981): 9–12.

Shoemaker, Linda. "Backstage at Beauport." *Historic New England* 5 (Summer 2004): 2–7.

Stanton, Lucia. *Free Some Day: The African-American Families of Monticello.* Charlottesville: Thomas Jefferson Foundation, 2000.

Sutherland, Daniel. *Americans and Their Servants: Domestic Service in the United States from 1800 to 1920.* Baton Rouge: Louisiana State University Press, 1981.

Thomson, Ron, and Marilyn Harper. "Telling the Stories: Planning Effective Interpretive Programs for Properties Listed in the National Register of Historic Places." *National Register Bulletin.* Washington, DC: National Park Service, 2000.

Tilden, Freeman. *Interpreting Our Heritage,* 3rd ed. Chapel Hill: University of North Carolina Press, 1977.

Truettner, William H., and Thomas Andrew Denenberg. "The Discreet Charm of the Colonial." In *Picturing Old New England: Image and Memory,* edited by William H. Truettner and Roger B. Stein, 79–110. New Haven: Yale University Press, 1999.

Villa Louis. Prairie du Chien, WI: Friends of Villa Louis, 2002.

Walker, Patricia Chambers. "A More Complete History: Interpreting Domestic Servants at Historic House Museums." Master's thesis, John F. Kennedy University, 1996.

Walker, Patricia Chambers, and Thomas Graham. *Directory of Historic House Museums in the United States.* Walnut Creek, CA: AltaMira Press, 2000.

Wallace, David. *Sagamore Hill Historic Furnishings Report,* vol. 2. Washington, DC: GPO, 1991.

Wallace, Michael. *Mickey Mouse History and Other Essays on American Memory.* Philadelphia: Temple University Press, 1996.

Webb, Amy, and Carolyn Brackett. "Cultural Heritage Tourism Trends Affecting Historic Sites." *Forum Journal* 22 (Spring 2008): 29–35.

West, Patricia. *Domesticating History: The Political Origins of America's House Museums.* Washington, DC: Smithsonian Institution Press, 1999.

———. "Irish Immigrant Workers in Antebellum New York: The Experience of Domestic Servants at Van Buren's Lindenwald." *Hudson Valley Regional Review* 9 (September 1992): 112–16.

———. "'The New Social History' and Historic House Museums: The Lindenwald Example." *Museum Studies Journal* 2 (Fall 1986): 22–26.

———. "Uncovering and Interpreting History at Historic House Museums." In *Restoring Women's History through Historic Preservation,* edited by Gail Lee Dubrow and Jennifer B. Goodman, 83–95. Baltimore: Johns Hopkins University Press, 2003.

Wheary, Dale. "Maymont: Gilded Age Estate." *Maymont Notes* 1 (Fall 2001): 9–14.

Wilkening, Susie. "Family Visitation at Museums: Historic Sites and History Museums." *Dispatch,* January 2008, 2, 4.

Wilkening, Susie, and Erica Donnis. "Authenticity? It Means Everything." *History News* 63 (Autumn 2008): 18–23.

Wiss, Janney, Elstner Associates, Inc., *Historic Structure Report for Brucemore, Cedar Rapids, Iowa,* 1991.

Index